The Ideological Origins of
Great Power Politics, 1789–1989

A volume in the series

CORNELL STUDIES IN SECURITY AFFAIRS

edited by Robert J. Art, Robert Jervis, *and* Stephen M. Walt

A full list of titles in the series appears at the end of the book.

The *Ideological Origins* *of* *Great Power Politics,* *1789–1989*

Mark L. Haas

Cornell University Press

Ithaca and London

First published 2005 by Cornell University Press

Printed in the United States of America

Library of Congress Cataloging-in-Publication Data

Haas, Mark L.
        The ideological origins of great power politics, 1789–1989 / Mark L.
Hass
            p. cm. — (Cornell studies in security affairs)
        Includes bibliographical references and index.
        ISBN 0-8014-4321-0 (cloth : alk. paper)
      1. International relations—Decision making.   2. Ideology.
3. World politics.   4. Great powers.   I. Title.   II. Series.
        JZ1253.H33 2005
        327.1'09—dc22   2005007514

Cornell University Press strives to use environmentally
responsible suppliers and materials to the fullest extent possible
in the publishing of its books. Such materials include vegetable-
based, low-VOC inks and acid-free papers that are recycled,
totally chlorine-free, or partly composed of nonwood fibers. For
further information, visit our website at
www.cornellpress.cornell.edu.

Cloth printing   10 9 8 7 6 5 4 3 2 1

To my father, Carl H. Haas,
who had the misfortune to leave this world far too soon;
and to my mother, Lorraine Haas,
who has had the courage to go on for so many years without him

Contents

Acknowledgments

The road to the completion of this book was a long one, though highly rewarding. I am grateful to numerous people and institutions that provided invaluable aid and support along the way.

The book has benefited immeasurably from the insights and constructive criticisms of many scholars. I am particularly indebted to Jeff Legro, Dale Copeland, John Owen, and Allen Lynch, all professors at the University of Virginia. I will always be extremely grateful for their steadfast support and assistance.

Many other colleagues provided valuable advice and criticisms on some or all of the book: Deborah Boucoyannis, Steve Brooks, Colin Dueck, John Duffield, David Edelstein, Kelly Erickson, Nisha Fazal, Arman Grigorian, Kurt Haas, Jacques Hymans, Iain Johnston, Whittle Johnston, Mark Kramer, Sean Lynn-Jones, Erez Manela, Chuck Mathewes, Rose McDermott, Steve Miller, Kevin Narizny, Jeremy Pressman, Brian Rathbun, Steve Rosen, Monica Duffy Toft, Kenneth W. Thompson, Chris Twomey, Will Walldorf, and Steve Walt. I am also grateful to the reviewers for Cornell University Press, who offered very detailed and thoughtful comments. Robert Jervis was particularly generous with his time. Bob read the entire manuscript twice, and each time he offered penetrating insights for improving the argument. Roger Haydon at Cornell University Press provided valuable editorial suggestions that greatly improved the final project. I must also thank Tom Spragens, Tim Lomperis, and Ole Holsti of Duke University for first inspiring me to begin the journey that ultimately led to the completion of the book.

This project would not have been possible without the generous financial and institutional support of several organizations: the Graduate School of Arts and Sciences and the Spicer Fellowships at the University

[ix]

of Virginia, the Institute for the Study of World Politics, the Earhart Foundation, the DuPont Foundation, the Presidential and the Philip H. and Betty L. Wimmer Family Foundation Fellowships at Duquesne University, and, most important, post-doctoral fellowships at the John M. Olin Institute for Strategic Studies and the International Security Program at the Belfer Center for Science and International Affairs, both at Harvard University. I thank the directors of the Olin Institute and the International Security Program at the Belfer Center, Steve Rosen, Steve Miller, and Steve Walt, for providing such supportive and stimulating environments in which to work.

Portions of this book were presented at seminars at the Olin Institute and Belfer Center at Harvard University, and the Center for International Studies at Princeton University. I thank the participants in these seminars for their suggestions.

Portions of Chapters 1 and 4 were published as "Ideology and Alliances: British and French External Balancing Decisions in the 1930s," *Security Studies* 12, no. 4 (Summer 2003): 34–79. I thank Taylor & Francis for permission to use the material here.

Finally, I thank many friends and family members who, in their own important ways, contributed to the completion of this work. Though the following list is by no means exhaustive, I offer my deepest gratitude to Kurt Haas, Denny and Gertrude Hixenbaugh, Carl and Helen Haas, Trudy and John Culberson, Lyle and Jean Hixenbaugh, Lynne and Peter Boorn, Sr., Nancy and John Traina, Mike Kusic, and Pete Boorn.

I am particularly indebted to three family members who made this book possible. My wife, Margaret Roosevelt Haas, always encouraged me during the many long months of research and writing, and she repeatedly sacrificed her interests to allow me more time to dedicate to the book. For her frequent examples of sacrificial love, I remain both grateful and humbled. I dedicate this book to my mother, Lorraine Haas, and my father, Carl H. Haas, the latter of whom died when I was in high school. They both instilled in me a profound love of knowledge, and encouraged me from the beginning to follow my heart's desires to the best of my God-given abilities. I cannot thank them enough.

M.L.H.

Pittsburgh, Pennsylvania

The Ideological Origins of
Great Power Politics, 1789–1989

Introduction

"Ideology" is one of the most frequently used concepts in the study of international politics. It is also one of the most contentious subjects in the field. Scholars disagree greatly in their answers to fundamental questions: What impact do political ideologies have in international relations? How do they do so? Do ideologies tend to have beneficial or harmful effects on states' security interests? What is the relationship between ideology and power?

This book advances these debates. My core hypothesis is that ideologies, or actors' foundational principles of domestic political legitimacy, are likely to impact leaders' foreign policies by affecting their *perceptions of the threats* that others pose to their central domestic and international interests. The greater the ideological differences dividing decision makers from different states, the more likely they are to view one another as substantial dangers to both their domestic power and the security of their respective countries. Conversely, the greater the ideological similarities uniting states' leaders, the higher the probability they will view one another as supports to their key domestic and international interests, and therefore as less of a threat. Leaders' perceptions of threat will, in turn, create powerful incentives that push them to adopt specific foreign policies in particular situations.

To express these statements in a slightly different way, leaders will judge the threats that other states pose to their interests by examining how the latter organize their societies. Perceived threats will largely be a product of how another state's domestic institutions and principles relate to one's own.

The claim that political ideologies tend to have profound, systematic effects on states' most important international security decisions is a controversial assertion among international relations scholars. Political realism, for example, explicitly denies the importance of ideological variables to states' international choices. To most realists, considerations of power will invariably trump ideological concerns. This perspective remains the dominant view in international relations scholarship.

Even among those scholars who assert that political ideologies do have important effects in international politics, there remain key theoretical and empirical holes to fill. Too often both the causal mechanisms explaining precisely how ideological variables shape outcomes and the use of systematic case-study evidence for hypothesis testing remain underdeveloped.

I correct these shortcomings by developing a causal logic that provides a comprehensive explanation of how political ideologies are likely to shape decision makers' international policies. My argument is comprehensive in two principal respects. First, it examines how ideologies shape the level of threats to both the domestic and the international security interests of states' leaders. Many examinations of the effects of ideologies in international relations examine only one of these sets of interests. Second, the argument applies to any political ideology and so is not restricted to the potentially idiosyncratic effects of a particular system of belief. By examining the effects of the degree of ideological differences—or the ideological "distance"—dividing states' leaders on their perceptions of threat, the causal logic applies to all ideological relationships, regardless of the unique qualities associated with any particular set of legitimating principles.

After developing the causal logic, I test its hypotheses in detailed case studies of great powers' relations during critical times over the last two hundred years: the 1790s in Europe, the era of the Concert of Europe (1815 to 1848), the 1930s in Europe, Sino-Soviet relations from 1949 to 1960, and the 1980s and the end of the Cold War. I find that the degree of ideological differences dividing decision makers across states had consistently critical effects on leaders' most important international security decisions, including during times when the very survival of their country was at risk.

In this book I do more than merely account for unexplained variance of issues that are of marginal significance to world politics. I demonstrate that ideological variables shape leaders' understandings of the security environment in which they operate, in terms of which states constitute the greatest threats to leaders' key interests and the level of this perceived threat. Given these relationships, ideological variables are likely to affect decision makers' most important foreign policy choices. The greater the ideological differences dividing leaders, the higher their perceptions of threat, and thus the greater the incentives pushing them to adopt aggressive, power-maximizing strategies. Conversely, the greater the ideological similarities uniting decision makers, the less threatening their relationships, and thus the greater the likelihood that amicable relations will develop. Examining the nature of the ideological relationships among states' leaders thus provides insight into some of the most important questions in the study of international politics: Which states are leaders likely to view as their primary international enemies and allies? When are major wars most likely? When are states most likely to cooperate?

These findings are of much more than historical interest to scholars and politicians alike. Given the relationship between ideological variables and states' security decisions, leaders should be able to predict to an important degree when others are likely to engage in either hostile or cooperative behavior. This foreknowledge of leaders' likely foreign policy decisions should provide insight as to when policies of deterrence or of reassurance are likely to be successful in attempts to protect states' safety. Thus underlying my theoretical and empirical analysis is a highly practical political objective: to provide policy guidance to statesmen that helps both to avoid unwanted military hostilities among states and to mitigate the severity of such conflicts if they come.

The book also provides important insights into key dimensions of contemporary international politics. Perhaps most important, the argument helps us understand the sources of hostility toward the Western powers expressed by Islamic fundamentalist organizations like Osama bin Laden's al Qaeda terrorist network, and why many U.S. leaders believe that America's security will be substantially enhanced by the spread and stabilization of liberal political institutions in China, Russia, Afghanistan, Iraq, and other key states around the world.

Although my primary objectives are to reveal the impact of political ideologies in international relations and the manner in which they have an effect, this does not mean that I fail to recognize the importance of power factors to leaders' foreign policies. I reject the now stale exercise of showing how realist theories and the power variables that ground them cannot explain every important outcome in international relations. Instead, the analysis illuminates particular ways in which ideologies and power, in combination, affect international politics, and the areas in which one set of variables provides superior analytic leverage in relation to the other. I ultimately seek to create a foundation upon which we might build a more integrated framework between ideological and power variables in order to understand the central dynamics of international relations.

[1]

Ideological Similarities and Differences and Leaders' Perceptions of Threat

How do ideological variables affect leaders' perceptions of threat and their consequent foreign policies? Although this book is by no means the first to examine the effects of political ideologies in international relations, it does differ in an important respect from most of its predecessors. Most analyses of ideologies in international politics examine the effects on foreign policy of the specific behavioral prescriptions associated with particular belief systems. Ideologies thus affect international relations by shaping leaders' primary foreign policy objectives and their preferred means for realizing these goals. Examples of behavioral prescriptions include political liberalism's injunction to resolve disputes peacefully, communism's command to support working-class movements around the world, and fascism's call for "superior" races to dominate "inferior" ones in a merciless struggle for existence. I label the unique prescriptions associated with particular systems of belief "ideological content."

I take a different approach. Instead of examining the international effects of the various contents of different ideologies, I examine the ideological *distance* among actors, which I define as the degree of ideological differences dividing them.[1] The core claim is that there exists a strong relationship between the ideological distance dividing states' leaders and their understandings of the level of threat they pose to one another's central domestic and international interests. The greater the ideological differences dividing decision makers across states, the higher the perceived level of threat; the greater the ideological similarities uniting leaders, the lower the perceived threat. These relationships should hold

1. Cf. Raymond Aron, *Peace and War, A Theory of International Relations* (Malabar, Fla.: Robert Krieger, 1981), 99–100; Hans J. Morgenthau, *Politics among Nations: The Struggle for Power and Peace* (New York: Knopf, 1961), 23, 58, 64, 190, 217, 221–223, 256, 509, 561, 562.

regardless of the varying behavioral prescriptions associated with different ideologies.

The evidence I present in the empirical chapters demonstrates the analytical advantages of an argument based on ideological distance rather than ideological content. In each period of history, large ideological differences among leaders led to high levels of threat. Conversely, ideological similarities contributed to cooperation among liberals, monarchists, communists, and fascists. Thus despite stark differences in ideological content, there were clear patterns of outcomes. These patterns are important because they reveal the influence of systemic forces that transcend the unique effects of any particular ideology.[2] This variable is the degree of ideological differences dividing decision makers across states, which is systemic because of its relational or distributional nature.[3]

I do not deny that the various contents of different ideologies often have important international effects, or that some ideologies support the argument more than others. My goal, however, is to determine to what extent a parsimonious understanding of leaders' ideological relationships—based solely on the ideological distance dividing decision makers—helps us understand states' core security policies.

The Causal Logic

The causal logic linking the degree of ideological differences dividing states' leaders to perceptions of threat and consequent foreign policy choices consists of three different causal mechanisms, each of which draws largely on insights from different research programs: demonstration effects, social psychology, and communications theories. The three mechanisms are united by the fact that they are "human nature" analyses that draw on well-established empirical findings with regards to how individuals tend to react to the ideological environments in which they operate. Because the causal mechanisms are based on universal human dispositions, we should expect their applicability to be both widespread and enduring.

I define political ideologies as the principles upon which a particular leadership group attempts to legitimate its claim to rule and the primary institutional, economic, and social goals to which it swears allegiance. Ideologies are, in short, particular visions for ordering *domestic* politics. For example, do leaders advocate representative or autocratic political institutions? Capitalist or socialist economies? Full rights of citizenship for some or all races and ethnic groups in their state?[4]

2. Kenneth N. Waltz, *Theory of International Politics* (New York: McGraw-Hill, 1979), 69.
3. Ibid., 98.
4. Throughout the book, I use such phrases as "ideological beliefs," "ideological objectives," and "legitimating principles" interchangeably.

Political ideologies as I define them have their most obvious impact with regard to domestic politics. Because elites who share a commitment to a particular way of ordering political life are likely to coalesce into groups, ideological differences will be at the heart of what divides one political party from another in a given country. As a result, interparty competition for political power within a state will be to an important extent ideological in nature. Outcomes that in some way support particular belief systems will very likely help the domestic interests of the parties associated with these beliefs and vice versa.

Related analysis applies to relations among politicians from different states. The most important international characteristic of political ideologies for our purposes is that they are inherently transnational phenomena, meaning that people from different states can claim allegiance to the same set of ideological beliefs.[5] In other words, no party's legitimating principles will be wholly unique to it. Instead, members of any given group in one state are bound to share ideological objectives with parties in other states. In the following sections, which develop the three causal mechanisms of the argument, I show how ideologies' transnational nature and the effects of this quality on leaders' political identities will tend to shape politicians' perceptions of the threats to both their *domestic power* and the *security interests* of their state.

Ideological Differences and the Fear of Subversion: The "Demonstrations Effects" Mechanism

The first causal mechanism shows how ideological variables shape politicians' perceptions of threats to their domestic interests. A core finding of the demonstration-effects literature is that political developments across states are in important ways interconnected (for our purposes, a demonstration effect refers to the process by which institutions, behaviors, or beliefs in one state are emulated in some manner in others).[6] To this body of research, the success or failure in one state of particular institutional structures, belief systems, or political actions (such as a coup or revolution) will affect how these phenomena are understood in other polities in the international system. When particular policies succeed in one state, the ideas grounding these policies will likely be looked on more favorably by other actors in the system. As a result, others are more likely to adopt them in their own country. Conversely, failure of specific policies in one state will likely create doubt

---

5. Bruce Cronin, *Community under Anarchy: Transnational Identity and the Evolution of Cooperation* (New York: Columbia University Press, 1999); John M. Owen, "Transnational Liberalism and U.S. Primacy," *International Security* 26, no. 3 (Winter 2001/2002): 117–152.

6. Benjamin A. Most and Harvey Starr, "Theoretical and Logical Issues in the Study of International Diffusion," *Journal of Theoretical Politics* 2, no. 4 (October 1990): 391–412.

in others concerning the viability and legitimacy of the ideas ground-ing these choices. Other actors in the system are therefore less likely to adopt them.

The fact that political developments in one state can inspire similar ones in others helps to explain, for example, why rulers in Europe's old regimes in the 1790s took so seriously the Marquis de Lafayette's and other French leaders' threat to present Europe with the "contagious example of a dethroned king,"[7] and why American leaders during the Cold War were concerned about the toppling of "dominoes" to commu-nism throughout the world. Both sets of individuals clearly believed that changes in one state were likely to inspire similar political outcomes elsewhere. Indeed, the very language of revolutionary "contagion" or "infection"—which is a virtual constant among leaders confronted with a state founded on opposing political principles[8]—reveals well the belief that the health of one's own regime can be profoundly affected by the *internal* political developments in other states (i.e., no external threats, such as armed aggression, need be involved). As the French diplomat Vicomte de Chateaubriand warned his government in 1822 about the emerging states in South America (which offered little, if any, power-political threat to the European powers): "All [France's] policy ought to be directed to bringing monarchies into existence in the New World rather than republics, which will send us their principles with the prod-ucts of their soil."[9]

The transnational nature of most political ideologies makes these vari-ables particularly susceptible to the impact of demonstration effects on their overall status. When people across states claim allegiance to the same set of ideological principles, the perceived legitimacy and effective-ness of these beliefs will likely be affected by events that take place in dif-ferent countries. When particular beliefs succeed and flourish in one state, these outcomes will likely enhance the standing of these principles as a whole, thereby providing a political boost to all parties dedicated to them regardless of the groups' states of origin. Conversely, when move-ments associated with particular political principles fail or languish in one state, this will likely be a setback for these principles as a whole, and thus for the domestic interests of all parties dedicated to these beliefs. In these ways, developments in other states become intertwined with par-ties' attempts to acquire and maintain political power in their own coun-try. This analysis helps to explain why, for example, liberal parties throughout Europe greeted the Whigs' ascension to power in Britain in

7. In Georges Lefebvre, *The French Revolution from Its Origins to 1793,* trans. Elizabeth Moss Evanson (New York: Columbia University Press, 1962), 211.

8. Stephen M. Walt, *Revolution and War* (Ithaca: Cornell University Press, 1996), 40.

9. In Charles Webster, *The Foreign Policy of Castlereagh, 1815–1822: Britain and the European Alliance* (London: G. Bell and Sons, 1963), 431.

[7]

1830 with renewed hope for their domestic political fortunes, while conservative parties were greatly concerned about the impact that this party change would have on domestic politics in their own state.[10] In the contemporary international system, demonstration effects created by the success of liberal regimes have played an important role in consolidating representative institutions in Eastern European states since the end of the Cold War.[11]

The relationships described in the previous paragraphs have key implications for decision makers' understandings of the threats that other states pose to their domestic legitimacy and power. When leaders from different states are dedicated to similar legitimating principles, each group should look sympathetically on one another's success since the achievement of each is likely to support the domestic interests of all. As we shall see in Chapter 3, this analysis goes far in explaining the cooperative policies among Austria, Prussia, and Russia throughout much of the nineteenth century. The key decision makers in each of these states believed they had to support one another in order to preserve their own domestic authority.

Conversely, when different states are governed by parties that are dedicated to rival legitimating ideals, the success of one group is likely to increase the legitimacy of other leaders' ideological enemies at home, thereby threatening these decision makers' domestic power. To this logic, the *mere presence* in the system of states governed by parties dedicated to different principles of political legitimacy will frequently be seen as powerful subversive threats to current decision makers' claim to rule. The greater the ideological differences dividing states' leaders, the more pressing these fears of subversion are likely to be. These concerns were ones that plagued decision makers throughout Europe in the 1790s and 1930s.

Leaders' fears of ideological subversion are likely to be exacerbated by a substantial mistrust of ideological rivals' international objectives. Specifically, decision makers will tend to worry that others dedicated to opposing legitimating principles will target their state for ideological conversion.[12] Thus when politicians confront ideological rivals, they will fear for their hold on domestic power not only due to the processes of ideological diffusion through demonstration effects, but to the deliberate subversive policies of other states' leaders.

10. Sir Charles Webster, *The Foreign Policy of Palmerston 1830–1841: Britain, the Liberal Movement, and the Eastern Question* (New York: Humanities Press, 1969), 2:854; W. Bruce Lincoln, *Nicholas I, Emperor and Autocrat of All the Russias* (Bloomington: Indiana University Press, 1978), 144–145.
11. Henry J. Nau, *At Home Abroad: Identity and Power in American Foreign Policy* (Ithaca: Cornell University Press, 2002), 134–147.
12. Walt, *Revolution and War*, chap. 2.

Social Identity Theory and the Likelihood of Conflict: The "Conflict Probability" Mechanism

The previous analysis demonstrates how the degree of ideological differences dividing states' leaders, when tied to the insights of the demonstration-effects literature, generates predictions concerning how leaders will tend to see their counterparts in other states in terms of threats or supports to their *domestic* power. In what follows, I show how the same variable, when filtered through the insights of social identity theory and related theories of social psychology, leads to predictions about how leaders tend to evaluate the *international-security* threats to their state posed by other actors in the system.

Social identity theory was first developed as a challenge to those arguments that attributed intergroup conflict to competition over scarce resources. Drawing on data from controlled experiments involving individual subjects, the creators of this theory discovered that even without material conflicts of interest among groups, disputes are still likely to result from psychological impulses that are universally shared among humans.

The starting point for social identity theory's analysis of intergroup conflict is the claim that humans have a universal need for a positive conception of themselves. This need is in large part satisfied through two means that are as universal as the impulses that led to them. First, individuals will invariably come to identify their sense of self with the fortunes of a group. Because the psychic and physical insecurity that individualism implies is unbearable, people take refuge in the common identity and mutual reassurance that define communities. Second, because people's desire for positive self-representation is only partially realized by identifying themselves with the possibilities and achievements of a particular group, this need must also be met with a favorable comparison of one's own group(s) to others. In short, people have a universal tendency both to categorize others into "ingroups" and "outgroups," and to desire their own group(s) to realize higher levels of achievement and status than others.[13]

A key implication of social identity theory's claims is that intergroup interactions will tend to be fundamentally conflictual in nature, regardless of disputes over material interests. Given individuals' needs to assert the superiority of their own group(s) in relation to others, people will confront powerful psychological incentives pushing them to understand their group(s) in highly favorable terms and others in a negative manner.

---

13. Michael A. Hogg, *The Social Psychology of Group Cohesiveness: From Attraction to Social Identity* (New York: New York University Press, 1992); Henri Tajfel, *Human Groups and Social Categories: Studies in Social Psychology* (Cambridge: Cambridge University Press, 1981); John C. Turner, *Rediscovering the Social Group: A Self-Categorization Theory* (New York: Basil Blackwell, 1987); Jonathan Mercer, "Anarchy and Identity," *International Organization* 49, no. 2 (Spring 1995): 237–246.

"The very factors that make ingroup attachment and allegiance important to individuals," as one scholar of the subject puts it, "also provide a fertile ground for antagonism and distrust of those outside the ingroup boundaries."[14] People will tend to see members of their own group(s) as virtuous, trustworthy, and reliable individuals who possess important common interests with one another.[15] Members of opposing groups will quite often be believed to possess the opposite qualities to the point where they become the objects of mistrust, scorn, and even hatred.[16] Given these last beliefs, conflictual relations among groups are highly likely, if not inevitable.

This analysis generates important implications for international relations. Most people, at least in part, make sense of the world that is beyond domestic politics by classifying people into two groups: fellow citizens of one's own state and those who belong to other political groupings. Social identity theory predicts that bifurcating the world in this manner will impel people to attribute positive images to one's fellow citizens and negative, even hostile, characteristics to all others. This manner of stereotyping in-group and out-group members in terms of negative and positive attributes implies that international politics must remain an inherently competitive and conflict-prone arena in which the interests of fellow citizens are given, in the aggregate, priority to those of all other individuals. Social identity theory therefore adds a psychological support to the predictions generated by realist theories.[17]

The problem with this analysis is that it is overly restrictive in its claims. There is little doubt that citizenship is an important determinant of leaders' political identities. But the claim that politicians will make no meaningful discriminations among all decision makers who are not members of their state will in most cases be inaccurate. Within the category of "non-citizen," decision makers are likely to make a distinction between those politicians who share their legitimating principles and those who do not. The greater the ideological similarities among states' leaders, the more their political identities will be believed to overlap. Conversely, politicians from different states who are dedicated to rival ideological objectives will view one another as the antithesis of their political identities; they will be rivals in terms of both state and ideological interests.

The transnational qualities of political ideologies provide the foundation upon which I ground these assertions. Ideologies' transnational

---

14. Marilynn B. Brewer, "The Psychology of Prejudice: Ingroup Love or Outgroup Hate?" *Journal of Social Issues* 55, no. 3 (Fall 1999): 442.

15. Turner, *Rediscovering the Social Group*, 65.

16. Hogg, *Social Psychology of Group Cohesiveness*, 104; Vamik Volkan, *The Need to Have Enemies and Allies: From Clinical Practice to International Relationships* (Northvale, N. J.: Aronson, 1988); Donald L. Horowitz, *Ethnic Groups in Conflict* (Berkeley: University of California Press, 1985).

17. Mercer, "Anarchy and Identity."

nature allows politicians from different states to claim allegiance to the same set of legitimating principles. Moreover, because dedication to particular ideological objectives necessarily implies the rejection of alternative systems of belief, people dedicated to the same ideological principles will have one or more ideological enemies in common. When leaders from different states recognize that they both share a commitment to the same ideological objectives and possess the same ideological enemies, they will tend to view one another as *closer* to their own political identities than those decision makers who do not meet these conditions. As one scholar expresses it, when politicians from different countries are dedicated to similar ideological objectives and share ideological adversaries, they form a "transnational ideological group" whose members will tend to identify with one another: they will "tend to derive positive utility from one another's gains vis-à-vis opposing ideological groups . . . [and] perceive losses in their own power from increases in the power of opposing ideological groups in other states."[18] The greater the overlap in ideological beliefs, the greater this transnational identification is likely to be. This analysis does not claim that participation in a transnational ideological group eliminates or even supersedes politicians' loyalties to the state in which they hold citizenship. These statements address how leaders will tend to categorize their counterparts in other states, and not their attitudes toward fellow citizens.

When filtered through the insights of social identity theory, the claim that the degree of ideological differences dividing states' leaders will play a central role in determining how close these individuals will judge one another to be to their defining political group yields testable hypotheses concerning decision makers' perceptions of threat. Given the above analysis, we would expect threat perceptions to vary significantly depending on which groups are in power in specific states at particular times. The greater the ideological similarities among states' leaders, the less threatening their relations are likely to be. This relationship is likely to hold because the greater the perceived overlap in politicians' political identities, the greater the tendency for these individuals to trust one another and to believe that they have similar interests. Conversely, the greater the ideological differences among states' leaders, the more their political identities will diverge, and thus the more likely it is that these individuals will both ascribe hostile intent to one another and believe that their interests are bound to conflict.

Expressed a little differently, the conflict-probability causal mechanism predicts that ideological variables will affect in critical ways how decision

18. Owen, "Transnational Liberalism and U.S. Primacy," 123. See also David Skidmore, "Introduction: Bringing Social Orders Back In," in *Contested Social Orders and International Politics*, ed. David Skidmore (Nashville: Vanderbilt University Press, 1997), 4–6; Cronin, *Community under Anarchy*.

makers respond to the ubiquitous problem of uncertainty about others' intentions. The greater the ideological differences dividing decision makers across states, the more likely they are to think the worst about one another's international objectives. Conversely, the greater the ideological similarities uniting states' leaders, the more likely they will give each other the benefit of the doubt and attribute benign motives to their counterparts' actions. As long as the condition of uncertainty is in effect, the degree of ideological differences dividing states' leaders will have a consistently greater impact on their perceptions of threat and consequent choices of allies and enemies than will issues of relative power.

Ideological Differences and Increases in Misperception: The "Communications" Mechanism

The final causal mechanism linking the degree of ideological differences dividing states' leaders and their perceptions of threat is based on an important claim of communications theory: the greater the ideological differences among actors, the greater the impediments to effective communication among them.[19] This relationship is likely to hold even if ideological rivals use (in the language of contemporary social science) "costly signals" in their communications efforts.

The relationship between ideological variables and leaders' ability to communicate effectively results because actors' identities affect profoundly critical elements of the communications process, such as individuals' modes of cognizing and the development of rules for both encoding and decoding various symbols, including the constitutive elements of language. As one scholar puts it: "For a message to be correctly understood there must be sufficient similarity, if not identity, between the intention of the sender and the meaning attributed by the receiver."[20] However, "since the encoder and the decoder are two separate individuals, their reactions are likely to be similar only to the extent that they . . . have similar frames of reference. The more different they are, the less isomorphism there will be between the encoded and the decoded content."[21]

To the extent that individuals' ideological beliefs affect their frames of reference (by, for example, impacting their perceptions of reality or generating unique expectations or experiences), we would expect leaders dedicated to different belief systems to tend to attribute different meanings to

19. Robert Jervis, *Perception and Misperception in International Politics* (Princeton: Princeton University Press, 1976), chaps. 4, 5; Albert Mehrabian and Henry Reed, "Some Determinants of Communication Accuracy," *Psychological Bulletin* 70, no. 5 (November 1968): 366, 373, 378.
20. Raymond Cohen, *Negotiating across Cultures: Communication Obstacles in International Diplomacy* (Washington, D.C.: U.S. Institute of Peace, 1991), 20.
21. Lorand B. Szalay, "Intercultural Communication—A Process Model," *International Journal of Intercultural Relations* 5, no. 2 (1981): 136.

the same symbols and events. This tendency will very likely significantly handicap ideological rivals' ability to communicate effectively with one another, especially with regards to the subtleties that are often involved in international diplomacy.

Again, these barriers to effective communication among ideological rivals are not a product of lack of effort or difficulties of translation, but of different identities that push people to interpret language and other signals in contrary ways. President John F. Kennedy expressed well precisely these points when he wrote to Soviet leader Nikita Khrushchev: "I am conscious of the difficulties you and I face in establishing full communication between our two minds. This is not a question of translation but a question of the context in which we hear and respond to what each other has to say. You and I have already recognized that neither of us will convince the other about our respective social systems and general philosophies of life. These differences create a great gulf in communications because language cannot mean the same thing on both sides unless it is related to some underlying purpose."[22]

Theories that emphasize the importance of "costly signaling" in demonstrating actors' intentions (i.e., the adoption of actions that individuals would find too costly to make if they were bluffing about their objectives) are likely to have trouble solving the problems described above. Actors dedicated to different legitimating principles simply have a tendency to interpret the same events and signals—even if they are costly—in very different ways. Historical examples of this tendency are not hard to find. Despite the fact that Nicholas I of Russia continued to forego opportunities for expansion in the Near East throughout the era of the Concert of Europe—decisions that according to rationalist accounts are supposed to be excellent costly signals of an actor's benign intent[23]—Britain's foreign minister, Lord Palmerston, and fellow Whigs continued to believe that Nicholas was bent on significant territorial aggrandizement. Britain's and France's commitment to defend Poland in 1939—a clear signal that their leaders had decided to confront Nazi Germany—was originally interpreted by Joseph Stalin as a hostile move against Soviet interests.[24] Similarly, Stalin's decision in the mid-1930s to shift to his "united front from above" policy and thereby increase his support for the capitalist governments in Britain and France (a costly signal because it meant that the Soviet Union was abandoning, or at least downplaying, the cause of the Comintern) was originally interpreted by many in the West as a new and more subtle

22. Letter of November 16, 1961, *Foreign Relations of the United States, 1961–1963, Kennedy–Khrushchev Exchanges*, vol. 6, virtual archive, 56. http://www.law.uh.edu/cdrom/USFAC/FRUS/Frus_V06.pdf.
23. Andrew Kydd, "Sheep in Sheep's Clothing: Why Security Seekers Do Not Fight Each Other," *Security Studies* 7, no. 1 (Autumn 1997): 143.
24. Donald Cameron Watt, *How War Came: The Immediate Origins of the Second World War, 1938–1939* (New York: Pantheon Books, 1989), 215–216, 236.

attempt at subversion.[25] Thus even costly signals can be interpreted in very different manners. The effectiveness of even these types of communications are therefore likely to be significantly handicapped when they take place among decision makers dedicated to rival ideological beliefs.[26]

Because misperception can lead to unexpected cooperation among leaders as well as conflict, there is not an inevitable connection between an inability to communicate effectively and increasing perceptions of international threats. Nevertheless, barriers to effective communication among ideological rivals will more often than not lead to increases rather than decreases in threat perceptions. Ideological rivals will tend to interpret one another's words and deeds in the worst possible light. As a result, these decision makers are likely both to perceive conflicts of interest with one another even when none exist, and to magnify the severity of existing disputes. In this environment, attempts to resolve conflicts in an efficient and crisis-free manner will be very difficult.

The opposite relationships to those described in the previous paragraphs should also hold true. Because similar ideological beliefs should impel individuals to ascribe similar meanings to the same symbols and events, the smaller the ideological differences among actors, the greater the likelihood of effective communication among them. Consequently, the greater the overlap in leaders' legitimating principles, the lower the likelihood of an international crisis resulting from either diplomatic misunderstanding or an inability to signal benign intent.

The three causal mechanisms linking the degree of ideological similarities and differences among leaders to their perceptions of threat generate the following hypothesis:

> Hypothesis 1: The greater the ideological differences dividing states' leaders, the more likely they are to see one another as threats to both their domestic power and the security of their state. The greater the ideological similarities uniting decision makers, the more likely they are to see one another as supports to their domestic and international interests, and therefore as less of a threat. These relationships will hold because the degree of ideological differences dividing leaders impacts their estimates of the likelihood of both domestic subversion and international conflict, as well as their ability to communicate effectively. (For a diagram of the linkages between ideological variables and perceptions of threat according to the three causal mechanisms, see Figure 1.)

25. Jonathan Haslam, *The Soviet Union and the Struggle for Collective Security in Europe, 1933–39* (New York: St. Martin's Press, 1984), 59.
26. For other historical examples of this problem, see Ole Holsti, "Cognitive Dynamics and Images of the Enemy," in *Image and Reality in World Politics,* ed. J. C. Farrell and A. P. Smith (New York: Columbia University Press, 1967), 16–39; Robert Jervis, "War and Misperceptions," in *The Origin and Prevention of Major Wars,* ed. Robert I. Rotberg and Theodore K. Rabb (New York: Cambridge University Press, 1988), 114–117.

The "demonstration-effects" mechanism (demonstration-effects literature)

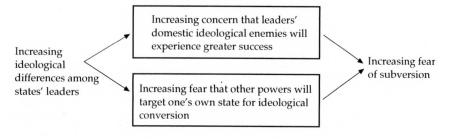

The "conflict-probability" mechanism (social identity theory)

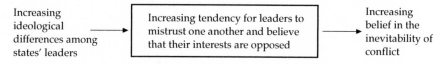

The "communications" mechanism (communications theories)

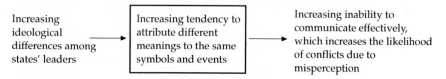

Figure 1. Summary of the causal mechanisms

Although I have combined the predictions generated by the three causal mechanisms into a single hypothesis, it is worth emphasizing that each affects leaders' perceptions of threat in very different ways. The conflict-probability mechanism predicts that ideological rivals will view one another as inevitably hostile to the security interests of their state. In this case, there is a direct connection between ideological variables and profound conflicts of interest among actors. We would therefore expect the effects of this mechanism on outcomes to be both strong and pervasive.

The demonstration-effects mechanism indicates how ideological differences will stimulate leaders' fears for their domestic power. Decision makers' fears of subversion, however, are likely to vary not only with the extent of the ideological dangers emanating from other states, but also with the extent of their domestic vulnerability, which will be a product of much more than international developments. Such factors as a state's economic well-being, the charisma and competence of its politicians, and the extent of party cleavages will all play a role in determining how susceptible a particular regime is to the subversive forces created by other actors in the system. For this reason, the impact

[15]

of ideological variables on leaders' perceptions of threat due to demonstration effects is likely to be less direct than the workings of the conflict-probability mechanism.

The communications mechanism makes similar predictions as the conflict-probability argument. Both predict that ideological rivals will tend to assume the worst about one another's intentions. The communication effect, however, is more restricted in its scope. Whereas the conflict-probability mechanism refers to a general presumption of enmity among ideological rivals, the communication effect most prominently refers to those specific instances when leaders dedicated to different ideological objectives are trying to communicate benign intent to one another, but cannot due to the effects of different perceptual schemata. Because those instances when ideological enemies are actively signaling benign intent to one another should be relatively rare, the universe of cases when the communications mechanism can be tested is likely to be fairly small, especially in relation to the other two mechanisms. We would therefore expect this component of the causal logic to be less robust than the other two linkages.

PERCEPTIONS OF THREAT, FOREIGN POLICY BEHAVIOR, AND THE PROBABILITY OF WAR

The causal logic generates important implications for states' foreign policies. Perhaps most powerful and significant are those incentives created by the conflict-probability mechanism. The tendency for ideological rivals to believe that conflict among them is inevitable will create very strong incentives for politicians to maximize their state's relative power in relation to their adversaries. These incentives will push decision makers both to join a system of alliances and increase their military spending in order to balance their rivals and, more dramatically, to adopt various hard-line policies—such as crisis initiation and even preventive hostilities—that are designed to diminish the power of their enemies. Ideological differences among leaders thus substantially increase the probability of international war.

Leaders' heightened concern over relative power comprises, however, only part of the foreign policies central to relations among ideological rivals. Because increasing ideological similarities among decision makers are likely to lower the security threats confronting their state, politicians will have an interest in seeing their ideological adversaries replaced with individuals whose legitimating principles are much closer in identity to their own. Thus in times of peace, leaders will likely engage in policies designed to destabilize their rivals to the point where an ideological revolution in these states becomes more likely.[27] In times of military conflict, leaders are likely to adopt total war aims designed to replace their enemy states' existing domestic structures and principles with ones more similar to their own. Wars among ideological rivals are therefore likely to be fought at the highest levels of intensity.

Politicians are likely to adopt very different policies toward those decision makers with whom they share important ideological beliefs. The greater the ideological similarities uniting leaders, the more likely they are to believe that their relations will be both peaceful and even cooperative. This presumption of amity will likely impel decision makers not to be overly fearful of positions of power inferiority in relation to states within their ideological community. As a result, leaders in these situations are likely to engage in policies of reassurance to manage interstate relations rather than adopting hard-line deterrent policies.

The ramifications of the demonstration-effects causal mechanism reinforce the policy incentives discussed in the previous paragraphs. In order to reduce the danger of subversion among ideological enemies, decision makers will likely adopt policies designed both to isolate rival regimes to prevent ideological contagion, and to lay stress upon their opponents to facilitate ideological changes in these states. Thus the demonstration-effects mechanism predicts, just like the conflict-probability causal mechanism, that leaders will try to destabilize their ideological rivals in times of peace, and to engage in policies of forcible regime exportation during times of war.

With regard to regimes that are already members of leaders' ideological community, the demonstration-effects causal mechanism predicts that decision makers should adopt largely cooperative policies. Politicians' domestic interests are likely to be furthered by the success in other states of parties dedicated to similar ideological objectives. Consequently, we would expect decision makers to eschew those actions (such as the threat or use of force) that would likely harm their international ideological allies' domestic power, and instead engage in policies that were designed to aid the others' interests, such as forming an alliance or offering various forms of diplomatic and economic support.

Finally, the communications causal mechanism predicts that the greater the ideological differences among leaders, the greater the difficulty they will have in communicating effectively with one another, and the more likely these individuals will interpret one another's actions and proclamations in the worst possible light. These dynamics will likely impel ideological rivals to adopt policies designed to guard very closely their state's relative power position.

27. To subvert a regime's political system, a state can engage in policies of containment (e.g., diplomatic, economic, and strategic isolation) or engagement (e.g., economic and political infiltration).

The opposite relationship should also hold true. The greater the ideological similarities among decision makers, the greater their ability to communicate effectively with one another. Effective communication allows statesmen the possibility of mitigating the pernicious effects of the security dilemma (the tendency for even non-aggressive states to frighten others when building up their capabilities for defense) by increasing the likelihood that status quo powers will be able to convey to one another the limited nature of their foreign policy ambitions. Thus among states within an ideological community, relative gains seeking is likely to be reduced because leaders' signals of benign intent have a greater chance of being understood and believed under these circumstances than in others.

The above analysis yields the following hypothesis linking the degree of ideological differences and similarities among leaders to particular foreign policies:

Hypothesis 2: The greater the ideological differences dividing decision makers of different states, the greater the emphasis they will place on issues of relative power (and thus the more likely they are to adopt various hard-line policies against their adversaries up to and including preventive war), and the more interested they will be in converting ideological rivals to legitimating ideals closer in identity with their own. The greater the ideological similarities uniting states' leaders, the less important issues of relative power will be to their relations, and the greater the incentives for them to adopt cooperative policies with one another. (For a diagram of the linkages among ideology, perceptions of threat, and foreign policy behavior, see Figure 2.)

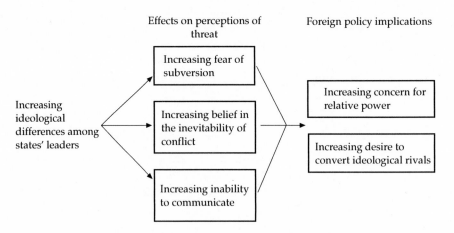

Figure 2. Summary of the causal links between ideology, threat, and foreign policy

CONTRIBUTIONS OF THE ARGUMENT

This book's principal theoretical contribution is the development of a causal logic that shows how political ideologies affect states' leaders' perceptions of threat and consequent foreign policies. Too often supporters of the idea that ideologies are of central importance to international politics have left the causal mechanisms linking these variables to outcomes underexplained.

Beyond this general advancement to the study of ideologies in international relations, I offer three primary contributions. First, I provide a different understanding of the relationship between political ideologies and leaders' most basic *security* concerns than described by many prominent examinations of this subject. Probably the dominant way in the literature of conceptualizing ideologies' relationship to security issues is in dichotomous terms: a leader can be predominantly either a security seeker or driven by ideological interests. To this view, ideologically motivated actors are willing to sacrifice their state's "true" interests for the sake of objectives derived from their beliefs. To this perspective there is an air of irrationality and fanaticism surrounding these types of leaders.[28]

I adopt the opposite approach. Instead of asserting that leaders' ideological and security concerns are in tension, the causal logic shows how the degree of ideological similarities uniting states' decision makers shapes how they understand other actors in the system *in terms of security threats.* Ideology therefore provides an important foundation for states' security since ideology informs how leaders understand their security environment. Because ideological similarities among leaders tend to result in peaceful relations, and because ideological differences tend to lead to hostile actions, the safety of states will most likely be augmented when they operate within an ideological community.

Second, the argument offers a different way of understanding how ideologies affect states' policies. Many studies that examine the impact of ideologies on outcomes conceptualize ideologies as unit-level (i.e., solely domestic) variables that affect policies primarily by impelling leaders both to possess specific interests and to adopt or eschew particular means for realizing these goals (what I have labeled "ideological content"). Consistent with this "inside-out" manner of theorizing, these studies assert that leaders should possess these preferences over ends and means regardless of external circumstances.

28. Cf. Jack Snyder, *Myths of Empire: Domestic Politics and International Ambition* (Ithaca: Cornell University Press, 1991); Alan Cassels, *Ideology and International Relations in the Modern World* (New York: Routledge, 1996); Stephen M. Walt, *The Origins of Alliances* (Ithaca: Cornell University Press, 1987).

I do not explore the impact of political ideologies on outcomes according to a strictly inside-out logic of decision making. Instead, I examine how the *ideological distance* separating actors impacts their foreign policy choices. The same actors are thus likely to adopt very different policies depending on the ideological nature of the *other* actors in the system. Strictly unit-level arguments cannot make this claim.

This distinction is important because it determines how we understand the ultimate sources of states' policies. Specifically, are some states by nature peaceful or aggressive (as many domestic theories of foreign policy assert), or do these states tend to be aggressive or peaceful depending on the ideological environment in which they operate? When we see leaders' behaviors dramatically altering due to domestic changes in other states, it is very likely that the effects of the ideological distances dividing them—rather than those of ideological content—are at work since ideological content in these instances is constant.

Similarly, I do not assert that the principal manner by which ideologies affect politicians' foreign policy choices is by giving them unique interests. I assume that leaders' key goals are the protection of both their domestic power and the security of their state. Ideologies do not alter these objectives. Instead, ideologies affect leaders' policies by pushing them to adopt particular international strategies for realizing these two sets of goals. Ideologies impact the strategy-formulation process by shaping decision makers' views as to which states are likely threats and supports to their interests. For example, the great powers' policies toward one another throughout the Concert of Europe were much more cooperative than they had been during the 1790s, not because their leaders' interests had radically changed, but because the ideological environment (defined in terms of the degree of ideological differences dividing states' leaders) in which they operated had substantially altered. This environmental change pushed decision makers to adopt very different strategies in order to realize their central domestic and international interests.

A third contribution of the argument is that it lays the foundation for the creation of a more integrative framework between ideological and power variables for the study of the central dynamics of international politics. Although the primary purpose of the book is to reveal the critical impact that ideologies have on states' foreign policies, the same causal logic—as I detail in a subsequent section in this chapter—also illuminates specific ways in which power variables are likely to have significant and independent effects on these decisions. Thus I point both to areas in which either power or ideological variables provide superior analytic leverage in relation to the other, and to particular ways in which both types of variables combine to affect outcomes.

OTHER "IDEATIONAL" INTERNATIONAL RELATIONS THEORIES

My argument differs in key ways from other prominent studies of international relations that assert an important role for ideational variables in the policy-formulation process, including democratic peace, constructivist, and balance-of-threat theories, as well as Samuel Huntington's "clash of civilizations" thesis.

The causal logic provides a more comprehensive argument for the role of ideological variables in international politics than democratic peace analyses (the proposition that established liberal democracies do not war with one another). Unlike these studies, my argument is neither limited to the foreign policies of liberal leaders, nor does it reduce politicians' ideological beliefs primarily to only those principles that determine regime type. Moreover, democratic peace analyses tend to concentrate exclusively on the threats to leaders' security interests that are posed by decision makers' ideological rivals, while ignoring the domestic threats posed by these actors. I correct these shortcomings.

My argument shares constructivism's emphasis on issues of identity as a key cause of states' foreign policies. However, I examine the effects of ideational variables that many of the most prominent constructivists exclude from their analyses. Systemic, or third-image, constructivists, led by Alexander Wendt, "bracket the corporate sources of state identity and interests [i.e., the domestic attributes of actors, including political ideologies], and concentrate entirely on the constitutive role of international social interaction, exploring how structural contexts, systemic processes, and strategic practice produce and reproduce . . . state identities."[29]

To a great extent I reverse this analytic strategy. My goal is to examine the effects of domestic-ideological variables on leaders' understandings of the international environment and their consequent foreign policy behavior. All that the causal logic requires are assessments made by statesmen of the ideological distances separating their legitimating principles from those of the other key actors in the system. Neither interaction among these decision makers nor participation in shared international social structures is necessary in making these determinations. Indeed, it is precisely the fact that ideological rivals do *not* share similar visions for ordering the political world that results in threatening relations among them. Moreover, when ideological rivals do interact, they will quite often misunderstand one another's communications. In these cases, interaction does not result in agreement or participation in shared social structures, but the opposite. Third-image constructivists and my analysis thus utilize different logics to explain the sources of states' foreign policies.

29. Christian Reus-Smit, *The Moral Purpose of the State* (Princeton: Princeton University Press, 1999), 166.

This book's causal logic possesses important differences and similarities with Stephen Walt's balance-of-threat theory, which is one of the more significant reformulations of realist theories in the literature. In Walt's first book, *The Origins of Alliances,* the differences between balance-of-threat theory and my argument are pronounced. In this work, Walt downplays the impact of ideological variables in affecting politicians' perceptions of threat and concomitant systemic outcomes (in the case of this book, alliance formation). In *The Origins of Alliances,* Walt describes the effects of ideological variables on states' alliances as either spurious or relatively unimportant when compared to the impact of other variables on these outcomes.[30]

Walt's understanding of the role of ideological variables in affecting leaders' perceptions of threat and related foreign policy choices changed significantly in *Revolution and War.* In this second version of balance-of-threat theory, Walt asserts that changes in the defining ideologies of states tend to increase their leaders' perceptions of threat and thus the likelihood of conflict by creating new interests in states; by shaping the perceptions that leaders have of the external environment; by increasing leaders' fears of subversion; and by increasing the likelihood of misperception among actors due to the rapid turnover of diplomatic personnel.[31] I complement this second version of balance-of-threat theory by developing in greater detail than Walt the theoretical foundations (e.g., demonstration effects, social identity, and communications theories) upon which the causal mechanisms common to Walt's argument and my own are based.

Despite some important similarities between my argument and Walt's balance-of-threat theory as articulated in *Revolution and War,* key analytical differences between the two arguments remain. Perhaps most important, Walt examines the international effects created by a specific and ephemeral situation: the distorting and ambiguous circumstances that are likely to arise in the immediate aftermath of a successful revolution. Consequently, according to Walt's argument, ideologies' most important international effects should in most cases last for only a few years after a revolutionary regime comes to power. Over time, "relations between the revolutionary states and the rest of the system will become increasingly 'normal'" as the former become socialized into accepting less ideological interpretations of the world.[32]

My causal logic, in contrast, applies to any relationship among actors dedicated to different legitimating principles, regardless of how a particular regime was created (i.e., through revolutionary or evolutionary means) or how long a current type of polity was in existence. As a result, I

---

30. Walt, *Origins of Alliances,* 39, 40, 139, 143, 182, 184, 185, 198, 200–202, 214, 217.
31. Walt, *Revolution and War,* chap. 2.
32. Ibid., 43.

am able to explain, for example, why key American and Soviet leaders continued to view their relationship in ideological terms seventy years after the Russian Revolution in 1917, and why a similar dynamic occurred between the old regime powers and France until the Bourbon restoration in 1815, which was twenty-six years after the French Revolution. If Walt's analysis is correct, surely these periods of time would be sufficient for these actors to become socialized into the workings of the international system to the point where neither they nor the other powers viewed one another as ideological threats.[33]

Finally, I offer very different predictions for the future of international relations from Samuel Huntington's "clash of civilizations" thesis. To Huntington, individuals' "civilizational," and not ideological, identities will be the principal determinant of the dominant patterns of international cooperation and conflict in the future.

Huntington defines a civilization as "the highest cultural grouping of people and the broadest level of cultural identity people have short of that which distinguishes humans from other species." He lists eight major civilizations in the contemporary system: Western, Confucian, Japanese, Islamic, Hindu, Slavic-Orthodox, Latin American, and possibly African.[34] If the "clash of civilizations" thesis is correct, states within the same civilization should be inclined to cooperate, and states from different civilizations should tend to develop conflictual relations.

I agree that leaders' transnational identities will be central to their foreign policies; I disagree over the key components of this identity. People within the same civilization (culture) can be dedicated to very different ideological objectives (e.g., the creation of different political and economic institutions), just as individuals from different civilizations can share ideological beliefs. This fact allows the two analyses to make very different predictions. For example, I predict that liberals in the Islamic world will tend to view the Western democracies as a much smaller threat to their key domestic and international interests than will nonliberal parties in the region. As a result, the spread of liberal regimes throughout the Middle East will tend to benefit the Western powers' interests. According to Huntington's thesis, in contrast, because civilizational identities trump ideological ones, Islamic leaders' dedication to political liberalism will do little to blunt the antagonism between Western and Islamic cultures. Contemporary developments in the international system will likely allow for a test of these different predictions.

33. My argument is more comprehensive than Walt's in another important way. I explain both how large ideological differences among leaders translate into high perceptions of threat, as well as how substantial ideological similarities tend to generate cooperative relations. Walt's analysis applies primarily only to the former relationship.
34. Samuel P. Huntington, "The Clash of Civilizations?" *Foreign Affairs* 72, no. 3 (Summer 1993): 24–25.

POWER VARIABLES AND THEORIES

Neo-realist theories offer the most direct challenge to my understanding of the sources of decision makers' perceptions of threat. Consequently, these theories constitute the principal competing arguments to my own.

To neo-realists, leaders' understanding of the dangers posed by the other actors in the system are almost exclusively a product of relative power distributions. The greater the power disparity among states, the greater the tendency for the weaker to fear the intentions of the stronger, and thus the greater the incentives to try to reduce this capabilities gap through internal and external balancing. In comparison to issues of relative power, decision makers will pay relatively little attention to ideological variables in making their most important security choices. As Kenneth Waltz explains, to realists "considerations of power dominate considerations of ideology."[35]

If neo-realists' understandings of the sources of leaders' threat perceptions are correct, then the evidence should reveal two prominent tendencies. First, we should see decision makers' perceptions of threat and behavior more consistently tracking changes in the international distribution of power than shifts in any other variable. Second, we should not see systematic, substantial differences in foreign policy strategies among different groups of leaders in the same state. Because the international power variables confronting all decision makers of the same state are identical, we should expect to see different parties of the same state adopt fairly similar security policies.

This book's hypotheses are falsified if these neo-realist predictions are confirmed. A primary goal is therefore to demonstrate the latter's inadequacies. This does not mean, however, that my ultimate objective is simply to demonstrate the empirical shortcomings of neo-realism in the study of international politics. This analytical approach is now a well-worn exercise in the international relations literature.

My ultimate goal is more positive than negative. Although I reject the strict materialist analyses of neo-realist theories by showing the systematic importance of ideological variables to states' security policies, I also recognize that realist theories do provide important insights into the study of international relations (though at some points in time more than at others). Consequently, after demonstrating that ideological variables should be considered central to the great powers' key foreign policies over the last two hundred years, my next objective is to provide a framework for the creation of a more synthetic analysis that combines insights of both realist and ideological arguments.

35. Kenneth N. Waltz, "Realist Thought, Neorealist Theory," *Journal of International Affairs* 44, no. 1 (Spring/Summer 1990): 31.

Power variables relate to my argument in two principal ways. First, the effects of relative power concerns combine with various dimensions of the causal logic to supplement and refine some of its predictions. In this scenario, realist arguments and my own provide complementary insights into core dynamics of international politics. Second, under particular conditions, the effects of power variables are likely to trump the impact of ideological distances on leaders' foreign policies. Thus I do not deny that realist theories are at times likely to provide a superior explanation of states' security policies than my own. The key is to determine under what conditions they are most likely to do so.

Power Variables as a Supplement to the Causal Logic

There are three principal ways in which power factors are likely to combine with my argument to supplement and refine its hypotheses. The first is tied to the central predictions of the conflict-probability causal mechanism, which asserts that ideological rivals are likely both to attribute hostile intent to one another and to believe that their interests are bound to conflict. This relationship, and its converse, should hold regardless of power relationships among states. Thus decision makers should possess hostile attitudes toward polities founded on rival legitimating ideals regardless if power configurations are ones of equality, superiority, or inferiority. An analogous claim can be made about cooperative relations that are likely to obtain among similarly legitimated regimes.

Relative power concerns will tend, however, to exacerbate the feelings of amity and enmity predicted by the patterns of ideological affinity in the system. If leaders believe that conflictual relations are highly likely with a state of great relative power capacity, these individuals will invariably be more fearful of this state than if this power condition did not exist. Thus increases in the relative power of an ideological enemy will tend to make a bad situation worse, but decreases in the same state's power will not eliminate antagonistic feelings. Similarly, if politicians believe that cooperative relations are likely with a great power, they are likely to view this state even more sympathetically since its power capabilities increase the likelihood of realizing the interests that unite these countries.

Second, although ideological variables will play a significant role in determining which states leaders view as likely enemies, power factors will largely affect what policies decision makers are able to adopt to address these threats. In order to sustain a geopolitical conflict, especially either hot or cold wars, states must possess a certain level of capabilities in relation to their adversaries. Without sufficient relative power, leaders cannot maintain highly coercive or effective deterrent policies against even those states that decision makers view as extremely threatening to their interests. Ideology largely determines the threat; relative power circumscribes the means available to deal with these dangers.

A third way in which the insights of realism unite with those of this book to provide a more accurate description of world politics revolves around the concept of uncertainty in international relations. A fundamental tenet of realist theory is that because state leaders can never be completely certain about the intentions of others, and because intentions can change in the future, relative power concerns must always be an important concern to decision makers. There are important elements of truth in these claims. Nevertheless, realist assertions in this area are too broad as currently formulated. I refine them by showing how the nature of the ideological relationships among actors limits the conditions under which uncertainty is likely to be a powerful stimulant to international conflict.

The conflict-probability causal mechanism asserts that ideological distance will be a key determinant of leaders' assessments of one another's intentions. The greater the ideological similarities among decision makers, the greater their tendency to attribute benign intentions to one another. Consequently, in situations of high ideological affinity, the potency of uncertainty as a catalyst of international conflict will be noticeably weakened because statesmen will tend to assume the best about the ambitions of those actors within their ideological community.

This insight generated by the conflict-probability mechanism is reinforced by the key hypothesis of the communications mechanism: the greater the ideological similarities among actors, the greater their ability of communicating effectively with one another. Effective communication allows statesmen the possibility of mitigating the pernicious consequences of the security dilemma by increasing the likelihood that status quo powers will be able to convey to one another the limited nature of their foreign policy ambitions. Thus among states within an ideological community, the problem of uncertainty is likely to be reduced because leaders' signals of benign intent have a greater chance of being understood and believed under these circumstances than in others.

This analysis does not mean that a high degree of ideological similarities among states' leaders will eliminate the problem of uncertainty in international relations. Statesmen can never be completely certain that high levels of ideological similarities will lead to peaceful interactions among them. Moreover, there is no guarantee that states will always remain within a particular ideological community; domestic revolutions are always a possibility. Consequently, leaders will in many cases hedge against the possibility that states' ideological identities, and thus their policies, can change in the future. It is worth noting that although this latter concern about states' future intentions is consistent with realist analyses, the foundation of this worry in this particular instance, i.e., that states' policies are predominantly a product of ideological variables, is not. Thus I add to realist logic by revealing an additional factor that should heighten the problem of uncertainty in international politics.

The facts that leaders can never be completely certain about the intentions of others and that revolutions are always a possibility means that realists are most likely correct when they claim that the problem of uncertainty will be a perennial one in international relations. This fact places an important limit on my argument, and points again to the need to integrate the effects generated by both ideological and power variables in international politics into a more synthetic analysis. Nevertheless, in the right ideological circumstances the potency of uncertainty as a cause of international conflict can be significantly mitigated. Although the *possibility* of intentions changing or leaders misunderstanding them will always remain, statesmen will tend to believe that the *probability* of their counterparts within their ideological community adopting highly aggressive policies will be low. Rational leaders will base their security decisions, especially such costly and risky actions as preventive hostilities, primarily on the probability of future conflict with other nations and not just the possibility that such conflict can result. Consequently, reducing decision makers' estimates of the likelihood of future conflict with particular states will most likely weaken the incentives to initiate confrontational policies with these states in the present.

Conditions for Confirming the Hypotheses

The previous section demonstrates how realist insights and my causal logic are likely to combine to shape outcomes. The hypotheses of these two sets of arguments will, however, frequently generate mutually exclusive predictions rather than symbiotic ones. My argument is likely to be most powerful relative to realist theories the greater the fragility of a particular regime. I define "regime fragility" by two criteria: a particular group of leaders' hold on power must be fairly tenuous, and the ideological shifts resulting from a change in leadership must be substantial (i.e., the ideological effects of this party change must in some way repudiate core legitimating principles of the previous rulers).

America today would not meet the test for regime fragility because shifts in power from Republicans to Democrats do not result in major ideological changes on core issues like regime type or economic institutions. France in the 1930s would pass the test because the parties of the left and right had nearly equal power and they vehemently opposed one another on key ideological issues, particularly whether France should replace its capitalist economy with a socialist one.

When both conditions of regime fragility are met, leaders' fears of subversion due to the success of their ideological enemies in other states will tend to be particularly acute. Conditions of regime fragility are also likely to make politicians' ideological identities more salient than under different

[27]

conditions. Periods of intense domestic struggles with ideological enemies will push leaders to be highly conscious of their ideological differences and similarities. The causal mechanisms are likely to be very robust in these situations since decision makers will be particularly inclined to identify closely with their ideological allies in other states and to oppose their international ideological enemies.

Realist arguments will tend to be increasingly powerful in relation to my own when one of the following three conditions is met. First, realist predictions are most likely to be upheld when leaders confront *unambiguous* and *substantial* threats to their state's security, such as occurs when a state is either under military attack or is highly likely to be so in the near future. In these circumstances, power-political concerns will tend to override the impact of ideological variables on outcomes. Perhaps most notably, in extremely threatening security environments, ideological antipathy to particular regimes is unlikely to provide an insurmountable barrier to an alliance. Thus when Britain was under attack by Germany in the 1940s, Britain's key leaders were desperate to conclude an alliance with the Soviet Union despite many of these individuals' continued aversion to communism. Similarly, when experience clearly demonstrates that decision makers' presumption of amity toward those actors with whom they share important ideological objectives is misplaced, these individuals are likely to stop basing their assessments of these other actors' intentions on their ideological similarities. For example, Germany's invasion of Czechoslovakia in March 1939 destroyed most British and French conservatives' belief that Adolf Hitler possessed limited international ambitions. A similar statement can be made about Soviet views of China after Mao Zedong's hostile rhetoric and actions after 1957.

Although these statements are important concessions to realist arguments, we must be very careful not to exaggerate the conditions under which realist variables are likely to supersede the effects of ideological distances on states' security policies. The assertions in the previous paragraph do *not* mean that ideological considerations are likely to shape leaders' foreign policies only when security threats are low, as realists claim.[36] The evidence presented in the following chapters demonstrates the centrality of ideological variables to leaders' security policies in such periods as the 1790s and 1930s in Europe, the 1950s in Asia, and the U.S.-Soviet relationship in the 1980s. No reasonable interpretation of these periods could view them as ones of benign security threats. The principal decision makers of the times clearly did not believe them to be so.

---

36. Walt, *Origins of Alliances*, 37–38; Kenneth Waltz, "Reflections on *Theory of International Politics:* A Response to My Critics," in *Neorealism and Its Critics*, ed. Robert O. Keohane (New York: Columbia University Press, 1986), 329.

A more accurate description of the conditions under which ideological distances are most likely to shape leaders' security policies is not when international threats are "low," but when they are *uncertain*, i.e., situations in which a state has not unambiguously demonstrated its enmity toward another. In the absence of a clear and substantial danger to a state's security, ideological variables will be central to how decision makers assess one another's international intentions. Thus under conditions of uncertainty, different groups of leaders will tend to interpret the same evidence in very different ways. For example, in the 1930s most Western conservatives required virtually unambiguous proof of Hitler's bellicose intentions before they understood him to be a probable hegemonic threat to the Western powers' security, while most British and French socialists required significantly less evidence before they reached the same conclusion. Similar statements can be made about British Tories' and Whigs' views of Russia during the Concert of Europe, the attitudes toward the Soviet Union held by Chinese proponents and opponents of the Great Leap Forward in the late 1950s, and Soviet old and New Thinkers' views of the United States in the 1980s. Because conditions of uncertainty will dominate most states' security relations most of the time, we can expect ideological differences to be central to how leaders understand their security environment in a correspondingly high percentage of the cases.

Similarly, there is no doubt that coalitions among ideological enemies during wartime (e.g., the Grand Alliance of Britain, America, and the Soviet Union during the 1940s, the Sino-U.S. alignment in the 1970s and 1980s, and America's alliances with various dictatorial regimes throughout the Cold War and during the current "war on terrorism") reveal the power of realist theories and the limits of ideological explanations of international threats. However, ideological distances will very often be central to why states find themselves in situations like these in the first place. For example, in the 1930s ideological factors were critical to both British and French leaders' failure to form alliances with the other great powers against Nazi Germany (outcomes that facilitated the outbreak of great power conflict) and to the Nazis' preference for waging a hegemonic war. Without the effects of ideological distances on outcomes throughout the 1930s, Britain very likely would not have been placed in a situation that necessitated forming an alliance with the USSR.

Furthermore, when necessity dictates that ideological enemies ally against a greater threat, these coalitions are likely to break apart as soon as the common enemy is defeated, as happened, for example, between the Soviet Union and America after the Second World War and the United States and China when the Cold War ended. In contrast, alliances among states dedicated to similar ideological objectives are likely to long outlive the power-political threat, as was the case for Austria, Prussia, and Russia after the Napoleonic Wars and the NATO alliance after the Cold War.

[29]

It is also important to recognize that even when states confront unambiguous threats to their safety, ideological variables are likely to continue to shape key dimensions of leaders' security policies. When states are at war with their ideological rivals, decision makers are likely both to attribute their enmity to their ideological differences and to designate regime change for their adversary to be a preeminent war-fighting objective. Wars among ideological enemies will therefore tend to become total conflicts as one side or both tries to convert the other to its own domestic institutions and principles. This was the case throughout the wars of the French Revolution, various attacks against minor powers by members of the Concert of Europe in the nineteenth century, during the Second World War, and America's attacks on Afghanistan and Iraq during the "war on terrorism." Realist theories cannot explain these policies.

The second condition under which realist arguments are likely to acquire greater saliency in relation to ideological variables occurs when there are no significant ideological differences among the principal actors in the system from the perspective of the key decision makers in a particular state (e.g., Soviet leaders' views of the other great powers during the interwar period or the Western democracies' views of one another in the contemporary system). In this situation, ideological variables become less useful in determining which of these states constitutes the greatest threat to a particular country's interests at any particular point in time. Some other factors, most notably power-political concerns, must of necessity fill this gap.

Given this analysis, it is not surprising that Soviet leaders in the 1930s tried to ally with the Western democracies against Nazi Germany or that throughout the Cold War America aligned with dictatorships, including communist China, against the Soviet Union. In these cases, leaders formed (or tried to form) alliances with ideological rivals against states that were both greater power-political threats and roughly *equal ideological dangers*. When states are equally threatening in ideological terms, it only makes sense that power-political considerations will become of greater importance in making differentiations among these actors in terms of the level and immediacy of the security threats confronting a particular country. "Realist" behavior, however, is most likely to obtain only as long as a given state's key leaders continue to see no significant ideological differences among the other major actors in the system. For example, although British Whigs for much of the 1820s adopted policies toward the other great powers that were consistent with realist balance-of-power theory, once France experienced the July Revolution of 1830—which made France a much more liberal regime and thus much ideologically closer to the Whigs' principles than the other continental powers—Whigs' policies changed substantially. After the regime change in France, Whigs for most of the remainder of the Concert of Europe pursued an alliance with France that was directed against the absolutist monarchies of Prussia, Austria, and Russia.

[30]

Furthermore, recognizing that State A's leaders are ideologically equidistant from the other key actors in the system tells us nothing about the size of the ideological gap separating these decision makers. State A's decision makers can perceive few ideological differences among their counterparts in the other great powers, but understand the distance separating their legitimating principles from those of the other key actors to be either small or large. In either case, power-political concerns are likely to be of increasing importance in determining which state(s) constitute the greatest threats to A's interests, but the size of the ideological differences dividing these decision makers will largely determine the magnitude of this threat. For example, France's current leaders may on any given issue move closer or farther apart to Britain, Germany, or Italy based largely on pertinent geopolitical concerns (just as Soviet politicians did in the 1930s), but French leaders' overall sense of the threats posed by these states will be much lower than that perceived by Soviet decision makers in the 1930s.

The third and final circumstance in which states' leaders are most likely to adhere to realist prescriptions in relation to my argument occurs when these individuals tend not to recognize that other political forms are plausible. If leaders currently confront no prominent rival to their own ideology, and if they believe that no such belief systems are likely to arise in the foreseeable future, the incentives pushing decision makers to view one another as participants in a transnational ideological community will likely attenuate. In short, without an ideological outgroup, there can be no ideological ingroup, even if states' leaders objectively share many ideological beliefs. This analysis helps explain why there was such a radical break in great power relations after the French Revolution. Before this time, Europe's key decision makers gave little thought to the notion that the European powers could be anything other than divine-right monarchies.[37] This lack of foresight limited the sense of community among the great powers' leaders, despite their substantial, objective ideological similarities. By demonstrating that the great powers could experience a change in regime type, the French Revolution was critical to the creation of a powerful sense of ideological solidarity among the old regime states in the years following the Napoleonic Wars, as we shall see in Chapter 3.

RESEARCH METHOD

The Independent Variable: The Degree of Ideological
Similarities among Decision Makers

The independent variable of the argument is the degree of ideological similarities among leaders across states. Operationalizing this variable

37. R. R. Palmer, *The World of the French Revolution* (New York: Harper and Row, 1971), 26.

requires a two-step process. The first objective is to understand the core ide-ological beliefs of a particular group of decision makers in any given state. Again, by "ideological beliefs" I am referring to leaders' central domestic political, economic, and social goals. Thus unlike most studies that examine the impact of political ideologies in international relations, this one does not reduce individuals' ideological beliefs primarily to only those principles that determine regime type (narrowly conceived in terms of institutional structures, e.g., democracy, republic, monarchy, autocracy, totalitarian). Any principle that is critical to politicians' vision for ordering domestic politics is included in my operationalization of political ideologies.

In addition to regime type, the two most important ideological goals of different groups of decision makers examined in the case studies involve views on the preferred system of political economy (e.g., laissez-faire cap-italism, welfare-state capitalism, socialism, and communism), and beliefs about which groups within a particular state should be eligible for the full rights of citizenship (i.e., do all groups in a particular society have equal rights, or are some systematically privileged over others).[38]

In order to capture the often substantial ideological differences among different groups of politicians in the same state, I operationalize decision makers' ideological beliefs by party ideology. I measure parties' core legitimating principles on the subjects discussed in the previous para-graphs by examining parties' political platforms and mission statements, and the writings and speeches made by party leaders.

This method of operationalizing leaders' ideological beliefs is not with-out potential analytical problems. Perhaps most notably, basing leaders' ideological principles on more than just institutional structures (or regime type narrowly defined) and including such considerations as the pre-ferred system of political economy and views on which domestic groups should be eligible for the full rights of citizenship means that invariably there will be cases in which leaders are torn by cross-cutting ideological loyalties. For example, both Nazi Germany and the Soviet Union pos-sessed similar institutional structures (both were totalitarian regimes), but the Nazis' racist, anti-communist belief system was in total opposi-tion to the Soviet Union's defining socioeconomic principles and the eth-nic composition of many of its peoples. In the same time period, British

---

38. Examining the relative statuses of different groups within a particular state has potential overlap with nationalistic beliefs. Core tenets of nationalism are that humanity is naturally divided into different nations, and that every nation should have its own state. Taken together, these tenets are an ideology as I have defined the term because they articulate a particular vision for ordering domestic politics. (Nationalism is sometimes defined in terms of international behavior, e.g., by acting aggressively or following realist prescriptions; in these cases, nationalism is not consistent with my definition of a political ideology.) When a nationalistic state confronts a multinational regime, threat perceptions are likely to be high, as are relations between states that systematically suppress the other's dominant ethnic group.

conservatives shared most French Socialists' commitment to republican-ism, but these parties' views on the preferred system of political economy were almost totally antithetical. In cases such as these, which dimension of parties' legitimating ideals wins out?

Because there is no compelling reason why we should *ex ante* privilege, for example, regime principles over socioeconomic ones, it is difficult to solve this problem of indeterminacy in a methodologically progressive manner. Yet some considerations with regard to my analysis are worth keeping in mind. In the five historical periods examined, there are rela-tively few examples of leaders being torn by cross-cutting ideological loy-alties. The large majority of the time either all the ideological "arrows" pointed in the same direction (i.e., leaders of different states opposed one another in all dimensions of their ideological beliefs), or one type of legit-imating principle was so preeminent in a particular era that it trumped any cross-cutting effects that other legitimating ideals may have created. Moreover, the problem of theoretical indeterminacy created by cross-cut-ting ideological loyalties does not imply that ideology is unimportant to the policy-making process, only that it is difficult to determine *ex ante* which ideological considerations will be most important in a given instance. Demonstrating that some set of ideological variables played a key role in systematically shaping leaders' foreign policy choices is still an important contribution to the literature.

After coding the ideological beliefs of different groups of decision mak-ers, I then make comparisons across states in order to ascertain the degree of ideological differences dividing them. It is worth reiterating that although I examine the *domestic* objectives of ideologies to operationalize the independent variable, I do not rely on ideologies' *international behav-ioral prescriptions* to inform the predictions of the causal logic. Hence the differences between ideological "distance" and ideological "content."

Determining the ideological distances dividing states' leaders is obvi-ously not an exact science since the variables involved are qualitative, not quantitative. To interpret the degree of ideological differences or similari-ties among decision makers across states, the following questions are par-ticularly important.[39] Do decision makers in State A explicitly emulate the ideological objectives of leaders in other regimes? Do different groups of decision makers use nearly identical language and speak of similar eco-nomic, social, and institutional objectives to legitimate their authority? Do groups of politicians in different states assert that they are members of the same transnational ideological group? How similar are states' meth-ods of political representation and economic institutions? Do decision

39. As an additional means of measuring ideological distance, and as a control for my cod-ing of this variable, I also rely on the judgments of other scholars who determined the ideo-logical distances among various actors for reasons other than testing my argument.

makers in a particular state espouse ideological objectives that leaders in other countries explicitly condemn for their own society? Do leaders in State A systematically violate the rights of groups that have equal or privileged statuses in State B?

Although it is difficult to determine precisely how wide the ideological distances are that divide various groups of decision makers in different states, a less daunting methodological exercise is to determine if the degree of ideological differences separating states' leaders becomes *greater* or *less* over time as a result of domestic-political shifts (e.g., party or regime changes) in one or more countries. When a party dedicated to different ideological goals from its predecessors comes to power, we can code in a relatively straightforward manner whether or not this party change led to an increase or decrease in the ideological distances dividing this state's key decision makers from the other actors in the system, and we can do so without having to ascertain precisely how wide these ideological distances are. We can then observe if these changes on the independent variable led to changes in politicians' perceptions of threat and behavior in ways consistent with my argument.

This method of operationalizing the argument's independent variable helps to control for two problems that are especially prominent in ideational analyses: those of tautology and spuriousness. The causal logic avoids the problem of tautology because it measures the degree of ideological similarities among states' leaders independently of behavior. I control for the problem of spuriousness, most notably the *realist counterhypothesis* that power variables are the ultimate source of both leaders' understandings of their ideological relationships and their foreign policy choices,[40] in three principal ways. First, throughout the empirical chapters, I demonstrate that decision makers' understandings of the ideological relationships among states were clearly and directly tied to objective domestic developments (in terms of constitutional, institutional, and party changes) in various countries. This pattern reduces the chances that changes in the independent variable were primarily a product of factors omitted from the analysis.

Second, throughout the case studies, I repeatedly point to the fact that outcomes diverged from what power-centered theories predict. Thus leaders' understandings of the ideological relationships among them and their foreign policy decisions frequently either did not alter when power factors fluctuated significantly, or the former variables changed when the distribution of power remained fairly constant. Demonstrating that states' key foreign policy choices consistently did not coincide with changes in power variables is important not only because this method

40. Cf. Ido Oren, "The Subjectivity of the 'Democratic' Peace: Changing U.S. Perceptions of Imperial Germany," *International Security* 20, no. 2 (Fall 1995): 147–184.

helps to control for the problem of spuriousness, but because it reveals the potency of ideological changes in affecting key outcomes even in potentially adverse material circumstances.

Third, I demonstrate that leaders' key foreign policy decisions frequently vary to a significant extent by party affiliation. If leaders' ideological beliefs were either inconsequential to their security policies or epiphenomenal of their state's placement in the international distribution of power, we would expect that decision makers from the same state would adopt similar security policies regardless of party affiliation since the international power variables confronting all citizens of the same state are identical.

The Dependent Variable: Leaders' Perceptions of Threat

There are two dominant dimensions to the operationalization of leaders' perceptions of threat. First, which state(s) were the principal objects of a particular group of leaders' security fears? Second, to what degree were these other powers feared? Both these components will be revealed primarily by examining leaders' public and private statements on these issues.

An important dimension of my analysis is to examine how perceptions of threat are translated into specific foreign policy strategies. In these cases, threat is an intervening variable between ideological differences among states' leaders and these other variables that are further down the causal chain. Because the particular behaviors and outcomes predicted by the causal logic are sufficiently specific and descriptive, most of these latter variables can be operationalized in a very straightforward manner. Specific behaviors and outcomes that fall into this category include the composition of alliances; the threat or use of force up to and including major war; trends in defense spending; if leaders tried to contain rival powers by strategically, culturally, and economically isolating them; if statesmen provided economic, diplomatic, or military support to particular countries; and if leaders attempted to export, especially by force, particular institutional structures and ideological beliefs to other actors in the system.

Contextual Variables: Objective and Subjective Measurements of Ideological Distance

I operationalize the degree of ideological differences dividing states' leaders primarily by examining objective measurements of this variable, not by actors' *perceptions* of it. In testing the argument's hypotheses, I assume that there is in most cases a high degree of correspondence between actors' perceptions and objective measurements of their ideological relationships.

Relying primarily on objective assessments of ideological distances rather than decision makers' perceptions of them helps to control for the problem of spuriousness that I discuss above.

There are, however, specific circumstances in which leaders' perceptions of the degree of ideological differences dividing them are likely to vary to a significant extent from objective measurements of this variable. In other words, in some cases decision makers are likely to view the same ideological distance dividing them (measured objectively) as smaller or larger depending on circumstance. By identifying the conditions in which there are most likely to be substantial differences between leaders' understanding of their ideological relationships and objective measurements of them, we can both predict when the argument's hypotheses are less likely to be supported, as well as better judge the significance of various violations of these hypotheses.

There are three prominent contextual variables that are likely to push decision makers to possess significantly different perceptions of ideological distances in relation to objective assessments of this variable.[41] The first of these variables is the number of prominent ideologies in the system. When states' key decision makers are divided into two primary ideological groupings, it is most often clear which leaders belong in which ideological group, as well as the size of the ideological differences dividing them. During the Cold War, for example, it was relatively easy to determine which of the great powers belonged in the liberal-capitalist camp and which belonged in the communist one. It was also clear that the ideological distance dividing the two groups was quite large.

Assessments of ideological distance become much more complicated if additional prominent ideologies are brought into the mix. When states' leaders are divided into three or more ideological groups, some of these groups will very likely be ideologically closer to one another than to others. When this occurs, there will be a natural tendency for decision makers to focus on the greatest ideological threat in the system, and discount (at least partially) differences with lesser ideological dangers.

A key implication of this claim is that the same ideological distance dividing two groups of decision makers in a strictly bilateral relationship might not appear as pronounced if a greater ideological threat is added into leaders' calculations. For example, many British and French socialists in the 1920s understood the ideological differences with the Soviet Union to be large because of the latter's totalitarian regime type. These differences, however, were to a greater extent downplayed after the fascist revolutions in Italy and Germany. Once there was a greater ideological

---

41. I mentioned a fourth such variable earlier: actors' judgments about the plausibility of different political ideologies arising to challenge their own. When leaders tend not to believe that rival ideologies are viable, they are more likely to discount the (objectively) high levels of ideological similarities uniting them.

danger in the system, British and French socialists were more likely to emphasize their ideological similarities with the Soviet Union than before. Objectively large ideological differences thus appeared smaller with the introduction of another, even more different, ideological group into the system.

A second variable that is likely to push decision makers to hold significantly different perceptions of ideological distances in relation to their objective measurements are actors' reference points. Ideological changes in other states may appear to be of greater or lesser consequence to outside observers depending on the latter's ideological expectations for these states. When leaders in State A expect the ideological differences with State B to continue to be large, an unanticipated narrowing of this gap may lead A's decision makers to perceive a greater amount of ideological affinity after the change than objectively exists. For example, the old regime powers in Europe after the French Revolution no doubt felt a much greater degree of ideological affinity for Napoleon's dictatorship in France from 1799 to 1802 because he succeeded a revolutionary regime. If Napoleon had supplanted the Bourbons instead of the Second Directory, the other great powers most likely would have viewed him as a much greater ideological threat than they originally did.

Similarly, when leaders in State A expect those in State B to remain close ideological allies, movement away from this reference point may result in perceptions of much larger ideological differences than actually exist. For example, Mao's move to the left ideologically in the late 1950s may have had a greater impact on Soviet leaders' views of the PRC because they expected China's ideology not to deviate substantially from the Soviet Union's. A similar outcome may have occurred between Britain's foreign secretary, Lord Palmerston, and King Louis-Philippe of France during the late 1830s when the latter refused to support aggressively the liberal cause in Spain. In these cases, unrealized expectations may have contributed to exaggerations of ideological differences.

A third contextual variable that is likely to impact leaders' assessments of ideological differences is what I label "wave of the future" effects. When a particular political ideology is on the march, meaning that it is gaining power and prestige at the expense of other belief systems, the differences separating this ideology from others may seem greater than in different circumstances. Thus the ideological differences separating liberal-capitalist and communist leaders may have seemed larger to Western leaders in the 1950s when communism was gaining converts than in the 1980s when this ideology had clearly lost much of its international appeal.

When any of these contextual variables are in play, the argument's hypotheses are less likely to be supported. Yet violations due to these variables are less significant than in other circumstances. When any of the contextual variables are in effect, ideological distances are still shaping outcomes, though it is actors' (somewhat distorted) perceptions of this variable, not objective assessments of it, that are the key to the process. As long as it can be demonstrated that leaders' perceptions of ideological distances are not epiphenomenal of power-political concerns, ideological variables in these instances should still be viewed as central determinants of policies.

Methodology and Case Study Selection

I test the argument's hypotheses by applying the methods of congruence procedure and process tracing to in-depth analyses of five historical systems. The purpose of the congruence procedure is to ascertain if outcomes correspond with my predictions. Process tracing examines leaders' decision-making processes in order to determine if they acted for the reasons hypothesized, or were instead motivated by some other considerations. Process tracing thus establishes causality and not just correlations among variables. An additional methodological benefit of process tracing is that it provides more tests for an argument (since each step in the policy-formulation process can be viewed as evidence that confirms or disconfirms various hypotheses) while maintaining a limited number of case studies.[42]

Given the broad scope of the case studies, especially in terms of both the number of years examined in each of the cases and the total number of great powers studied (with the language barriers that such an endeavor implies), I rely primarily on the numerous excellent secondary sources as the foundation to evaluate the hypotheses' validity, though primary sources are also included in the analysis. I have tried to mitigate any bias that may occur as a result of this method by using numerous sources, including those most widely respected, that describe the same events from several different perspectives.

The five international systems investigated are the 1790s in Europe, the era of the Concert of Europe (ca. 1815–48), the decade of the 1930s, Sino-Soviet relations from 1949 to 1960, and the period marking the end of the Cold War in the 1980s. I choose these cases for the following reasons. First, in each period at least one of the great powers experienced a change in regime type and/or the ascension to power of a political party dedicated to affecting major ideological changes in its state. These developments resulted in either an increase or decrease in the ideological distances separating the great powers' leaders. Such changes in the independent variable allow for tests of my hypotheses while attempting to

---

42. Gary King, Robert O. Keohane, and Sidney Verba, *Designing Social Inquiry: Scientific Inference in Qualitative Research* (Princeton: Princeton University Press, 1994), 226–227.

control for the effects of power variables on outcomes. The cases also provide variation in the types of ideologies in question (liberalism, monarchism, aristocratism, fascism, and communism are all represented), the states involved in the analysis, the time period examined, polarity, and perceptions of the offense-defense balance.

Second, power variables in these systems were quite often configured in ways that make for fairly easy tests of realist hypotheses. Most notably, power was frequently distributed such that it should have made for fairly straightforward predictions as to which state was the dominant threat in the system, as well as the level of the threat, and thus the balancing strategies that the other powers should have adopted to protect their security. Moreover, all the cases examine great powers' relations during either hot or cold wars, which are the times when realist explanations of states' foreign policies (according to realists' own accounts) are supposed to be the most potent. By implication of these facts, great power relations in these periods of history likely represent "hard cases" for my claims. This fact allows for a more rigorous testing of the argument's explanatory power.

Finally, these cases are worthy of examination because the intrinsic importance of each demands that we have an accurate understanding of their key dynamics.

I now turn to my case study examinations. I begin with an analysis of great power relations in Europe after the French Revolution in 1789. My central question in this and subsequent chapters is always the same: What impact did the degree of ideological similarities and differences among decision makers have on their perceptions of threats and consequent foreign policy choices?

[2]

The Three Wars of the French Revolution

On the eve of the French Revolution in 1789, the likelihood of war between France and the other great powers of Europe was very small. Austria was racked with rising debt, faced open rebellion in its possessions in the Netherlands, and was bogged down in a war with the Ottoman Empire. Russia was involved in two wars of its own: one with Sweden and one with Turkey, and its leaders desired to dismember a third state, Poland. A primary foreign policy objective of Great Britain's decision makers was to maintain their country's position of neutrality vis-à-vis continental affairs. Although Frederick William II, king of Prussia, had an insatiable desire for territorial acquisitions, he was much more interested in augmenting his possessions from the east (especially from Poland) than from France.[1] Finally, before the Revolution, France was "paralyzed by political chaos and financial bankruptcy," which were conditions that made its leaders' desire for peace especially acute.[2]

This favorable strategic climate for peace on the continent was obviously the calm before the storm, since within three years of the Revolution Europe would experience the first of a series of devastating wars that would continue for most of the subsequent twenty-three years. Although scholars are virtually unanimous in their collective belief that the French Revolution was in large part responsible for these wars, they are in disagreement as to which factors created by the Revolution are most responsible for the conflagrations that were to follow. An important divide

1. J. H. Clapham, *The Causes of the War of 1792* (New York: Octagon Books, 1969), 11.
2. T. C. W. Blanning, *The Origins of the French Revolutionary Wars* (New York: Longman, 1986), 50.

[40]

among scholars is whether the primary motives for hostility and war among the powers in the 1790s were primarily due to ideological variables or traditional conflicts of interest and power.

This chapter contributes to this debate by showing that the degree of ideological differences separating revolutionary France's leaders from their counterparts in the old regime powers was the key variable shaping these politicians' perceptions of the threats that the other countries posed to both their domestic interests and the security of their state. Although power variables did impact outcomes in significant ways, ideological concerns had the more profound effects on the key actors' most important international policies, including those that led to each of the major wars of the 1790s: the War of 1792 and the Wars of the First and Second Coalitions (1793–97 and 1798–1802, respectively), as well as those that brought the Wars of the French Revolution to an end.

THE ORIGINS OF THE WAR OF 1792

At first glance, it may appear unlikely that this book's argument can provide an adequate explanation of the origins of the Wars of the French Revolution. The Revolution occurred in the summer of 1789, yet war among the great powers did not break out until almost three years later in April of 1792. Moreover, there were not unusually high levels of threat and hostility among the powers until the summer of 1791. Because of the fairly long lag time between the ideological changes in France that accompanied the Revolution and high levels of hostility among the great powers, it appears unlikely that the ideological differences dividing the powers' leaders can explain the origins of their conflicts.[3]

This critique of an ideological explanation of the origins of the Wars of the French Revolution is flawed, however. From 1789 to 1791, the domestic developments in France represented a significant ideological threat to the nobility of the other great powers, but *not* particularly to the monarchs of these states. In fact, the monarchs in each of the other great powers to an important degree sympathized with the ideological changes in France that transpired from 1789 to 1791. It is therefore not surprising that hostility levels between the powers' heads of state remained fairly low in this period.

It was only after various domestic developments in France in the summer of 1791 that resulted in threats to the power and life of the French king that the monarchs of the other great powers viewed France as a significant ideological danger. Their relations with France quickly degenerated after this point, just as the argument predicts.

---

3. Ibid., 82, 122; Stephen M. Walt, *Revolution and War* (Ithaca: Cornell University Press, 1996), 62.

Pre-revolutionary France was a semi-feudal society that granted massive political and economic privileges to its nobility. Since the time of Louis XIV, the French aristocracy was given special access to key positions in government, the military, and the judiciary. As a result, nobility had monopolized the most important positions in these institutions. French nobility also enjoyed important economic benefits, including widespread seigneurial rights and tax exemptions.[4]

At its inception, the French Revolution was predominantly anti-aristocratic in nature. "The first meaning of equality in the Revolution," according to the historian R. R. Palmer, "was that the difference between noble and nonnoble should be abolished."[5] The Revolution ended many of the economic and political privileges enjoyed by the aristocratic classes, including the entire seigneurial system, many tax exemptions, the system of inequality of legal rights, and, above all, much of the special access to positions of political power.[6] Thus as a consequence of the Revolution, "the old regime had been in principle destroyed; equality of taxation and equality of opportunity had been in principle established."[7]

The most important French revolutionary leaders from 1789 to 1791 were not nearly as opposed to the French monarchy as they were to the aristocracy. These individuals did demand that France become a constitutional monarchy. This outcome limited the power of the king by granting more power to the representative branch of government and by enumerating various rights of citizenship that could not be violated even by the monarch. Nevertheless, the dominant group of revolutionary leaders from 1789 to 1791 (who for the most part were members of the moderate Patriot Party) wanted the king to retain significant political power. It was not until 1791 that groups dedicated to the overthrow of the monarchy started to gain ascendancy in French domestic politics. As a result, even after the Revolution the king "held hereditary office, was responsible to no one, and was inviolable" (no constitutional measure was adopted to address treason by the king).[8] In foreign affairs, the king possessed diplomatic initiative and the right to appoint ambassadors, military leaders, and cabinet officials. Domestically, he possessed a "suspensive" veto that could block legislation for two legislatures, or at least four years.

---

4. Theda Skocpol, *States and Social Revolutions: A Comparative Analysis of France, Russia, and China* (Cambridge: Cambridge University Press, 1979), 51–67; Crane Brinton, *A Decade of Revolution, 1789–1799* (New York: Harper and Row, 1934), 1–28.

5. R. R. Palmer, *The World of the French Revolution* (New York: Harper and Row, 1971), 57.

6. D. M. G. Sutherland, *France 1789–1815: Revolution and Counterrevolution* (Oxford: Oxford University Press, 1986), 36, 79, 105–106; Skocpol, *States and Social Revolutions*, 178; Palmer, *World of the French Revolution*, 57–64; Georges Lefebvre, *The French Revolution from Its Origins to 1793*, trans. Elizabeth Moss Evanson (New York: Columbia University Press, 1962), 1:130.

7. Brinton, *Decade of Revolution*, 37.

8. Lefebvre, *French Revolution*, 1:152.

The constitutional power of the French monarch was reinforced by the actions of Louis XVI in the two years subsequent to the Revolution. The king on several occasions adopted policies that seemed to indicate support for the political changes in France created by the Revolution. These included offering concessions at the beginning of the revolutionary process that transformed France from an absolute to a constitutional monarchy, and swearing allegiance to the constitution and promising to further its objectives.[9] Louis's public approval of the effects of the Revolution no doubt owed in no small measure to the strength of the revolutionary forces in France and the king's fear of antagonizing them. Yet Louis privately admitted that his concessions to transform France into a constitutional monarchy were a "free act."[10] Moreover, Louis—unlike the French nobility—did not ardently lobby the other great powers to try to return France's political situation to the one that existed before the Revolution. The king believed that he had more to lose by such efforts than he was likely to gain.[11] This reasoning indicates that Louis, unlike the large majority of the aristocratic classes, was to an important degree satisfied with the outcome of the Revolution.

Given the facts that the dominant group of French revolutionary leaders from 1789 to 1791 desired that the French monarchy retain considerable power, that the evolution of France's institutions in the first two years after the Revolution reflected this preference, and that Louis appeared to an important degree to approve the political outcomes of the Revolution, there seemed every reason, especially for foreign observers, "to predict the success of the monarchical experiment" in France in the years immediately following the Revolution.[12]

These same considerations lead us to expect that the ideological distance separating revolutionary French leaders from those in the old regime states would vary by the latter's political position. Since the legitimating principles of the French revolutionaries—even the moderates who wielded power until 1791—were antithetical to the power and authority of the French nobility, we would expect the aristocratic classes in the other powers to view France after 1789 as a very serious ideological threat. In contrast, because the French Revolution's challenge to monarchical authority in France was not nearly as great as it was to aristocratic power (both in terms of the stated goals of the Patriot Party's leaders and

9. Ibid., 1:134, 136; Brinton, *Decade of Revolution*, 7, 32.

10. Sutherland, *France 1789–1815*, 46; Lord Acton, *Lectures on the French Revolution*, ed. John Figgis and Reginald Laurence (New York: The Noonday Press, 1959), chap. 3.

11. Louis's chief fears on this subject were that pressure from the other powers to return to the status quo ante would likely result either in civil war or the ascendancy of the aristocracy at the expense of the monarchy (Sutherland, *France 1789–1815*, 107; Lefebvre, *French Revolution*, 1:194).

12. Brinton, *Decade of Revolution*, 27.

the actual changes in France's political system), we would expect that the other monarchs in the system would not see France after 1789 as a state unambiguously opposed to their foundational principles. We would therefore predict that the hostility of the monarchs toward France would be noticeably less than that of European aristocrats.

This is the pattern that emerged among the great powers from 1789 to 1791. The large majority of nobles in the other continental powers worried that the demise of the nobility in France would ultimately contribute to the diminishment of their own power and privilege. It is largely on account of this fear—and not out of a selfless concern for their ideological brethren in France—that "with few exceptions the nobles [of Europe] swung to counter-revolution."[13] Aristocrats throughout continental Europe pushed for their states to adopt policies designed to restore the old regime in France, including by war if necessary.

The reaction to the Revolution by the monarchs in the other powers was for the most part very different from that of the aristocratic classes. Because monarchical power in post-revolutionary France was preserved to a much greater extent than was aristocratic authority, the Revolution simply did not represent as great an ideological challenge to monarchs as it did to nobles. Joseph II and Leopold II of Austria, Frederick William II of Prussia, and Catherine of Russia all acknowledged that as long as Louis continued to wield considerable power, the threat of the Revolution to their own domestic interests was not very great.[14]

In fact, instead of being unalterably opposed to the French revolutionaries, the monarchs in each of the other continental powers to varying degrees sympathized with the revolutionaries' objectives. Joseph, Leopold, Frederick William, and Catherine all claimed allegiance to the principles of the Enlightenment, including the tenets articulated and espoused by the French *philosophes*. This common philosophical heritage between the old regime monarchs and the French revolutionaries meant that the former in important instances advocated domestic policies for their own states that were similar to ones advocated by the revolutionaries in France. These facts are important for my argument because the continental monarchs' commitment to "enlightened despotism" made the ideological distance dividing these rulers from the original leaders of the French Revolution not as large as we might otherwise expect.

13. Lefebvre, *French Revolution*, 1:187. Prussia's nobility, which was likely the strongest of any in the great powers, was particularly hostile to the Revolution (G. P. Gooch, *Germany and the French Revolution* [New York: Longmans, Green, 1920], 372, 378, 396).
14. L. P. Segur, *History of the Principal Events of the Reign of Frederick William of Prussia* (London: Longman and Rees, 1801), 2:361; Lefebvre, *French Revolution*, 1:195; Isabel de Madariaga, *Russia in the Age of Catherine the Great* (New Haven: Yale University Press, 1981), 541.

In Austria, for example, "the subjects of the Habsburg monarchy had no need to follow [the] example [of the French Revolution,] since a benevolent monarchical government [under Joseph II] had decided to amend such conditions of its own accord."[15] Similarly, Joseph's successor, Leopold, sought to "liberalize the constitutional arrangements" in his own empire in manners similar to the political developments in France from 1789 to 1791.[16] Indeed, the French Revolution was to some degree an aid to Leopold's domestic interests because it helped to justify his alliance with the Third Estate in order to limit the power of the Austrian nobility.[17] Thus "far from seeking to extirpate the Revolution, Leopold sympathized with and himself sought to realize many of its aims."[18]

Similarly, in the late 1780s and early 1790s, King Frederick William of Prussia approved of various codes of legal conduct and rights for Prussia and its people. The purpose of the great Codes (or Landrecht) was to substitute reason for tradition as the foundation of Prussian politics, which was a standard Enlightenment goal.[19] Moreover, the language of the Codes was very similar to that used by the French revolutionaries. According to this legislation, "the laws and ordinances of the State must not limit the natural liberty and the rights of citizens more than the general interest requires. The universal rights of man are based on the natural liberty to seek his own welfare without injuring the rights of others." Title 13 of Part ii denied by implication the unlimited power of the monarch by drawing up a list of his rights, and the authors made a practice of employing the word "citizens" in place of subjects.[20] According to the logic of the Code, "Prussia would become . . . a state founded on law, not on undefined prerogative."[21]

---

15. Ernst Wangermann, *From Joseph II to the Jacobin Trials: Government Policy and Public Opinion in the Habsburg Dominions in the Period of the French Revolution* (New York: Oxford University Press, 1969), 74.

16. Blanning, *Origins of the French Revolutionary Wars*, 72.

17. Wangermann, *From Joseph II to the Jacobin Trials*, 83–84, 86–87.

18. Blanning, *Origins of the French Revolutionary Wars*, 72; see also 71, 82–83; T. C. W. Blanning, *The French Revolutionary Wars 1787–1802* (New York: Arnold, 1996), 52, 64; Lefebvre, *French Revolution*, 1:195. Consistent with this analysis, Leopold urged Louis and Marie Antoinette to accept the outcomes of the Revolution (Palmer, *World of the French Revolution*, 74).

19. One of the most distinguished and experienced statesmen in Prussia, Count von Hertzberg (who had aided Frederick the Great for a generation in conducting foreign policy), spoke favorably of the Revolution because it embodied the Enlightenment principles that he, and the Prussian monarch, admired: "France, enlightened and stimulated by the newer philosophers, desires to create the best possible constitution and to surpass the English, inasmuch as it combines monarchy and republic" (in Gooch, *Germany and the French Revolution*, 373).

20. Ibid., 387.

21. Ibid. On Frederick William's sympathy for the Revolution, see ibid., 373, 387, 389; Segur, *History of the Principal Events*, 2:28–30, 359–367. The assertion that Frederick William approved of the French Revolution as long as monarchical power was preserved is corroborated by an edict issued by the Prussian government two months after the War of 1792

Although Empress Catherine of Russia was more hostile to the Revolution from its inception than any of the other great power monarchs, she too had the potential to see the Revolution resulting in a move toward her legitimating ideals. Catherine possessed a sincere admiration for many of the central political tenets of French philosophers, especially those of Montesquieu. As recently as the 1780s she had envisioned initiating "profound political changes [in Russia, including] . . . the participation of elected representatives in an advisory capacity in judicial and legislative institutions."[22] It is perhaps on account of her sympathy for the political ideals of the Enlightenment that Catherine permitted news of the Revolution to circulate freely in Russia, including the publication of the Declaration of the Rights of Man in the *St. Petersburg Gazette* and a number of speeches and decrees of the French National Assembly, as well as a great amount of revolutionary literature.[23]

Finally, the reaction to the Revolution by British decision makers was especially favorable. Many revolutionary French leaders openly recognized that they desired to create a constitutional monarchy in France that was explicitly based on the British model. As a result, British statesmen from across the political spectrum—including Prime Minister William Pitt, King George III, and opposition leader Charles James Fox—widely believed that the Revolution would result in a significant diminishment in the ideological distance separating the two states' key decision makers.[24] Even many British aristocrats tended not to see the French Revolution as a very large ideological threat since the political and economic changes the French revolutionaries were adopting to curb the power of the French

---

began. According to this statement, "his Prussian Majesty long cherished a hope that at length . . . the persons who direct the French Administration *would revert to the principles of prudence and moderation* [exhibited in France for the first two years after the Revolution,] and thus avoid the extremities to which matters have unhappily arrived" (in Segur, *History of the Principal Events*, 2:361 [emphasis added]).

22. de Madariaga, *Russia in the Age of Catherine the Great*, 306. Leading enlightenment figures in the West had long perceived Catherine to be "the most progressive monarch of Europe" (Martin Malia, *Russia under Western Eyes* [Cambridge, Mass.: Harvard University Press, 1999], 49 and chap. 1; de Madariaga, *Russia in the Age of Catherine the Great*, 547, 540). Catherine had even crafted legislation that the king of France forbade to have published in his realm for fear of its subversive effects on his subjects (Malia, *Russia under Western Eyes*, 50). These facts are important because if Catherine believed herself to be more enlightened than her fellow monarchs—including Louis XVI—then forcing the French king to rule in a manner more consistent with Enlightenment principles would imply that the Revolution resulted in a diminishment in the ideological distance separating Russian and French leaders.

23. de Madariaga, *Russia in the Age of Catherine the Great*, 421, 540–541. There was even in this time the creation of a special room for the reading of French newspapers established at the Military School of Aspirant Officers (Andrei Lobanov-Rostovsky, *Russia and Europe, 1789–1825* [New York: Greenwood Press, 1968], 4).

24. Pitt, for example, stated in the House of Commons in February 1790 that he could not "regard with envious eyes, an approximation in neighboring states to those sentiments which are the characteristic features of every British subject" (in Walt, *Revolution and War*,

nobility were ones that Britain had to an important degree already implemented.[25] Thus from the point of view of all the key groups of leaders in
Britain, "the French appeared to be imitating Britain, and this was universally regarded with approval."[26]

The key point to be taken from the above analysis is that those individuals most responsible for making foreign policy in the great powers of
Europe (the monarchs in Austria, Prussia, and Russia, and cabinet members and the king in Britain) tended not to view the ideological differences with France for the first two years after the Revolution as terribly
large. This is important because it means that the powers' mild reaction to
the revolutionary French regime from 1789 to 1791 is consistent with an
ideological interpretation of threats. Conversely, those individuals for
whom the Revolution created the largest ideological divide—continental
aristocrats—favored much more aggressive policies toward the new
French regime in these years.

In order to understand more fully the importance of the degree of ideological differences dividing the great powers' leaders to their relations,
we must examine the effects of domestic changes in France subsequent to
the 1789–91 period. When France's domestic situation took a much more
radical turn in the summer of 1791, the ideological gap separating
France's leaders from their counterparts in the other powers became
increasingly large. The wider this divide, the higher leaders' perceptions
of threat became. War between France, Austria, and Prussia in 1792 was
the ultimate consequence of this process.

Virtually all historians agree that the turning point that pushed the powers down the road to war was Louis XVI's infamous "flight to Varennes" in
June 1791, at which time the king attempted to emigrate from France.[27] The
attempt failed, and Louis was forced, under guard, to return to Paris.

Until this point in time, Emperor Leopold of Austria had been stead-
fastly opposed to war against France. Almost immediately after the flight

---

58). See also Ian Christie, *Wars and Revolutions: Britain 1760–1815* (London: Edward Arnold,
1982), 212; Blanning, *French Revolutionary Wars*, 42; Archibald Alison, *History of Europe: From
the Commencement of the French Revolution in 1789, to the Restoration of the Bourbons in 1815*
(New York: Harper and Brothers, 1860), 1:161; Lefebvre, *French Revolution*, 1:185. These sentiments were reciprocated by key leaders of the French Revolution. Clapham, *Causes of the
War of 1792*, 5.
25. Lefebvre, *French Revolution*, 1:49; Palmer, *World of the French Revolution*, 14.
26. John W. Derry, *Politics in the Age of Fox, Pitt, and Liverpool: Continuity and Transformation*
(New York: St. Martin's Press, 1990), 71. Edmund Burke and his supporters were the primary exceptions to the belief that the Revolution would increase the ideological similarities
uniting the British and French regimes. Yet this faction lacked sufficient power to affect
British policy.
27. Blanning, *Origins of the French Revolutionary Wars*, 84; Clapham, *Causes of the War of 1792*,
36; Lefebvre, *French Revolution*, 1:179; Brinton, *Decade of Revolution*, 52; Clive Emsley, *British
Society and the French Wars, 1793–1815* (London: Macmillan Press, 1979), 13; Sutherland,
France 1789–1815, 122.

to Varennes, however, the emperor became convinced that conflict with France was "not only unavoidable but desirable."[28] From this point on, Leopold took the lead in pushing the German powers to war against the revolutionary regime in France. Because neither French power nor the content of the German monarchs' ideologies had changed as a result of Louis's failed attempt to emigrate from France, neither realist theories nor arguments that examine the effects of ideologies' unique policy prescriptions can explain why this event had such dramatic effects on the great powers' foreign policies.

The flight to Varennes had such an important impact on the powers' relations because this event was the catalyst that greatly changed the ideological relationships among these states' key decision makers. The continental monarchs, including Leopold, asserted that the French Revolution did not represent a significant ideological threat only as long as Louis continued to wield considerable power in France. After the French king's flight and recapture, this precondition was no longer met. More radical parties that were determined to destroy the French monarchy became much more powerful after this event (these groups were led by members of the Brissotin Party, named after their leader, Brissot de Warville).[29] Thus the flight to Varennes and the king's subsequent recapture resulted in a substantial widening of the ideological distance separating France's leaders from those in the other powers.

This change in the ideological distance dividing the great powers' leaders pushed decision makers on both sides of the divide to view one another as severe dangers to both the security of their state and their domestic interests, just as the conflict-probability and demonstration-effects mechanisms predict. After the flight to Varennes, leaders in both revolutionary France and the old regime states increasingly believed that military conflict with the other was inevitable. Many revolutionary French statesmen, especially members of the increasingly powerful Brissotin Party, simply did not believe that peace with monarchical states was possible. In fact, the dominant theme in French political discourse in the months leading up to the War of 1792 was the assertion of "the existence of a gigantic international conspiracy designed to restore the old regime."[30]

28. Blanning, *Origins of the French Revolutionary Wars*, 84.
29. By the standards of the old regime powers, the Brissotins were a "shockingly radical group." The constitution proposed by the Brissotins in February 1793 was based on universal suffrage, direct election of representatives, and national referenda on certain acts of the central government (Brinton, *Decade of Revolution*, 109, 113).
30. Blanning, *Origins of the French Revolutionary Wars*, 99. See also Clapham, *Causes of the War of 1792*, 26–27, 198. Moreover, most French leaders spoke of the need for war for preventive reasons, which is a position that is entirely consistent with the belief that war with the old regime powers was inevitable. See Jacques Sole, *Questions of the French Revolution*, trans.Shelley Temchin (New York: Pantheon Books, 1989), 101–102; Walt, *Revolution and War*, 65; Blanning, *French Revolutionary Wars*, 62; David Armstrong, *Revolution and World Order:*

These views were reciprocated by key decision makers in the German powers, especially Leopold. The more radical French domestic politics became, the more the Austrian monarch believed that hostilities between the two sets of powers were unavoidable.[31]

Leaders' fears of the international intentions of their ideological rivals were matched by worries that their adversaries would both stimulate and/or deliberately provoke subversive activities in their states. From the perspective of the old regimes, "the universal quality of [France's] revolutionary principles and the strident presence in Paris of foreign refugees could not help but alert [other states] to the danger of international contagion."[32] After the flight to Varennes, the Marquis de Lafayette and other French leaders warned that if the German powers pushed France too far, they would expose the system to the "contagious example of a dethroned king."[33] This warning was not viewed as an empty threat. Leopold and his closest advisors, for example, "stated unequivocally that the danger of unrest spreading from France to the rest of Europe . . . influenced their decision to seek to form an anti-revolutionary bloc."[34] Perhaps no other fact demonstrates the importance of the fear of subversion in the minds of the leaders of the old regime powers than the numerous prophylactic measures enacted to reduce the possibility of ideological contagion. The most prevalent of these measures were attempts to restrict access of all things French into their polities (including French diplomats), and by increasing repressive measures at home in order to try to prevent popular uprisings.[35]

French politicians' fears of ideological subversion (in the form of counter-revolution) were probably even more powerful and widely held than was this fear in the old regime powers. Indeed, scholars invariably

---

The Revolutionary State in International Society (Oxford: Clarendon Press, 1993), 97; Clapham, *Causes of the War of 1792*, 65, 119, 135.

31. Clapham, *Causes of the War of 1792*, 150.

32. Blanning, *Origins of the French Revolutionary Wars*, 85.

33. In Lefebvre, *French Revolution*, 1:211.

34. Blanning, *Origins of the French Revolutionary Wars*, 86; also see 85. Austria's foreign minister, Anton Kaunitz, wrote in a note to Austrian diplomats in July 1791 that the spread of the "spirit of insubordination and revolt" was so menacing that all governments needed to "make common cause in order to preserve the public peace, the tranquillity of states, the inviolability of possessions and the good faith of treaties" (in Armstrong, *Revolution and World Order*, 101).

35. Russia, for example, expelled the French ambassador after the Revolution (as did Savoy and the Sublime Porte), and Austria thought about doing so. Britain took such action after Louis's execution in January 1793. Spain, Holland, and Venice did so when the French monarchy was suspended four months earlier. Even if French representatives were received, they were watched carefully by the home state's authorities. The French representative in Munich described his (hardly atypical) diplomatic experiences with a revealing metaphor: "A plague-stricken person whom the police have sequestered for the security of all is not more watched and dreaded than I am" (in Linda Frey and Marsha Frey, "'The Reign of the Charlatans Is Over': The French Revolutionary Attack on Diplomatic Practice," *Journal of Modern History* 65, no. 4 (December 1993): 720).

describe leaders of the Brissotin Party and similar groups as "paranoid" about the likelihood of the revolutionary regime's survival in a monarchical world.[36] Members of these parties believed that the conservative powers were firmly committed to counter-revolutionary efforts, both through external force and sponsoring ideological fifth columnists in France.

Growing fears of domestic subversion and others' aggressiveness among Austrian, Prussian, and French leaders after the flight to Varennes quickly resulted in increasingly hostile relations between the two sides. In the summer of 1791, the Austrian and Prussian governments issued a series of diplomatic circulars that, in the name of the monarchies of Europe, threatened France with war unless the French monarchy retained its authority. The most important of these was the Declaration of Pillnitz, which was issued on August 28, 1791. The document asserted that the authority and welfare of the king of France was "a matter of common concern to all the sovereigns of Europe," and it proposed that the powers unite to restore monarchical power in France. If all the other powers agreed to this, then Austria and Prussia would proceed "with the forces necessary to attain the proposed common objective."[37]

Although for a time the German powers' threats of war unless Louis's authority were preserved appeared to succeed, ultimately these threats helped to increase the Brissotins' domestic power until they were the de facto rulers of France by the end of 1791.[38] Prussian and Austrian pressure designed to reduce the ideological distance dividing the great powers' leaders thus ultimately resulted in a significant widening of this gap. After 1791, policies short of war were therefore no longer advancing the

36. Walt, *Revolution and War*, 62, 73; Blanning, *French Revolutionary Wars*, 49; Kyung-Won Kim, *Revolution and International System* (New York: New York University Press, 1970), 29.

37. "The Declaration of Pillnitz," in John Hall Stewart, *A Documentary Survey of the French Revolution* (New York: Macmillan, 1951), 223–224.

38. On September 14, 1791, Louis was restored to the throne, and he accepted the constitution offered by the National Assembly. As the domestic situation in France moved to the right, thereby decreasing the ideological differences among the powers, the German powers' leaders' perceptions of the threat posed by France noticeably declined. It therefore appeared that peace between the powers would continue. For example, upon hearing that Louis had accepted the new Constitution, Frederick William proclaimed: "The peace of Europe is at last assured" (in Gunther Rothenberg, "The Origins, Causes, and Extension of the Wars of the French Revolution and Napoleon," in *The Origin and Prevention of Major Wars*, ed. Robert Rotberg and Theodore Rabb [Cambridge: Cambridge University Press, 1988], 209). See also Clapham, *Causes of the War of 1792*, 96; Lefebvre, *French Revolution*, 1:212; Steven Ross, *European Diplomatic History, 1789–1815: France against Europe* (New York: Anchor Books, 1969), 39. Frederick William's push for peace after Louis accepted the new constitution is problematic for those who claim that a desire to exploit French weakness was the Prussian king's primary motive for war. Later in the decade, Frederick William told Lord Malmesbury of Britain about his "invariable abhorrence of the French principles" and his "thorough conviction that if they were not checked, all government and order would be overthrown" (in Sydney Seymour Biro, *The German Policy of Revolutionary France: A Study in French Diplomacy during the War of the First Coalition* [Cambridge: Harvard University Press, 1957], 1:340, 354).

German powers' interests. The incentives pushing Austria and Prussia to attack France were therefore becoming increasingly powerful after this year. In preparation for a military offensive, Austria and Prussia agreed to an alliance on February 7, 1792.[39]

The Brissotins reciprocated the German powers' fears and hostilities. Because these individuals believed that conflict with monarchical states was inevitable, they argued that France's security would best be protected by seizing the initiative and attacking the old regime powers at a time of France's choosing. As Brissot told the Assembly in October 1791, "It is not merely necessary to think of defense, the [counterrevolutionary] attack must be anticipated; you yourselves must attack."[40] If the monarchs were determined to "stir up a war of kings against France," France, as Convention member and ally of Brissot, Maximin Isnard, proclaimed, would "stir up for them a war of peoples against kings." These views were greeted with near universal approval in the French Assembly.[41] Given the hostile beliefs and policies adopted by the key leaders on both sides of the conflict, military conflicts between these powers were virtually unavoidable after 1791.

Although the belief in the inevitability of conflict with ideological enemies and the fear of subversion were the factors most responsible for the increasingly hostile relationship between France and the German powers after June 1791, revolutionary French leaders' inability to understand at critical times the diplomatic signals sent by Austria and Prussia contributed to their deteriorating relations, as the communication mechanism predicts.

The most important example of diplomatic misunderstanding brought about by ideological differences in this period concerned the true meaning of the Pillnitz Declaration. As explained, this declaration, which was jointly issued by Leopold and Frederick William II, threatened to preserve the French monarchy through intervention of a concert of old regime powers. There was, however, a critical caveat to this threat. The concert would act against France *only if* (the infamous *alors et dans ce cas* or "then and in that case" clause) all the great powers agreed to joint action. Because Britain was unlikely to abandon its policy of neutrality, unanimity was similarly unlikely, and thus the entire concept of a concert was abortive. Leopold understood this. He wrote to Austria's foreign minister, Anton Kaunitz, that this clause released

---

39. Blanning, *Origins of the French Revolutionary Wars*, 114; Clapham, *Causes of the War of 1792*, 157–159. Defeating France at this time was so important to Austria's and Prussia's leaders that they were willing to sacrifice long-standing geopolitical interests to realize this objective. Their actions, designed to destroy the revolutionary French regime, allowed Russia to make disproportionate gains in the second partition of Poland (Lefebvre, *French Revolution*, 1:221).

40. In Clapham, *Causes of the War of 1792*, 115; see also 135.

41. Ibid., 119.

him from any immediate commitment.[42] The British held a similar view.[43] The leaders of revolutionary France, however, possessed a very different understanding of this declaration. They took the German powers' threats at face value and mistakenly believed that invasion was imminent.

This does not mean that Austrian and Prussian leaders had no long-run intentions of attacking France if French domestic politics did not evolve in ways consistent with their preferences. It simply means that the German powers were not planning to do so as imminently as many French revolutionaries believed. Thus France's leaders correctly anticipated Austria's and Prussia's long-run, but not their short-run, ambitions.

French leaders' misunderstanding of the German powers' short-run intentions resulted directly from the effects created by the increasing ideological gap separating the powers' key decision makers. The ideological beliefs to which revolutionary French leaders were dedicated impelled them to interpret events in very different ways than did their predecessors. "In the normal practice of classical diplomacy," as Kyung-Won Kim explains, "it would not have taken great ingenuity to interpret correctly what was really meant by the well-known conditional clause of the [Pillnitz] declaration. But the fact was that the French were no longer attached to the normal practice of classical diplomacy. There had been [an] ideological revolution in France, and as a result the French tended to view the outside world in radically different terms than before."[44]

Given their ideological differences with the old regime states, the key decision makers in France after 1791 did not believe that the overtures made by the German powers could be anything but revealing of intended immediate physical hostility. Any diplomatic subtleties to the contrary were simply dismissed as contrary to the actual state of affairs. French politicians' misperception of the German powers' diplomacy enflamed an already highly volatile situation, and virtually eliminated any remaining chances of avoiding war among these states. Without the radicalization of French domestic politics after the summer of 1791 and the subsequent creation of a huge ideological gulf among the great powers' key decision makers, peace among these states—which had looked so promising before the French Revolution—most likely would have continued well into the 1790s and for the foreseeable future.

---

42. Blanning, *Origins of the French Revolutionary Wars*, 87.
43. Jennifer Mori, *William Pitt and the French Revolution, 1785–1795* (Edinburgh: Keele University Press, 1997), 100.
44. Kim, *Revolution and International System*, 124; also see 30–32; Blanning, *Origins of the French Revolutionary Wars*, 73.

THE ORIGINS OF THE WAR OF THE FIRST COALITION, 1793–97

The key features of the origins of the War of the First Coalition, most notably Britain's entry into the wars against France, were to an important extent a product of French expansion.[45] Few, however, would have anticipated that French conquests would have been an issue based on France's performance during the first five months of the War of 1792. From the war's beginning in April until September, the German powers' triumph over the revolutionary state looked assured. After several victories, the road to Paris looked open and the collapse of the French regime appeared to be imminent.

By the fall of 1792, however, the French had completely reversed the battlefield situation. Most important, on September 20, the French won the battle of Valmy, which stopped the allied armies one hundred miles from Paris. After Valmy, the Austrian and Prussian armies were forced to retreat from France.

The armed forces of the French Republic did not, however, stop when France was liberated. In November 1792, France won the battle of Jemappes, which placed Belgium under French control. Immediately after this victory, French leaders, including Brissot, asserted that France should expand to its "natural frontiers," which in the north meant that France should occupy territory to the Rhine River.[46] With this objective in mind, on November 16, 1792, the French Convention declared the Scheldt River (which flowed from Antwerp to the sea) open to navigation. This action sent a very clear signal that France desired to extend its control over both Belgium and a significant portion of the United Provinces.

Because the independence of the Low Countries of northwest Europe was a long-standing strategic interest to Britain, France's expansionary aims in this region were a clear threat to Britain's security. Britain's efforts to safeguard the Low Countries from French control were a critical reason for Britain's entry into the wars against France in February 1793.[47]

Although Britain's response to French expansion can be understood largely as a product of traditional balancing behavior, French leaders'

45. Because Britain was France's most determined foe during the War of the First Coalition, I concentrate almost exclusively on Anglo-French relations in this period. Austria continued to fight France for most of the remainder of the decade. Prussia, however, was knocked out of the wars in 1795 due to military defeat, financial exhaustion, and widespread fear of ideological subversion if it remained in the conflicts. Although Prussia was forced to recognize the French Republic at this time, Frederick William's ideological antipathy to France did not waver. Most notably, he refused to ally with France even when such a coalition could have helped Prussia acquire more territory in the third partition of Poland in 1795 (Biro, *German Policy of Revolutionary France*, 268, 313, 340–341, 353–354, 412).
46. Blanning, *French Revolutionary Wars*, 91.
47. Walt, *Revolution and War*, 77–89; Blanning, *Origins of the French Revolutionary Wars*, 158–159.

decision to invade northwest Europe is not best understood as a product of realist calculations. No doubt several factors contributed to France's expanding war aims in the fall of 1792, including realist calculations for power expansion, the ambitions of its military commanders, and the sheer headiness of a situation in which France's armies appeared to be invincible. But the key factor pushing France's decision makers to expand the war to foreign soil was their substantial ideological differences with the other powers. "The policy of revolutionary expansion," as Stephen Walt explains, "resulted from the same influences that had driven France to war seven months earlier. French foreign policy was in the hands of leaders who . . . saw themselves as part of a universal movement for liberty [and who were highly hostile] to monarchical institutions."[48]

When war broke out between France and the German powers in April 1792, France was still a constitutional monarchy, at least titularly. On August 10, 1792, however, the French political system dramatically changed. On this date, not only was the French monarchy suspended, but it also marked the day that formally "brought the radical democrats to power. They advocated a form of government in which every (male) citizen exercised his share of sovereignty collectively and directly. . . . The contrast with the elected commune of notables of 1789 was massive."[49] On September 21, the deputies of the National Convention voted to abolish the monarchy and place the king on trial. The First Republic of France was officially created at this time.

The Republic's revolutionary leaders were convinced that their ideological differences with the other powers made these states inevitable adversaries of the new French regime. As Foreign Minister Pierre LeBrun explained to the deputies of the Convention: "The moment of greatest danger will arrive next spring [of 1793], when allied tyranny will make its last effort, and then we must repel the combined force of all the kings." Similarly, Georges Danton (head of the Executive Council) warned that as long as France remained surrounded by monarchies, these states "would furnish us with an endless series of tyrants to confront."[50]

French leaders' belief in the inevitable enmity of all monarchical states created powerful incentives both to continue the war as long as France's armies were winning and to convert conquered states into republics on the French model. As Brissot wrote in November 1792: "We cannot be calm until Europe, all Europe, is in flames."[51] Because of the security threats to the Republic posed by monarchies, France, as Danton exclaimed

---

48. Walt, *Revolution and War*, 78–79; see also Blanning, *French Revolutionary Wars*, 88; Lefebvre, *French Revolution*, 1:271–272, 274.
49. Sutherland, *France 1789–1815*, 156.
50. Both in Walt, *Revolution and War*, 79.
51. In Lefebvre, *French Revolution*, 1:274.

to the Convention, had "the right to say to the peoples [of Europe]: you shall have no more kings!"[52]

The Republic wasted little time acting on these beliefs. On November 19, 1792, Paris issued a decree which stated that "the National Convention declares, in the name of the French nation, that it will grant fraternity and aid to all peoples who wish to recover their liberty."[53] A second decree, issued December 15, 1792, committed France to overturning the existing institutions in conquered territories in favor of a political system based on the revolutionary French system.[54] Only when conquered territories established republics like France's would warfare end. These statements constituted France's declaration of total war against all polities not like France. French leaders' ideological differences with other states pushed them to believe that they had to export their political institutions in order to protect their security.

French politicians' ideological beliefs and pronouncements were central to the other powers' enmity to the revolutionary regime, including Britain's leaders. Although British statesmen would have been hostile to any country that was conquering the Low Countries, most of Britain's key decision makers did not understand their conflict with Republican France as at root a geopolitical one. Instead, British leaders consistently asserted that France in the 1790s was a geopolitical danger *because it was an ideological threat*.[55] No one was more clear than Prime Minister Pitt in his belief that the revolutionaries' ideological differences with the other powers were the key factor responsible for France's aggressive policies that threatened Britain's safety. To Pitt, the principles of the French revolutionaries and the ideological gulf these beliefs created in relation to the other European powers pushed these individuals "to sow the seeds of rebellion and civil contention, and to spread war from one end of Europe to the other."[56] Moreover, Pitt and other key British decision makers

52. Similarly, the president of the Assembly, Henri Gregoire, proclaimed at this time: "All Governments are our enemies, all Peoples are our allies; either we shall fall or all peoples shall become free" (both in Walt, *Revolution and War,* 79).

53. "The First Propagandist Decree, 19 November, 1792," in Stewart, *Documentary Survey,* 381.

54. "The Second Propagandist Decree, 15 December, 1792," in Stewart, *Documentary Survey,* 381–384. See also Blanning, *French Revolutionary Wars,* 88.

55. William Pitt, "French Ambitions and the Liberty of Europe" (speech delivered to Parliament February 1, 1793), 51, and William Pitt, "On a Motion for Peace" (speech delivered to Parliament June 17, 1793), 98, both in R. Coupland, *The War Speeches of William Pitt* (Oxford: Clarendon Press, 1915).

56. William Pitt, "The French Declaration of War" (speech delivered to Parliament February 12, 1793), in Coupland, *War Speeches of William Pitt,* 56. The linkage between the ideological divide separating France from the other great powers and military conflict was an important theme of Pitt's speeches. At another time the prime minister claimed that the French "will not accept . . . any model of government but that which is conformable to their own opinions and ideas; and all men must learn from the mouth of their cannon the propagation of their system in every part of the world" (Pitt, "French Ambitions and the Liberty of Europe," 37). Although these statements demonstrating the importance of ideological variables to Pitt's views of

believed that as long as France remained committed to different ideological goals than the other powers, conflict among them would not end. As the prime minister put it, the domestic institutions of the republican French regime render "negotiation useless, and must entirely deprive of stability any peace which could be concluded in such circumstances. Where is our security for the performance of a treaty where we have neither the good faith of a nation, nor the responsibility of a monarch?"[57] Because the French Republic was so very different from Britain in terms of political institutions, French politicians, to Pitt, simply could not be trusted to possess limited international objectives.

Ideological variables were also pushing Britain into conflictual relations with France independently of either France's expansionary policies or British decision makers' anticipation of French international aggressiveness. Most notably, increasing ideological differences between British and French leaders over the course of 1792 caused Britain's decision makers to be increasingly worried about the likelihood of ideological subversion to French principles. These fears significantly exacerbated Anglo-French tensions, thereby making conflict between these states even more likely.

As previously discussed, the dominant sentiment among British leaders immediately after the French Revolution was that this event had resulted in a move by France toward the British political system. This belief was more than a passing interest to the most important decision makers in Britain. Most of these individuals asserted that because the institutional changes in France in the early 1790s were modeled on Britain's political system, Britain's security would be noticeably enhanced as a result of these domestic developments. Most notably, British leaders believed that the greater France's resemblance to Britain's political system, the more their counterparts in France could be trusted to possess more limited foreign policy ambitions than did previous French statesmen. As opposition leader Charles James Fox expressed this line of reasoning: "I was formerly the strenuous advocate for the balance of power, when France was that intriguing, restless nation which she had formerly proved. Now that the situation of France is altered, and that she *has erected a government from which neither insult nor injury can be apprehended by her neighbors*, I am extremely indifferent concerning the balance of power, and shall continue so till I see other nations combine the same

---

France are from his parliamentary speeches, the prime minister's private writings mirror his public pronouncements. See Mori, *William Pitt and the French Revolution,* 198; Frank O'Gorman, "Pitt and the 'Tory' Reaction to the French Revolution 1789–1815," in *Britain and the French Revolution, 1789–1815,* ed. H. T. Dickinson (London: Macmillan Education, 1989), 35, 37.

57. Pitt, "On a Motion for Peace," 99; see also Pitt, "French Ambitions and the Liberty of Europe," 49, 47, 48; William Pitt, "The Folly of a Premature Peace" (speech delivered to Parliament December 30, 1794), 121, 122, all in Coupland, *War Speeches of William Pitt.*

power with the same principles of government as that of Old France."[58] Prime Minister Pitt shared this optimism. He asserted on several occasions that even if the effects of the domestic changes in France made it a more powerful state, the creation of "good government" in France (i.e., government on the British model) would likely make it a "less objectionable neighbor" to Britain.[59] Realist theories of international relations cannot explain these sentiments.

Seventeen ninety-two marked the end of the widespread belief among British decision makers that France's domestic institutions after the Revolution were moving closer to those in Britain. The destruction of the French monarchy and the creation of the Republic created an immense ideological gap between the two states. Moreover, these developments were not the only manifestations of the increasing radicalism of French politics. In early September 1792, popular agitation in Paris led to a series of lynchings, known as the September Massacres, which left between 1,100 and 1,400 dead. In January 1793, Louis XVI was executed. To many outside observers, revolutionary France seemed to be drifting into anarchy.

The increasingly radical nature of France's internal politics over the course of 1792 significantly increased British leaders' hostility toward and fears of the French regime, including worries about the likelihood of domestic subversion. As the prime minister explained in a speech to Parliament days before Britain's entry into the war in February 1793, the principles of the French revolutionaries "strike directly against the authority of all regular government and the inviolable personal situation of every lawful sovereign."[60]

Numerous policies adopted by Britain in this period reflect this fear of ideological contagion. In November 1792, the British government fortified the Tower of London, called out the militia, sent troops to Scotland, and started debating a bill entitled "Suspension of Habeus Corpus and Power to take Security at least as to Foreigners." The British passed the Alien Act in January 1793, and in March of the same year the Traitorous Correspondence Bill.

In addition to the passage of these prophylactic measures, the fear of ideological subversion also resulted in the joining of the conservative or

58. In Alison, *History of Europe*, 161 (emphasis in original). In February 1990, Fox asserted that "the new form which the government of France was likely to assume . . . would render her a better neighbor, and less disposed to hostility, than when she was subject to the cabal and intrigues of ambitious and interested statesmen" (in Blanning, *French Revolutionary Wars*, 2).
59. In Mori, *William Pitt and the French Revolution*, 86; see also 90.
60. Pitt, "French Ambitions and the Liberty of Europe," 28. Similarly, in November 1792 Pitt stated that "the unexpected turn of events in France is but too much likely to give encouragement to the forces of disorder in every part of the world." Home Secretary Henry Dundas warned that "if the spirit of liberty and equality continues to spread with the same rapidity . . . it must soon break out in open sedition" (both in Walt, *Revolution and War*, 84; see also Mori, *William Pitt and the French Revolution*, 128).

Portland Whigs (named after their leader) with the Pitt government. Although this coalition was critical for the war-fighting potential of Britain, it is significant that the primary reason for this union was *not* concern with the French danger to the Low Countries. The gradual process by which the Portland Whigs deserted their former allies started in April 1792, *well before France offered a physical threat to Belgium and Holland.* The timing of this process corroborates the claim that ideological variables were having an independent effect on British leaders' perceptions of threat independent of France's territorial expansion.

Moreover, from the time the Portland Whigs began to make overtures to join the Pitt government until July 1794 when the union became official, the proclaimed reason for the coalition was always the same: the fear of domestic subversion to the principles espoused by the revolutionary French government. In April 1792, the proposed coalition was described as a "union of all parties in opposing sedition."[61] In November of that year, the Portland Whigs spoke of the need to repel "French cabals in this country."[62] When the coalition finally became official, Portland exposed the driving motive for this decision: "the expulsion of the Soul and Spirit of Jacobinism as a point of Union for us all."[63]

The impact of ideological differences with France on Britain's foreign policies became even more pronounced after Britain entered the war. Perhaps most notably, British leaders' belief that conflict with France was inevitable as long as it remained a revolutionary regime, coupled with these individuals' fears of ideological subversion, pushed the Pitt government from early in the conflicts to adopt total war-fighting objectives designed to promote counter-revolution in France. In other words, Britain's primary military objectives once war began were not simply to repulse France from the Low Countries and to keep these states free of French control, but to overthrow the existing French government and to replace it with one closer to the British system. These goals, in combination with policies designed to prevent domestic subversion, created the impression that by the summer of 1794 "the British government had . . . become a crusading zealot for the old order at home and abroad."[64]

Significantly, because most British leaders did not advocate the territorial dismemberment of France but only the reestablishment of the prewar boundaries, the strategy of promoting counter-revolution would not have significantly reduced France's power.[65] These objectives indicate not only that Britain took the French ideological threat very seriously, but that

61. In Mori, *William Pitt and the French Revolution*, 115.
62. Ibid., 125.
63. Ibid., 197.
64. Ibid., 196.
65. Piers Mackesy, *Statesmen at War: The Strategy of Overthrow, 1798–1799* (New York: Longman, 1974), 49; Ross, *European Diplomatic History*, 187–188.

British leaders believed that the strategic threat in large part resulted from the current ideological situation in France. If British leaders did not believe this, then changing the institutions and political principles of France without changing its power potential would not have resulted in a significant augmentation of British security.

Pitt's call for total war was neither a rhetorical aim that he was ready to sacrifice when it came into conflict with maintaining or augmenting Britain's relative power position, nor was this strategy a product of favorable battlefield conditions that lasted only as long as Britain was winning the war.[66] Instead, the strategy of counter-revolution remained central to Britain's war-fighting policies from within a year of its entry into the wars. For example, the fact that Britain's key leaders chose to siphon off significant resources that could have greatly added to their state's colonial possessions, and thus its relative power, in favor of counter-revolutionary efforts is substantial evidence supporting the claim that these individuals attributed the ultimate source of Anglo-French antagonism in the 1790s to their ideological differences.[67]

Pitt's strategy of total war created the additional cost of increasing the domestic opposition to the government's policies. Because of their more liberal ideological objectives than Tories, the Foxite Whigs "opposed the ministry on the grounds, not only that the allied Powers intended to destroy the French republic and restore the monarchy, but also that the power of the crown in Britain would know no bounds if the cause of monarchy triumphed on the Continent."[68] However, the opposition newspaper, *The Morning Chronicle,* stated that "fighting for security, in support of allies, or to oppose aggrandizement" was permissible.[69] Thus if Pitt had limited the war to preventing French territorial expansion, much of the Foxite Whigs' opposition to the conflict would have disappeared. Britain would therefore have been able to prosecute the war even more effectively than it did. That Pitt was willing to incur this cost further reveals the importance of counter-revolutionary policies to his prosecution of the war.

66. Emsley, *British Society and the French Wars,* 23; Christie, *Wars and Revolutions,* 230–231.
67. As Jennifer Mori explains, by the end of 1793 "Pitt [had] denuded the West Indian expedition of eight regiments for service in Toulon and the Vendee [and counterrevolutionary efforts]" (Mori, *William Pitt and the French Revolution,* 162). As early as February 1, 1793, on the eve of Britain's entry into the wars against France, Pitt asserted in Parliament that "there can be no consideration more deserving the attention of this House, than to crush and destroy [those] principles which are so dangerous and destructive of every blessing this country enjoys under its free and excellent constitution." To stop the "growth and progress" of French revolutionary principles in Britain and "other states of Europe" should be Britain's "first duty and principal concern" (Pitt, "French Ambitions and the Liberty of Europe," 29, 30). In June 1793, the prime minister stated that "the best security we could obtain, would be the end of that wild ungoverned system [in France], from which have resulted those injuries against which it is necessary to guard" (Pitt, "On a Motion for Peace," 98).
68. Christie, *Wars and Revolutions,* 218. See also Emsley, *British Society and the French Wars,* 17.
69. Emsley, *British Society and the French Wars,* 17.

The call for total war and the restoration of the French monarchy as a primary aim of British war-fighting objectives should also not be seen as a product of the allies' favorable military situation. Pitt maintained this policy regardless of the fluctuations on the battlefield. Even in the fall of 1794, when the war was going very badly for the allies, Pitt was adamant that he had "no idea of any peace being secure, unless France returned to the monarchical system."[70] As one of Pitt's opponents put it (according to Pitt's account): "If you will not treat for peace when you are successful, nor treat for it when you are unfortunate, there must be some secret cause which induces us to believe you are not disposed to treat at all."[71] This was precisely the point. Pitt believed that British security was to a significant degree founded upon increasing the degree of ideological similarities uniting the great powers' leaders. Consequently, his policy of total war toward France did not fluctuate according to changes on the battlefield.[72] As we shall see in the next section, however, what *did* cause Britain's policies during the wars to fluctuate significantly were ideological shifts in France that moved the revolutionary regime closer or farther away from Britain's domestic-political system.

FRENCH DOMESTIC CHANGES AND THE CONDUCT OF THE WAR OF THE FIRST COALITION

From the origins of the War of the First Coalition in 1793 until its end in 1797, the domestic situation in France underwent several dramatic changes that affected in critical ways the ideological distances dividing the key antagonists, Britain and France. Each time French politics shifted to the left, invariably feelings of threat between Britain and France increased. Conversely, the more conservative French politics became in

70. Pitt, "Folly of a Premature Peace," 118; see also Pitt, "French Ambitions and the Liberty of Europe," 28–30. Later in the decade Foreign Minister William Grenville in private correspondence described the republican government of France as "the real root and origin of all [France's] wickedness" and that "Europe can never be restored to tranquillity but by the restoration of monarchy in France." He would also state that "nothing will terminate this war but such success in France as enables us to restore the monarchy" (all in Mackesy, *Statesmen at War*, 69, 150; see also 231).

71. William Pitt, "The War Policy of the Government Reviewed and Defended" (speech delivered to Parliament May 10, 1796), in Coupland, *War Speeches of William Pitt*, 147–148.

72. France reciprocated this strategy of total war. As a member of the Committee of Public Safety stated in June 1794: "In ordinary wars after [military] successes, one would have sought . . . peace. . . . But in the war of liberty, they are only a means . . . of exterminating despots. . . . Neither peace nor truce nor armistice nor any treaty can be made with despots except in the name of a consolidated, triumphant republic . . . dictating the peace" (in Armstrong, *Revolution and World Order*, 88). See also Georges Lefebvre, *The French Revolution from 1793 to 1799*, trans. from the French by John Hall Stewart and James Friguglietti (New York: Columbia University Press, 1964), 2:12; Walt, *Revolution and War*, 79, 80; Blanning, *French Revolutionary Wars*, 165.

Table 1. Changes in Threat Perception during Britain's Wars with France
(all predictions and outcomes are from British leaders' perspective)

Period of Time/Changes in French Political System	This Book's Predictions/Outcomes	Problem That This Particular Outcome Poses for Realist Theories
May–August 1793 (Institutionalization of Gouvernement Revolutionnaire in France)	Large increase in threat	Major French victories of this period (e.g., in the Battles of Hondschoote and Wattignies and over France's internal enemies) had yet to take place (fall of 1793)
July 1794 to spring 1795 (Thermidor Reaction; Implementation of the conservative Constitution of 1795)	Marked decrease in threat perception; increased willingness to negotiate	France gained control of the Netherlands in this period
Summer of 1795 (Regicides gain control of French Legislature and Directory)	Perceptions of threat increased; peace negotiations with France deemphasized	No major change in the distribution of power that can explain these changes in threat perceptions
Spring 1797 to September 1797 (Royalists gain control of French Legislature and Directory)	Perceptions of threat decreased; increased willingness to negotiate	Bonaparte won major battles in Italy and threatened Austria, Britain's most important fighting ally
September 1797 (Coup of Fructidor and subsequent re-radicalization of French politics)	Increased perceptions of threat; negotiations are broken off immediately	No major change in the distribution of power that can explain these changes in threat perceptions
December 1799 to March 1802 (Napoleon's coup and subsequent consolidation of power, which included the repudiation of Jacobin principles)	Lower perceptions of threat; Treaty of Amiens ending the Wars of the French Revolution signed; Britain substantially cut defense spending	France held a hegemonic position in western Europe, including control of the Low Countries

this period, the more the levels of Franco-British fear declined. (For a summary of findings, see Table 1.)

These outcomes are problematic for both realist theories and arguments that are based on the specific behavioral prescriptions of different political ideologies. Contra realism, neither British leaders' core security policies nor their understandings of their ideological relationships corresponded very well with changes in French power or in battlefield conditions. Instead, British perceptions of threat and behavior closely tracked objective domestic developments in France. Similarly, if ideological content—and not distance—were the principal determinants of British policies, French domestic changes should not have resulted in such significant shifts in Britain's international decisions as occurred throughout the 1790s since the content of British leaders' ideological beliefs remained constant.

The first critical change in French politics that occurred after Britain's entry into the wars came in the spring of 1793. By this time, France had suffered a series of setbacks, most notably military defeat in Belgium, the outbreak of violent counter-revolution in the west, and a series of popular uprisings brought on by a continually deteriorating economy.

The ultimate effect of this political atmosphere was the discrediting of the Brissotins, which led to their expulsion from the Convention on May 31, 1793. A more radical party, known as the Mountain, subsequently took control of the French government and gave it a new direction and purpose (it was at this time that institutions such as the infamous Committees of Public Safety and General Security were formed). The French state under the Mountain's leadership was "to be openly and proudly revolutionary."[73] Calling itself *"gouvernement revolutionnaire,"* the Mountain "rushed through a constitution . . . with universal suffrage, an omnipotent unicameral legislature, and a Bill of Rights rather more collectivist than orthodox eighteenth-century Bills of Rights in Europe and America, submitted [it] to the people . . . [and then] suspended its application until the end of the war."[74] The *"gouvernement revolutionnaire"* was dedicated to large-scale income redistribution, de-Christianization of society, the governmental regulation of religion and virtue, and an official program of repression and intimidation that would become known as the "Reign of Terror."[75]

The rise of the radical Mountain party, with Maximilien Robespierre as its leader, had a dramatic impact on British perceptions of the French state. According to Pitt, "the Revolution of 31 May introduced an entirely new Government in France more atrocious than any of the former Systems and one which is *more incompatible with the safety of other Countries"* (and this perception of threat existed despite the fact that at the time of this revolution, France's internal and external situation was near chaos).[76] After this change in government, any significant doubts among British rulers about the principal objects of the war being those of overthrow and restoration were removed. As Lord Malmesbury (an experienced diplomat and one of the chief negotiators with France) put it, the chief object of the European

---

73. Brinton, *Decade of Revolution*, 120.
74. Ibid.
75. Palmer, *World of the French Revolution*, 111–120; R. R. Palmer, *The Age of Democratic Revolution: A Political History of Europe and America* (Princeton: Princeton University Press, 1964), 112–131.
76. In Mori, *William Pitt and the French Revolution*, 166 (emphasis added). At another time, Pitt described the revolutionary government instituted on May 31 as "a new Government, more dreadful in its character and more fatal in its effects than any which preceded it" (William Pitt, "The Jacobin Government of France" [speech delivered to Parliament January 21, 1794], in Coupland, *War Speeches of William Pitt*, 105).

conflict had become "the destruction of the atrocious system now prevalent in France."[77] Significantly, this commitment came before the important French victories of Hondschoote and Wattignies (which occurred in September and October, respectively, and impelled the allies to begin their retreat from French territory), and major victories over the regime's internal enemies, including in Toulon (which took place in December) and over the Vendean army (the revolutionary regime's most dangerous internal foe), which did not happen until November. In other words, the solidifying of British objectives did not correspond with changes in French capabilities or changes in battlefield conditions. Instead, they correlated with the increasing radicalization of France's domestic politics.

The next major domestic changes in France were the Thermidorian reaction of July 1794 and the subsequent adoption of the Constitution of 1795. After Thermidor, revolutionary fervor in France ebbed and politics shifted to the right. Newspapers enjoyed much greater freedom. Theaters increased their satire of Jacobin personalities and principles. Amnesty and clemency were granted to political opponents as jails were emptied of many of their political prisoners. By the spring of 1795, amnesty had been extended even to the surviving Brissotins. May 31 was dropped from the list of national holidays. Religious freedom was increased, which was meant to be a large concession to the rebellious Vendee. The Committee of Public Safety was stripped of its dictatorial powers, and the Thermidorian government ordered the Jacobin clubs closed. As in 1791 (and also as in Britain), the Constitution of 1795 required that suffrage depend upon relatively high levels of property ownership. There was even much hope that monarchical interests would be restored since royalists could be elected to the Convention. The results of all these measures was the "liquidation of the Jacobin venture in democratic republicanism."[78]

The fact that France after Thermidor to an important extent abandoned its most revolutionary principles clearly resulted in a narrowing of the ideological differences separating British and French decision makers.[79] This ideological shift was important because it impelled British statesmen to believe that current French leaders, unlike their immediate predecessors, would in "good faith" (as Foreign Minister Grenville put it) help bring peace back to the continent.[80] In other words, just as the conflict-probability causal mechanism predicts, there was a clear relationship between the domestic-political makeup of the French state and British

---

77. In Mori, *William Pitt and the French Revolution,* 166.
78. Brinton, *Decade of Revolution,* 199.
79. According to Foreign Minister Grenville, the government established in France after the Thermidor reaction was "unquestionably less dangerous in its principles than the former revolutionary government that preceded it" (in Mori, *William Pitt and the French Revolution,* 227).
80. Ibid., 228.

decision makers' tendency to trust that their French counterparts would honor their international commitments. The more radical French domestic politics became, the more British leaders regarded French statesmen as so untrustworthy that the former could not believe that negotiations could be conducted in good faith or that any peace on the battlefield could be anything more than a temporary truce.[81] Conversely, the more the nature of France's system of political representation resembled Britain's, the greater the tendency among British statesmen to believe that France would honor its international obligations. Hence the Pitt government's willingness to negotiate a peace treaty with France after Thermidor, which the prime minister had sworn never to do with the previous French regime. The historian R. Coupland explains the forces that pushed Pitt to come to the diplomatic table after Thermidor: "It seemed as if at last France had obtained a reputable and a settled Government, as if at last the obstacle in the way of peace, which Pitt had regarded as insuperable, had been broken down. Before the end of 1795, therefore, Pitt had decided to come to terms with the Directory."[82] Significantly, this change in Britain's policy was made in the context of French expansion, including into the presumably sacrosanct (from Britain's perspective) Low Countries, since in this period France conquered the Netherlands and turned the region into the Batavian Republic.

Even before peace negotiations had commenced, however, changes within France once again impelled British officials to rethink the likelihood of peace. Although the Constitution of 1795 appeared to be anti-revolutionary and even potentially friendly to royalist interests (because even royalist supporters could be elected to the Convention), additional legislation precluded this possibility. In order to minimize royalist influence, the Convention passed the Two-thirds Decree, which required that two-thirds of the members of the new legislative body be elected from the previous one, which was anti-monarchical in disposition. This legislation marked a turning point in French politics as revolutionary leaders mounted a campaign to push French politics back to the left. In addition to the Two-thirds Decree, the most important result of this campaign was that all five of the Directors elected at this time were regicides who had served on either the Committee of Public Safety or of General Security. The ideological effects of these outcomes were clear: "[the] past [of the

---

81. Pitt, "On a Motion for Peace," 99; Pitt, "French Ambitions and the Liberty of Europe," 49, 47, 48; Pitt, "Folly of a Premature Peace," 121, 122.
82. Coupland, *War Speeches of William Pitt*, 136. The French under the Directory reciprocated these overtures by adopting a less dogmatic stance to the rest of Europe in terms of its diplomacy. Starting in 1795, negotiations with non-republics became permissible, and for this task the French government "selected either career diplomats or those of moderate opinions, rather than those who had voted for the death of the king" (Frey and Frey, "Reign of the Charlatans Is Over," 736).

Directors] would be a guarantee of their future. The constitutional regime would be revolutionary."[83]

The British reaction to this development was immediate. In a letter to Morton Eden, Britain's ambassador to Berlin, Grenville stated that "the Nomination both to the Directory and to the Ministry, seem to make it much less likely than it had before appeared, that the present Government of France will apply themselves with good faith, to the restoration of peace."[84] Thus, even though Britain would engage in peace talks beginning in early 1796, key leaders were pessimistic that they would succeed. France was still revolutionary and therefore not to be trusted as having limited foreign policy aims.[85]

There were two more major shifts in French domestic politics leading up to the War of the Second Coalition. Once again, these changes, and the resulting shifts in the degree of ideological differences separating the powers' key decision makers, affected the policies of France's most determined rival in critical ways. The first change was a surge in royalist participation in the French government in the spring of 1797. In the election to the National Convention of March 1797, royalists won 180 of the 260 contested seats, bringing their total strength out of a possible 500 to 330.[86] The proportion of regicides in this new legislature dropped to less than one in five. By May of the same year, royalists had gained a majority in the Directory as well. This shift to the right in French politics made an immediate impact on domestic legislation. In June, the government removed both the electoral penalties on the relatives of émigrés and all the legislation against refractory priests. In July, the Legislature voted to close political clubs, including those of the Jacobins. These domestic changes in France had a direct effect on Franco-British relations. Probably most important, peace talks between the two states accelerated during this period. Significantly, this change occurred despite the fact of continued French military expansion, since Bonaparte won several major battles in Italy at this time. These victories threatened the security of Austria, which was Britain's most important ally.

This resurgence of royalism and its effects would not last the year, however. On 18 Fructidor (September 4), 1797, a coup, supported by the military, pushed France back in a revolutionary direction. A new government, known as the Second Directory, was formed. Royalists were purged from both the Directory and the Legislature. The law against émigrés and refractory priests was reinstated. Ex-nobles were deprived of their citizenship. Émigrés who had returned to France were ordered to leave the country,

---

83. Sutherland, *France 1789–1815*, 278.
84. In Mori, *William Pitt and the French Revolution*, 228.
85. Ibid., 231.
86. Sutherland, *France 1789–1815*, 302–304. This was possible because by this point in time the anti-monarchical Two-thirds Decree of the Constitution of 1795 was no longer in effect.

under penalty of death. An oath of hatred of monarchy was required for priests, and religious persecution increased. Diplomats tainted with aristocratic blood or monarchical service were dismissed and replaced with regicides and other anti-aristocrats. In short, France had moved yet again in a revolutionary direction, resulting in an increase in the ideological distance separating France's key leaders from those in the other great powers.[87]

As a direct result of this shift to the left, peace talks with Britain, which had been going on for months, were broken off within a week. In short, the coup of 1797 "provoked a rupture with England, and permitted Bonaparte to dictate to Austria the terms of a peace that could be nothing more than a truce."[88] Thus the coup of 1797 set the stage for the formation of the Second Coalition and the last of the major wars of the pre-Napoleonic period.

THE ORIGINS OF THE WAR OF THE SECOND COALITION, 1798–1802

The most important development in the War of the Second Coalition in relation to the previous two wars of the decade was Russia's entry into the fighting against France. Russia's position toward revolutionary France had been one of hostility since the fall of 1792. As with every other great power, Russia's leaders had pursued a policy of containment vis-à-vis France (by adopting initiatives designed to diplomatically, economically, and culturally isolate the French regime) as soon as French politics took a radical turn to the left.[89] Moreover, Russia had come close to entering the wars against France in 1796. In the fall of this year, Catherine had ordered an army of 64,000 men to be assembled and sent west against the French. She died, however, before this order could be executed. Her successor, Paul, though equally opposed to the Revolution for ideological reasons, refused to carry out his mother's plan. Most likely the dominant reason for Paul's decision to rescind Catherine's orders was so that Russian authorities could more effectively address increasingly prevalent serf revolts that were occurring at this time.[90] In 1798, Russia's leaders overcame their hesitancy (at least temporarily) and engaged France in battle.

Russian willingness to enter the wars against France was primarily a product of two changes that took place after the summer of 1797. First, the coalition against France had collapsed. By the fall of 1797 Britain was the only great power still engaged in the wars against the French (Austria was temporarily knocked out of the wars at this time when it signed the

87. Lefebvre, *French Revolution from 1793 to 1799*, 2:201.
88. Ibid., 2:197.
89. For details, see Blanning, *Origins of the French Revolutionary Wars*, 185–186; de Madariaga, *Russia in the Age of Catherine the Great*, 547; Brinton, *Decade of Revolution*, 180, 181.
90. Blanning, *Origins of the French Revolutionary Wars*, 187–188; Roderick McGrew, *Paul I of Russia, 1754–1801* (Oxford: Clarendon Press, 1992), 288.

Treaty of Campo Formio; Prussia had permanently exited the wars in 1795 after suffering military defeat and financial exhaustion). As a result, Russia could no longer rely on others to bear the costs in an action that its leaders repeatedly stated was in Russian interests: the destruction of the revolutionary regime in Paris. In this scenario, what had inhibited Russian ideological hostility to revolutionary France from being translated into war was Russia's ability to free-ride on the war-fighting efforts of other great powers. In this instance, the independent effects of both power (the system's multipolar structure) and ideological variables must be examined if we are to understand outcomes in this period.

The second factor that had changed in the period preceding Russia's entry into the wars was that France came closer to encroaching on Russian zones of interest than it had in previous years. Seventeen ninety-eight saw a significant increase in French expansion, including in the eastern Mediterranean and central Europe, as France increased its military efforts in Italy, Switzerland, and Egypt. With this expansion, Russia moved from overt diplomatic hostility toward revolutionary France to military belligerency. Russian behavior thus corresponds with the predictions of power-based theories. It appears that Russia responded to expanding French power by balancing against it.

While Tsar Paul's decision to enter the war against France was most likely a response to French expansion in the east, this does not mean, however, that concern over French power, per se, was the primary variable motivating Russian behavior. To begin with, Russian leaders believed that French aggression was derived from French principles. In fact, Paul "clearly identified Jacobinism with French expansion and a direct threat to political stability in Europe."[91] This belief, just as it did for British and Austrian decision makers, impelled Paul to adopt total war-fighting objectives that were explicitly designed to overthrow the revolutionary French regime and restore the French monarchy.[92]

A second reason why Russia's response to French expansion in the late 1790s should be to a great degree attributed to ideological variables is that Russian leaders, especially Paul, interpreted French actions as threatening to Russian interests, *not* primarily because they increased France's relative power, but because they threatened the political order of which Paul and fellow conservatives viewed themselves as champions. Why Paul

---

91. McGrew, *Paul I of Russia*, 279; Blanning, *French Revolutionary Wars*, 228–229.

92. On Paul's commitment to restore the French monarchy, see McGrew, *Paul I of Russia*, 301, 290–291, 295; Blanning, *French Revolutionary Wars*, 249, 252; Lobanov-Rostovsky, *Russia and Europe*, 19–21. On Britain's commitment to this goal in the War of the Second Coalition, see Mackesy, *Statesmen at War*, 69, 86–87, 150, 231; Michael Duffy, "British Policy in the War against Revolutionary France," in *Britain and Revolutionary France: Conflict, Subversion, and Propaganda*, ed. Colin Jones (Exeter: University of Exeter, 1983), 22. On Austria's commitment to counter-revolution in France in this period, see Blanning, *French Revolutionary Wars*, 130; Ross, *European Diplomatic History*, 191, 194.

viewed the consequences of French actions in these terms is the principal focus of this section.

On July 8, 1798, Paul had decided to send an army of 60,000 to 70,000 men west to join the war against France.[93] Significantly, this decision was made three weeks before the fall of Cairo at the hands of Napoleon's troops. Paul's decision to engage France in battle instead corresponds precisely with Napoleon's capture of the island of Malta. This event took place on June 12, 1798, but news of it did not reach Russia until early July, which was the time Russian policy changed. This timing is not just coincidental. Paul regarded the capture of Malta as the reason for entering the war.[94] The tsar saw this event as a casus belli for Russia not because of the strategic value of the island, but because of the ideological threat generated by the demise of the Knights of this territory.[95]

The Knights of Malta, for whom Paul had been named a protector in the previous year (joining the Holy Roman Emperor and the King of the Two Sicilies), were a vivid symbol of the monarchical order of the old regime. Indeed, the protection of this order was the Knights' *raison d'être*.

The purpose and aristocratic heritage of the Knights appealed greatly to Paul, who had always considered himself a protector of Europe's traditional political mores. The tsar had even established and placed under his guidance a priory in Russia that was linked to this group.[96] Paul hoped that his association with the Knights would help protect in Russia their shared ideological goals. According to Roderick McGrew, through Paul's links with the Knights the tsar hoped to "provide the base for a powerful and revived institution with which to defend monarchy and traditional values. . . . The Knights of Malta would provide an organizational center and an ideological form with which to shape the Russian nobility to the contours of Paul's own particular version of absolutism, and thus prepare them for the struggle in which they would have to play a leading role. In Russia, the Knights of Malta would become the *centerpiece* in a reformed and newly powerful monarchical society."[97]

By conquering Malta, Napoleon therefore did much more than simply enhance France's power-projection capabilities in the Mediterranean. France's behavior helped convince Paul that France under revolutionary

93. K. Waliszewski, *Paul the First of Russia, the Son of Catherine the Great* (London: William Heineman, 1913), 235.

94. Ibid., 238; Roderick McGrew, "Paul I and the Knights of Malta," in *Paul I: A Reassessment of His Life and Reign*, ed. Hugh Ragsdale (Pittsburgh: University Center for International Studies, University of Pittsburgh, 1979), 60.

95. Norman Saul, *Russia and the Mediterranean, 1797–1807* (Chicago: University of Chicago Press 1970), 35–36; Lobanov-Rostovsky, *Russia and Europe*, 21–22; Waliszewski, *Paul the First of Russia*, 240–245; McGrew, "Paul I and the Knights of Malta," 61.

96. McGrew, "Paul I and the Knights of Malta," 50, 48.

97. Ibid., 62 (emphasis added). These claims are corroborated by various associates of Paul's, including his son, Nicholas I (Waliszewski, *Paul the First of Russia*, 242).

leadership was an insatiable state that was bound to conflict with Russia. Just as important, the demise of the Knights of Malta called into question the viability of the ideological cause to which these individuals subscribed, which Paul had sworn to protect, and which the tsar had hoped to advance in his own state in the near future. Consequently, although the immediate cause of Russia's entrance into the war was France's territorial expansion, the nature of the threat generated by this expansion was not primarily a strategic one, but one of identity. Indeed, the strategic—but not the ideological—value of the island to Russia's interests (as Paul defined them) in all likelihood would not have justified the tsar's violent reaction to its capture by France.

The second prominent reason that Paul claimed had pushed him into war with France was a fear that French principles would spread to the Polish territories that Russia had acquired in the previous partitions of this state. Just as with the capture of Malta, this second fear was a result of French military activities, yet it, too, was more ideological than power-political in nature. Russian leaders feared that the presence of Polish soldiers in the French military (it was well known that a "Polish legion" of about 7,000 men was serving in the French army from about 1797 onward) would help to disseminate French ideas of nationalism and republicanism throughout Poland (and even Russia), thereby stimulating subversion and revolt against Russian control. The contributions of the Polish legion to the French cause "naturally led to a revival of agitation in Poland, and [Prince Alexander Andreevich] Bezborodko [who was Catherine's secretary of state and Paul's chancellor] was alarmed by its progress on all the south-west frontier of the Empire. The Chancellor feared that if it were favored by France it might receive a further impetus from the spread of republican ideas and might invade Russian territory, which, he said, 'would be the end of all things.'"[98]

Significantly, this fear of subversion manifested itself at a time when France's power-political threat to Russia's interests in eastern Europe was a relatively small one. Bezborodko asserted that there was no significant geostrategic conflict of interests between Russia and France at this time, and that the only factors preventing the creation of a modus vivendi between the two powers were due to their ideological differences.[99] Without the fears of subversion described in the previous paragraphs that accompanied France's territorial expansion in the east in the late 1790s, Russian leaders' perceptions of the French threat—and thus the incentives to join the war against it—would have been much lower.

98. In Waliszewski, *Paul the First of Russia,* 246.
99. Ibid.

THE END OF THE WARS OF THE FRENCH REVOLUTION

The twists and turns of the battlefield conditions and the ever-changing political situation in France during the War of the Second Coalition need not concern us. What is significant is how this war came to an end. Realist theories predict that the war would end either when one side defeated the other and established a hegemonic position in the system, or when a balance of power had been restored. With such an equilibrium, the source of threat and thus the cause of the war would have been removed. In contrast, I predict that hostilities would end when the ideological gap separating the powers' key decision makers significantly decreased, thereby lowering these individuals' perceptions of the threats that the other actors posed to their interests.

The last of the great powers to terminate hostilities with France, thereby ending the Wars of the French Revolution, was Great Britain, which did so by signing the Treaty of Amiens in March 1802. This treaty is puzzling from the point of view of realist theories since the agreement recognized French hegemony on the continent, including control over the Low Countries (which to realist arguments was Britain's casus belli in the first place). According to the terms of the treaty, France was to keep all its continental conquests. Of all Britain's territorial war booty in the Mediterranean, Caribbean, and Indian Ocean, it was to keep only Ceylon and Trinidad.[100]

Although Britain was undeniably war-weary and alone (since its allies had deserted it), these conditions were nothing new to this state. On several occasions during the previous war, it had soldiered on without allies and in spite of civil unrest. What made 1802 qualitatively different than, say, 1797? Although Britain was *more* fatigued in 1802 than 1797—a fact that might allow a power-centered theory to plausibly explain Britain's desire to exit the war—the great strategic vulnerability created by the treaty in combination with the fact that Britain significantly cut its defense spending after this time (more about this below) remains problematic for theories that stress that the imperative of maintaining the balance of power will invariably take precedence over all other concerns.

The major political change that occurred in France in this period was the coup in December 1799 that brought Napoleon to power. From Britain's perspective, it was far from certain that this event would mean the end of hostility between the two states. Pitt stated immediately after Napoleon's ascension to power that it was unwise to trust any person who held absolute power, and Napoleon appeared especially suspect on

---

100. According to the Treaty of Amiens, Britain recognized France's annexation of both Belgium and the Rhineland, as well as the Batavian, Legurian, Cisalpine, and Helvetian republics. Britain also agreed to return Malta, Minorca, Elba, Egypt, the French Caribbean islands, and South Africa to their original owners.

account of his past aggressive activities.[101] Yet even at this early date, Pitt did not hold back all hope that the political change in France would lead to an increase in international peace. Unlike a state guided by Jacobin principles, with which Pitt swore never to compromise, Napoleon's dictatorship was qualitatively different. According to Pitt: "In the first place, we see . . . a change in the description and form of the sovereign authority. . . . The different institutions, republican in their form and appearance . . . *are now annihilated;* they have given way to the absolute power of one man . . . and *differing from other monarchs only in this,* that . . . he wields a sword instead of a scepter."[102] In the prime minister's mind, peace was more likely after 1799 because France under Napoleon's dictatorship had the potential to be much more similar ideologically to the old regime powers ("differing from other monarchs only by wielding a sword instead of a scepter") than previous French regimes in the 1790s.

In order for my argument to explain the peace of Amiens from Britain's perspective, in the two years after Napoleon's coup he must have sufficiently demonstrated his repudiation of revolutionary France's core ideological objectives. By so doing, British leaders' perceptions of threat posed by France should have significantly decreased, thereby allowing for peace on terms that were unacceptable throughout the previous decade.

A strong case can be made that this is precisely what happened. After assuming power, Napoleon passed several anti-Jacobin measures, including executing several of those who participated in the "crime" of the September Massacres; he eased restrictions and penalties on émigrés; and he greatly increased religious freedom. Finally, in December 1800 Napoleon declared to the nation: "The Revolution is established upon the principles which began it: It is ended."[103]

With Napoleon's repudiation of many of revolutionary France's core ideological beliefs, Britain's leaders' perceptions of the French threat were substantially reduced. According to the historian A. B. Rodger, Britain was able to make the extremely generous offer of peace to France that ended the Wars of the French Revolution because its leaders, like many in Europe, "assumed that Bonaparte, unlike the Jacobins was someone with whom one could deal. All the monarchies would have preferred a Bourbon restoration . . . but the First Consul was strong, he had the reputation of being prudent, and he was at least preferable to the left-wingers."[104]

---

101. William Pitt, "Bonaparte" (speech delivered to Parliament February 3, 1800), in Coupland, *War Speeches of William Pitt,* 263–265.
102. Pitt, "Bonaparte," 263 (emphasis added). Paul viewed Napoleon in similar terms: "Paul saw Bonaparte as liquidating the revolution [and] re-establishing a sound conventional political and social order in France—a monarchy in everything but name" (McGrew, *Paul I and the Knights of Malta,* 314–315).
103. In Sutherland, *France 1789–1815,* 342.
104. A. B. Rodger, *The War of the Second Coalition, 1798–1801* (Oxford: Clarendon Press, 1964), 291. See also Mori, *William Pitt and the French Revolution,* 282.

Moreover, British leaders did not seem to believe that the peace of Amiens would be nothing more than a mere truce (as other old regime powers had assumed about previous agreements with revolutionary France).[105] As the ideological similarities uniting the powers' key decision makers increased, so, too, did the estimated likelihood of long-term peace. The accurateness of this assertion is demonstrated by the dramatic decline in British military spending that occurred after the treaty. After Amiens the British "set about disarmament with a frenzy that would have been justified only if Britain never had to face the possibility of war for a decade. Income-tax was abolished, naval expenditure reduced by two million, and St. Vincent at the Admiralty put on half-pay."[106] Theories that look only at the distribution of power can explain neither British leaders' high hopes for peace nor their corresponding policies of disarmament, especially given the military preponderance that France enjoyed on the continent at this time. That British statesmen misjudged Napoleon's extreme ambition in no way discounts the fact that it was increasing ideological similarities between British and French leaders that impelled the former to possess high hopes for prolonged peace in the first place.

105. Rodger, *War of the Second Coalition,* 291.
106. Ibid., 292.

[3]

The Concert of Europe, 1815–48

The years 1815 to 1848, known as the era of the Concert of Europe, are in important ways anomalous in the history of international relations over the last two hundred years. In contrast to the periods that preceded and succeeded it, great powers relations during this era were extremely peaceful.[1]

Scholars have offered various arguments to explain the peacefulness of the Concert system. Realists assert that the stability of this era owed primarily to the creation of a stable balance of power in the wake of the Napoleonic Wars. To this view, Concert leaders' fears of provoking balancing coalitions formed by the other powers pushed decision makers to adopt limited foreign policy goals that respected the vital interests of the other key actors. This restraint reduced the likelihood of great power conflict.[2] Other scholars have described the Concert in institutionalist terms. To this view, the peacefulness of the years in question was largely due to the establishment of institutionalized congress diplomacy, which both allowed the great powers' leaders to better understand one another's interests and intentions so as to avoid unwanted conflict, and created through various mechanisms incentives for sustained cooperation.[3]

1. For statistical analyses confirming this point, see Paul Schroeder, "Containment Nineteenth-Century Style: How Russia Was Restrained," *South Atlantic Quarterly* 82, no. 1 (Winter 1983): 11; Jack Levy, *War in the Modern Great Power System, 1495–1975* (Lexington: University Press of Kentucky, 1983), 113, 117, 144.

2. Hans Morgenthau, *Politics among Nations: The Struggle for Power and Peace* (New York: Alfred A. Knopf, 1961), chaps. 14, 27; Henry Kissinger, *A World Restored: Metternich, Castlereagh, and the Problems of Peace, 1812–1822* (Boston: Houghton Mifflin, 1973); Korina Kagan, "The Myth of the European Concert: The Realist-Institutionalist Debate and Great Power Behavior in the Eastern Question, 1821–41," *Security Studies* 7, no. 2 (Winter 1997/98): 1–57.

3. Robert Jervis, "From Balance to Concert: A Study of International Security Cooperation," *World Politics* 38, no. 1 (October 1985): 58–79; Richard Elrod, "The Concert of Europe: A Fresh Look at an International System," *World Politics* 28, no. 2 (January 1976): 159–174.

Finally, some scholars have explained the stability of the Concert in terms of complex learning that resulted in a new era of statecraft. To this way of thinking, the leaders of the great powers of the Concert, after emerging from the horrors of the Napoleonic Wars, came to realize that following short-run goals of power maximization was in the long run suicidal. They therefore came to identify their respective national interests with the preservation of the stability of the international system. It is this "shift in collective mentality" that explains the peacefulness of the period.[4]

This chapter challenges these explanations of the great powers' foreign policies during the Concert era, as well as the meaning of the statistical studies that reveal the great peacefulness of this time. I argue that great power relations during the years 1815 to 1848 should be divided analytically into two different periods. The first, from 1815 to 1830, was one of considerable great power cooperation. In these years, the key leaders in each of the powers were more likely to view the others as reliable allies than likely enemies. As a result, decision makers were not terribly concerned about issues of relative power for the first fifteen years of the Concert period. The great powers in these years neither started arms races (in fact they unilaterally cut military forces) nor developed war plans for fighting one another.[5]

Great powers relations underwent a considerable change after 1830. Instead of all five of the great powers, Britain, Russia, France, Austria, and Prussia, viewing each other as likely allies, after 1830 these states were for many years divided into two coalitions, with Britain and France on one side and Russia, Austria, and Prussia on the other.

There was considerable hostility and rivalry between these two groups. British Foreign Minister Lord Palmerston, for example, was determined to roll back the power of the three eastern monarchies (especially Russia's), while Tsar Nicholas of Russia wanted nothing more than the strategic isolation and humiliation of France. Although statistical examinations of the Concert era are correct that there was no hot war between the great powers during this period, relations between the two groups of alliances after 1830 could be considered for much of this period of time a cold war. Studies that make no distinctions between the 1815–30 and 1830–48 periods thus miss critical dynamics of great power relations during these years.

Analyses that rely on complex learning or the creation of effective institutions to explain states' foreign policies in the Concert period cannot

4. Paul Schroeder, "The Transformation of Political Thinking, 1787–1848," in *Coping with Complexity in the International System*, ed. Jack Snyder and Robert Jervis (Boulder: Westview, 1993), 47, quoted in Kagan, "Myth of the European Concert," 17. See also Paul Schroeder, *The Transformation of European Politics, 1763–1848* (Oxford: Clarendon Press, 1994), viii.

5. Reinhard Wolf, "How Partners Become Rivals: Testing Neorealist and Liberal Hypotheses," *Security Studies* 12, no. 2 (Winter 2002/3): 12.

account for the transformation in great power relations that occurred after 1830. If complex learning was the principal cause of great power cooperation from 1815 to 1830, why did statesmen all of a sudden unlearn what they had been practicing for the previous fifteen years? If institutions deserve the credit for great power cooperation in the wake of the Napoleonic Wars, why did actors shift to much more hostile policies when the institutional structure was still largely in place?

This book does not confront an analogous problem. From 1815 to 1830, the ideological similarities uniting the great powers leaders were substantial. With Napoleon's ultimate defeat at Waterloo and the subsequent restoration of the Bourbons to the French throne, the ideological gap that had existed in Europe since the French Revolution had been closed. As in 1789, the great powers of the system were all long-standing monarchies grounded on the principle of hereditary right. As the ideological distance separating the great powers' leaders narrowed significantly, their perceptions of the threats that the other states posed to their domestic and international interests shrunk to a substantial degree. Statesmen in this period therefore confronted strong incentives pushing them to eschew hostile policies toward one another in favor of cooperative ones.

In 1830, however, both Britain and France experienced party and institutional changes that significantly widened the ideological distances dividing these states' leaders from their counterparts in the eastern monarchies. It was these domestic changes in Britain and France that resulted in the division of Europe into two hostile camps, with the two constitutional monarchies on one side and the three absolutist powers on the other. In order to test these hypotheses against the evidence of the Concert, my analysis will concentrate primarily on the policies of the two strongest and most influential of the era's great powers: Russia and Britain.[6]

RUSSIA'S FOREIGN POLICIES

Russia emerged from the Napoleonic Wars as by far the greatest land power in Europe. In 1816 Russia had 60,000 more military personnel than did Britain, France, Austria, and Prussia combined![7] The key question for our purposes is: To what ends would Russia's leaders devote their state's advantageous position?

6. The system was almost a bipolar one according to some scholars' estimates. Enno Kraehe, "A Bipolar Balance of Power," *American Historical Review* 97, no. 3 (June 1992): 707–715; Paul Kennedy, *The Rise and Fall of the Great Powers: Economic Change and Military Conflict from 1500 to 2000* (New York: Random House, 1987), chap. 4.

7. Kennedy, *Rise and Fall of the Great Powers*, 154.

Realist theories can explain important elements of Russia's foreign policies in the years immediately following the end of the Napoleonic Wars. In this period, Tsar Alexander and his closest advisors were very aware that Britain was Russia's most powerful rival in terms of both power capacity and a relative lack of vulnerabilities due to its insular position. As a consequence Alexander believed that the other powers should attempt to balance against British strength. In order to accomplish this goal, the tsar sought to rehabilitate Russia's former enemy: France. He pushed for the termination of the Quadruple Alliance, which was directed against France, and the subsequent reincorporation of France into the councils of Europe. Alexander hoped that these strategies would both break Britain's and Austria's control over the Alliance, and would allow Russia a freer hand to make use of French naval power to counter Britain's. This seems to be balance-of-power politics at its best. As changes in the distribution of power occurred, a recent enemy was converted into an ally as a potential balance against the new most powerful state in comparison to one's own.

Alexander in this period was also interested in increasing Russia's power through territorial acquisitions. Specifically, Alexander wanted to bring a significant portion of the existing Polish regime (the Duchy of Warsaw) under Russian control. In order to buy Prussia's support for this goal, this state was offered territory from Saxony.

Leaders in Austria, Britain, and France were alarmed by the growth of Russian and Prussian power that the Poland-Saxony transfer would constitute, and they tried to prevent it through various means, including by (largely implicit) threats of military force. The fact that Prussia abandoned its ambitions in Saxony is often described as a victory for balance-of-power politics.[8] As Paul Schroeder points out, however, only Prussia and not Russia was forced to retreat on this issue. Russia did not capitulate because it possessed overwhelming power in comparison to that of Austria and France, and because British naval power could not be brought to bear in this region. According to Schroeder: "Balance-of-power tactics [over the Poland-Saxony issue] were tried and failed. The initial confrontation, which pitted Russia against Austria supported by Britain and France . . . was won by Russia hands down, as it forced Prussia back into line and compelled the others to accept its basic territorial and constitutional aims in Poland."[9] In short, just as many realist theories predict (especially the power-maximizing arguments from the "offensive realist" school), Alexander desired to increase Russia's relative power position on

---

8. Harold Nicolson, *The Congress of Vienna: A Study in Allied Unity, 1812–1822* (New York: Harvest/HBJ, 1946), 149; Edward Vose Gulick, *Europe's Classical Balance of Power* (New York: W. W. Norton, 1955), chaps. 7–9.

9. Schroeder, *Transformation of European Politics*, 537.

the continent, and neither previous commitments nor the fear of great power opposition could dissuade him from attempting to realize this aim.

The problem that Russian foreign policy in the Concert period poses for realist theories is that Russian behavior over Poland was the exception, not the rule, to its international decisions. Virtually all scholars agree that Russia's foreign policies in Europe and particularly in the Near East were ones of considerable moderation, especially when the opportunities for aggrandizement and the forces impelling Russian leaders to expand are considered. Poland was the only region in which such restraint was lacking.

There were four major international developments in the Near East in the Concert era in which Russian actions were a critical determinant of outcomes: the Greek rebellion against Turkey in the 1820s, the Russo-Turkish War of 1828–29, and the First and Second Egyptian Crises of 1833 and 1839, respectively. In each of these conflicts, Russian statesmen consistently adopted limited foreign policy aims despite opportunities for much more significant expansion. The high degree of ideological similarities uniting the great powers' leaders was primarily responsible for these outcomes.[10]

The Greek rebellion against Turkey became a prominent international issue in the spring of 1821 when a member of a leading Greek family, Alexander Hypsilantis (who was also a member of the Russian army), initiated a revolt in Greece against its Turkish oppressors. The event set off what was to be a decade of bloody and extremely cruel warfare. On the surface, Russia's interests in this matter appear to be clear. In terms of its effect on the international distribution of power, the creation of an independent Greek state would be doubly advantageous for Russian power aggrandizement. This outcome would both weaken the Ottoman Empire—a state that had been the object of Russian encroachment for generations—and increase Russian influence in the Balkans since an independent Greece would be tied to Russia through religious bonds. Russia's position vis-à-vis Austria would thus be advanced. Russia's key leaders also had considerable domestic pressures pushing them toward war with Turkey. Alexander had long portrayed himself as a defender of the Orthodox religion, and the atrocities committed by a Muslim power against fellow believers were more than many could stand.

Thus the domestic and international pressures pushing Alexander to war with Turkey were tremendous. As the tsar stated to Vicomte de Chateaubriand (the French representative at the Verona Congress in 1822): "Nothing, without doubt, appeared more agreeable to my interests,

10. It is appropriate to concentrate on Russia's policies in the Near East because the "Eastern Question" was probably the most important one for Russia's leaders throughout the Concert.

to the interests of my peoples, to the public opinion of my country, than a religious war with Turkey."[11] Yet until his death in 1825, Alexander continued to resist the forces impelling his state toward war.[12]

The other three Near Eastern crises that took place during the Concert era occurred during the reign of Nicholas I, who became tsar in 1825 after Alexander's death. In each of these crises, Nicholas continued his brother's policies of adopting moderate foreign policy goals despite significant opportunities for expansion.

The first of these key events was the Russo-Turkish War of 1828–29. By the end of this war, the Russian army had captured Adrianople and the road to Constantinople lay open. Despite these developments, and despite the fact that Russian aims of aggrandizement at the expense of the Ottoman Empire had been long-standing, the Treaty of Adrianople that ended the war had by virtually all accounts a very modest impact on the European balance of power.[13] Nicholas even returned many conquered territories to the sultan.

The Treaty of Adrianople should not be considered anomalous for Russian foreign policies in this period. Even before this agreement was signed, Nicholas had appointed a special committee of advisors to determine what direction Russia's foreign policy should take in the Near East in the foreseeable future. The Protocol of September 16, 1829, which was the report unanimously agreed to by the committee, "became the fundamental basis of Russian policy in the Near East for over two decades."[14] The most important decision reached by the group was that the Ottoman Empire must be preserved if at all possible, even if this outcome meant forgoing opportunities for Russian territorial aggrandizement. The report explicitly stated that Russia's past expansionary policies in this region of the world did not further Russia's current interests.[15]

Nicholas's key policies for the remainder of the Concert reflected these views. The central foreign policy achievement of Russian diplomacy after the Treaty of Adrianople was the Treaty of Unkiar-Skelessi signed with the Ottoman Empire in June 1833. This treaty ended the so-called First Egyptian Crisis, which resulted from rebellion within the Ottoman

11. In Matthew Anderson, "Russia and the Eastern Question, 1821–41," in *Europe's Balance of Power, 1815–1848*, ed. Alan Sked (London: Macmillan Press, 1979), 83.

12. Irby C. Nichols, Jr., "Tsar Alexander I: Pacifist, Aggressor, or Vacillator?" *East European Quarterly* 16, no. 1 (March 1982): 33–44.

13. Kenneth Bourne, *The Foreign Policy of Victorian England, 1830–1902* (Oxford: Clarendon Press, 1970), 23; David Gillard, *The Struggle for Asia, 1828–1914: A Study in British and Russian Imperialism* (London: Methuen, 1977), 25; Anderson, "Russia and the Eastern Question," 86; W. Bruce Lincoln, *Nicholas I, Emperor and Autocrat of All the Russias* (Bloomington: Indiana University Press, 1978), 201; Schroeder, "Containment Nineteenth-Century Style," 2–5.

14. Robert Kerner, "Russia's New Policy in the Near East after the Peace of Adrianople: Including the Text of the Protocol of 16 September 1829," *Cambridge Historical Journal* 5 (1935–37): 280.

15. Ibid., 283.

Empire. Mehemet Ali, Pasha of Egypt, had decided to wage war against Mahmud II, Sultan of the Empire, in an attempt to increase his regional power base and possibly replace Mahmud as sultan. When the British and French ignored Mahmud's appeal for aid against the increasingly successful rebel, the sultan had no choice but to appeal to his Empire's ancient foe: Russia. As the price for Russia's aid, Turkey was compelled to sign the Treaty of Unkiar-Skelessi. The most important provision in the treaty recommitted Turkey to close the Bosporus and Dardanelles straits to all foreign warships.

Despite this concession, the overall terms of this treaty were very lenient. The sultan was in a desperate condition. Yet despite the opportunity for territorial expansion, Nicholas continued his moderate foreign policies of the previous decade. Not only did he not seek to acquire any increase in territory at Turkey's expense, but within six months of the signing of the document, he had ordered the withdrawal of Russian troops from the Danubian principalities, re-recognized the suzerainty of Turkey in border regions of its empire, and significantly decreased the indemnities Turkey owed Russia as a result of their War of 1828–29. These actions offer concrete support to Nicholas's frequently made claim that he did "not claim one inch of Turkish soil" (as long as no other power claimed any of it as well).[16] In short, the tsar desired only the maintenance of his sphere of interest and the status quo, not new territorial acquisitions.

The final important event for Russia's foreign policies in the Near East during the Concert era is similar to the third. In 1839, the sultan of Turkey sought revenge against the rebellious Mehemet Ali by invading Syria, which Mehemet had acquired as a result of the first crisis six years earlier. The sultan's armies were quickly defeated in this attack, and his navy defected to the cause of the pasha. It looked highly likely that either the Ottoman Empire would collapse, or that it would be preserved under Mehemet's more forceful leadership.

The Second Egyptian Crisis was resolved largely due to the efforts of the great powers, especially Britain and Russia. These two powers, with support from Austria and Prussia, forced Mehemet to abandon much of his gains (including the Turkish fleet) and stipulated that Syria would not be a hereditary possession of the pasha, but would instead remain under his control only as long as he lived (Mehemet was already seventy-one years old). More important for the future of great power relations, all these states signed the July Convention of 1840. This accord stipulated that in peace time, Turkey would not allow any warships to pass through either the Bosphorus or the Dardenelles. When Turkey was at war, if one power's warships were permitted to pass through the straits, all the other powers would have the same right. Significantly, although France

---

16. In Lincoln, *Nicholas I,* 116.

eventually signed the convention of 1840 in the next year, it was originally not a part of the negotiations. Because of past and contemporary ties to Egypt, France was much more sympathetic to Mehemet than any of the other powers. The crisis was thus resolved over French objections.

The Convention of 1840 marked a setback for Russia's power-political interests in the region. The 1833 Treaty of Unkiar-Skelessi had committed the Porte—in an agreement with Russia alone—to close the straits to warships of all foreign states. The Convention of 1840 renewed this pledge, but it did so by an agreement with other great powers. The ultimate significance of this multilateral accord was that "the Straits were . . . made, explicitly and unmistakably, an object of European concern; their status was now regulated by an international agreement which was to last until the First World War."[17] The Convention of 1840 thus superseded the unilateral advantages that Russia had achieved in previous negotiations with the Ottoman Empire, and replaced them with a multilateral protectorate that explicitly recognized the other powers' rights and concerns in the region.

Realist theories offer some insight into explaining why Russia's leaders adopted consistently moderate foreign policies in each of the Near Eastern crises during the Concert period. Most notably, the authors of the aforementioned report (the Protocol of September 16, 1829) that guided Russia's foreign policies vis-à-vis Turkey for much of the Concert explicitly justified their call for moderation with reference to power-political considerations. The authors claimed that taking actions that would precipitate the collapse and subsequent partition of the Ottoman Empire was not in Russia's interests, both because other powers might benefit more from this outcome than would Russia, and because these events might trigger a war in which the other powers would likely be united against Russia.[18] These reasons for pursuing limited foreign policy objectives in the Near East are consistent with realist logic.

Although power-political concerns likely played a role in deterring Russia from adopting more expansionary objectives in the Near East, the evidence indicates that these considerations were not paramount. In each of the four Near Eastern crises of the period, Russia's leaders did not forgo more expansionary policies primarily because they were fearful of provoking a counterbalancing coalition formed by the other powers. For example, during the Greek rebellion in the early 1820s, Russia's key decision makers believed that the other powers would have difficulty preventing either Russian aid to the Greeks or the creation of an independent Greek state that would be in Russia's sphere of influence. This was not an unreasonable view. Key British leaders, including George Canning (who

17. Anderson, "Russia and the Eastern Question," 96.
18. Kerner, "Russia's New Policy in the Near East," 283; Lincoln, *Nicholas I*, 200, 201; Kagan, "Myth of the European Concert," 33, 34.

became foreign minister in 1822) believed that Russian power could not be restrained in the Balkans at this point in time.[19]

Similarly, at the time of the Russo-Turkish War of 1828–29, not only did Russia possess a significantly greater number of troops in the region than did France and Britain, but "Britain, France and Austria all . . . admitted Russia's right to enforce its bilateral treaties with Turkey," even if this meant war (the cause of the war from Russian leaders' perspective was Turkey's failure to honor various treaty commitments it had established with Russia in previous decades, most notably various commercial obligations and the promise to protect the Christian religion and its churches in territories within the Ottoman Empire).[20] The fact that the other powers explicitly recognized that Russia was justified to start a war with Turkey meant that Russia's leaders had even less reason to fear opposition to its policies by the other powers than an analysis of theater power variables indicated. Consistent with the claim that the chances were low that the other powers would form a balancing coalition against Russia are the facts that Britain's leaders were in this period committed to trying to restrain Russia by allying with, not against it; and at the beginning of the Russo-Turkish War, Britain and France clashed with Turkey, thereby helping Russia's war efforts instead of aiding the Ottoman Empire defend itself from the Russian threat.[21]

At the time Russia signed the Treaty of Unkiar-Skelessi with Turkey in 1833, the British and French were the powers that were deterred by superior Russian force, and not the reverse. The French fleet remained in the Mediterranean after Nicholas informed the French government that passage through the straits would be an act of war, and the British ambassador to the Porte (and a significant Russophobe), Lord Ponsonby, refused to allow the British fleet to enter the Dardanelles.[22] In other words, it appears that at this point in time the western powers were more afraid of a confrontation with Russia, at least in this region of the world, than the reverse. The claim that Russian moderation at this time resulted from a fear of a countervailing coalition is thus problematic.[23]

19. Schroeder, *Transformation of European Politics*, 642; Loyal Cowles, "The Failure to Restrain Russia: Canning, Nesselrode, and the Greek Question, 1825–1827," *International History Review* 12, no. 4 (November 1990): 697, 706, 707.

20. Matthew Rendall, "Russia, the Concert of Europe, and Greece, 1821–29: A Test of Hypotheses about the Vienna System," *Security Studies* 9, no. 4 (Summer 2000): 62; Barbara Jelavich, *Russia's Balkan Entanglements, 1806–1914* (New York: Cambridge University Press, 1991), 4–5, 39–41.

21. J. A. R. Marriott, *The Eastern Question: An Historical Study in European Diplomacy* (Oxford: Clarendon Press, 1917), 197–198.

22. Lincoln, *Nicholas I*, 205.

23. This claim is corroborated by the fact that the British fleet, as British Foreign Minister Lord Palmerston readily admitted, was "fully occupied" in other areas at this time (most notably in the North Sea and off the shores of Holland and Portugal) (Harold Temperley, *England and the Near East*, vol. 1: *The Crimea* [New York: Archon Books, 1964], 64).

The resolution of the Second Egyptian Crisis of 1838–41 is doubly puzzling for realist arguments. As with the first Mehemet crisis of 1833, there is little evidence to suggest that Nicholas signed the Convention of 1840 out of fear of a coalition of the other great powers. Austria and Prussia would most likely not have abandoned their traditional ally, and the liberal entente that united France and Britain for much of the 1830s was near collapse. The threat of war by the Western powers against Russia was thus (at least from Russia's perspective) not very credible. Moreover, this crisis marked the culmination of a policy that Nicholas had ardently pursued for much of his reign: an alignment with Britain that isolated France from the other great powers. This strategy is problematic for realism because from the beginning of the Concert to its end, Britain was the greatest power-political threat to Russian interests in the Baltic, the Near East, and Central Asia, while France, because of its naval strength and geographical position, was the state that could offer Russia the most valuable aid against Britain. A Franco-Russian alliance therefore made great sense according to the logic of power politics. The fact that both Russian and French nationalists and military strategists wanted such an alliance speaks to the validity of this claim.[24] Yet Nicholas and his closest advisors consistently pursued the exact opposite strategy.

Finally, it should be noted that the incentives pushing Russia's leaders to adopt expansionary policies during the Concert period should have been particularly strong according to realist analyses because this period was one of perceived offense dominance (this belief resulted from the revolution in war-fighting tactics demonstrated throughout the Napoleonic Wars).[25] This perception of offense dominance should have pushed decision makers to believe that security was scarce and thus the need to adopt power-maximizing strategies high. These considerations make Russia's continued international restraint in the face of opportunities for expansion even more puzzling to realist theories.

Two ideological variables were critical to the development of Russia's foreign policies throughout the Concert period: Russian leaders' great ideological antipathy to liberal-revolutionary groups throughout the system, and the high degree of ideological similarities uniting Russia's most important decision makers with their counterparts in other great powers.

24. Harold Ingle, *Nesselrode and the Russian Rapprochement with Britain, 1836–1844* (Berkeley: University of California Press, 1976), 34, 35, 61; Alan Palmer, *The Chancelleries of Europe* (London: George Allen and Unwin, 1983), 21.

25. Jack S. Levy, "The Offensive/Defensive Balance of Military Technology: A Theoretical and Historical Analysis," *International Studies Quarterly* 28, no. 2 (June 1984): 232. Although Stephen Van Evera labels the Concert era a defense-dominant one, he also asserts that because "subversion is a form of offense," leaders that fear subversion are likely to believe they are in an offense-dominant world. Fears of ideological subversion dominated the great powers' leaders thoughts throughout the Concert (Stephen Van Evera, "Offense, Defense, and the Causes of War," *International Security* 22, no. 4 [Spring 1998]: 20).

These two considerations were not unrelated. The existence in the system of revolutionary forces that posed a plausible threat to Russia's system of governance made its leaders more aware than ever of their large, objective ideological similarities with the other monarchical states. In the language of social-psychological studies of group formation, Russia's decision makers' fixation during the Concert era on an ideological outgroup (revolutionary forces) pushed them to identify even more closely with their ideological ingroup (fellow monarchical powers based on the principle of hereditary right).

Alexander's and Nicholas's great ideological antipathy to liberal-revolutionary actors pushed them to oppose all such groups in the system, even if doing so meant forgoing opportunities for power aggrandizement in favor of more moderate foreign policies. Alexander, Nicholas, and their key foreign policy advisors, including Count Karl Nesselrode (who was Russia's foreign minister for much of the Concert) and the Grand Duke Constantine (Alexander's viceroy in Poland and the tsars' brother), repeatedly asserted that the Greek revolt and the sultan's conflicts with Mehemet Ali were examples of the ongoing battle between revolutionary forces and monarchical authority that had plagued Europe since the French Revolution. To their minds, if Russia's leaders were to weaken the sultan by pursuing expansionary policies, they would be aiding the forces of revolution not only in the Ottoman Empire, but throughout Europe and even in Russia. As Alexander stated to one of his own ministers concerning the Greek crisis: "If we reply to the Turks with war, [revolutionary forces] will triumph and no government will be left standing. I do not intend to leave a free field to the enemies of order."[26] To aid the Greeks in their conflict with Turkey "would assist the game of the revolutionists in every country in Europe, to whom and to whom alone the late events [of the Greek rebellion] are to be attributed."[27]

Nicholas wholly concurred with these sentiments. In reference to the Greek rebellion he asserted: "I abhor the Greeks, although they are my co-religionists. . . . I look upon them as subjects in open revolt against their legitimate sovereign; I do not desire their enfranchisement; they do not deserve it, and it would be a very bad example for all other countries if they succeeded in establishing it."[28] With regard to the Egyptian crises, Nicholas wrote in a letter to his special emissary to the sultan that the "entire war [between Mehemet Ali and Mahmud II] is nothing other than a consequence of the subversive spirit reigning at the moment in Europe and especially in France. . . . With the conquest of [Constantinople by

26. In Anderson, "Russia and the Eastern Question," 81.
27. In Kagan, "Myth of the European Concert," 27. See also Matthew Smith Anderson, *The Eastern Question, 1774–1923* (London: Macmillan, 1966), 61.
28. In Lincoln, *Nicholas I,* 118. See also Anderson, *Eastern Question,* 74, 80. Britain, not Russia, was the power most responsible for Greek independence.

Mehemet] we will have right in our own back yard a nest of all those homeless individuals, men without a country, who have been banished from all well-ordered societies."[29]

Both Alexander and Nicholas recognized the geopolitical benefits to Russia that would result from the weakening of the Ottoman Empire. But the tsars' fierce ideological hatred of all liberal-revolutionary groups transformed how they viewed the sultan. Instead of primarily viewing the Ottoman Empire as a geopolitical rival, Alexander and Nicholas came to see the Porte as an ally against their common ideological enemies. Consequently, the tsars believed that adopting policies which weakened the Ottoman Empire would ultimately harm their own interests. To put this analysis another way, Russia's key leaders believed that domestic developments in different states were to an important degree interconnected. These individuals feared that when revolutionary forces triumphed in one country, this outcome made it more likely that similar groups would succeed elsewhere, including potentially in Russia. Given these views, it was more important to Alexander and Nicholas not to harm a transnational ideological ally than it was to increase Russia's relative power position at the Porte's expense. "Nicholas's strict view of dynastic legitimacy," as the historian Bruce Lincoln expresses related analysis, "would not allow him to violate the territorial integrity nor the dynastic order of a legitimate state," including the Ottoman Empire, even if this meant forgoing opportunities of power augmentation.[30]

Ideological considerations affected Russian leaders' foreign policies in important ways other than limiting their ambitions during various Near Eastern crises. Ideological variables also pushed Russia's most important decision makers to adopt very cooperative policies toward the other great powers, especially from 1815 to 1830. Consistent with the predictions of the conflict-probability causal mechanism, the high degree of ideological similarities uniting the great powers' leaders after the Napoleonic Wars pushed Alexander and Nicholas to see their counterparts in the other monarchical states as trustworthy individuals who shared key interests as their own, most notably containing the power of liberal-revolutionary groups throughout Europe. These feelings of trust and commonalty of interests were important because they allowed the tsars not to be overly concerned about Russia's relative power position in relation to the other key actors in the system. This view not only further reduced the incentives pushing Russia's decision makers to expand in the Near East, but

---

29. Similarly, Nesselrode wrote: "With the victory of Mehemet Ali, French influence would increase in Constantinople, which would very soon become a hot-bed where all those without principles and without a country, who conspire against Russia, would gather" (both in Lincoln, *Nicholas I*, 203). See also Ingle, *Nesselrode and the Russian Rapprochement with Britain*, 12; Rendall, "Russia, the Concert of Europe, and Greece," 83.

30. Lincoln, *Nicholas I*, 114. See also Anderson, "Russia and the Eastern Question," 89.

made them less concerned about the geopolitical expansion of the other powers. In fact, the tsars *encouraged* the other powers to increase their geopolitical influence in neighboring territories. Alexander, for example, pushed Austria and Prussia to increase their influence in leading the German Confederation, Austria to invade Italy when revolution broke out in Piedmont, France to invade Spain after the latter's revolution in 1820, and was even acquiescent when Britain established protectorates over Corfu and the Ionian islands.[31]

Alexander was thus willing both to forgo relative power increases for Russia if this outcome aided revolutionary groups in the system, and to push the other powers to increase their relative power if this benefited the cause of conservatism throughout Europe. These foreign policies are doubly puzzling for realist analyses. They are, however, explicable to the argument of this book. Because Alexander viewed the other powers as ideological allies against a common ideological enemy, increases in the other states' relative power positions were not nearly as threatening as they would have been under different ideological circumstances. To Alexander, "the supreme [foreign policy] necessity was to preserve the structure of conservative and monarchical solidarity which had . . . been created at the end of the struggle with Napoleon I."[32] To the tsar, "ideological loyalties were more important than material advantage."[33]

The importance of ideological distances to Russia's relations with the other great powers is even more clearly revealed by examining Nicholas's policies. The ideological relationships among the powers during Nicholas's reign contained elements of similarity and distinction in comparison to these relationships during Alexander's time in power. Throughout the Concert, Austria and Prussia remained fellow autocratic states that were dedicated to virtually identical legitimating principles as Russia. As a result, the degree of ideological similarities uniting the three eastern monarchies remained very high throughout both Nicholas's and Alexander's reigns.

The same cannot be said, however, about Russia's relationships with Britain and France. In 1830, the western powers experienced important domestic changes. In July 1830, the autocratic Charles X of France was swept from power and was replaced on the throne by his cousin Louis-Philippe,

---

31. Schroeder, "Containment Nineteenth-Century Style"; Schroeder, *Transformation of European Politics*, 558–59, 573, 613, 626.

32. Anderson, "Russia and the Eastern Question," 81. See also Schroeder, *Transformation of European Politics*, 621.

33. Anderson, "Russia and the Eastern Question," 82. Alexander expressed to Chateaubriand his beliefs in the commonalty of interests among the great powers that existed after Napoleon's defeat: "Now there no longer exists an English policy, a French, Russian, Prussian, or Austrian policy; there is now only one common policy which, for the welfare of all, ought to be adopted in common by all states and all peoples" (in Lincoln, *Nicholas I*, 105).

though the latter was not next in succession to acquire power. The July Revolution made France a more genuine constitutional monarchy than it had been the previous fifteen years. The powers of the king were somewhat circumscribed, ministerial authority was enhanced, the electorate was broadened, and the federal government's heretofore highly aristocratic bureaucracy was replaced by a more middle class one.[34]

Britain, in large part inspired by the success and peacefulness of the July Revolution, also underwent a liberalizing process. In 1832, the Reform Bill (which widened the electoral base and created more pro-reform peers in the House of Lords) was passed, and as a result British leaders were made even more beholden to public opinion. Eighteen thirty also witnessed the Whigs gaining control in the lower House for the first time in fifty years. They would govern for thirteen of the next eighteen years.

These domestic changes in Britain and France had important effects on the ideological distances dividing the western powers' leaders from those in Russia. This was especially so with regard to the July Monarchy in France. Although Nicholas actually liked Louis-Philippe as a person, he hated him for what he represented: a violation of the principle of dynastic succession. The French king therefore violated a keystone principle upon which the Russian monarchy was founded.

The shift in power in Britain in 1830 from the Tories to the more liberal Whigs meant that the ideological distance separating the key British and Russian decision makers had also increased. Yet because the political changes in Britain in the early 1830s did not originate from revolutionary political processes that resulted in a violation of the principle of dynastic succession—as had the developments in France in this period—we would expect the ideological differences dividing Russia's leaders from those in Britain to be *smaller* than with regard to Russia's relations with France. Nicholas recognized this to be the case. One of Nicholas's ministers reported that the tsar made "an invariable distinction between France [of the July Monarchy] and England. The former is not a regular power upon which one can rely; the latter is a power with which one can negotiate because, *since it is founded on lawful bases*, it will always fulfill and respect the agreements which it makes." Nicholas later wrote that these were his "very words."[35]

---

34. Frederick Artz, *Reaction and Revolution, 1814–1832* (New York: Harper and Row, 1934), 290; H. A. C. Collingham, *The July Monarchy: A Political History of France, 1830–1848* (London: Longman, 1988), 131.

35. Both in Lincoln, *Nicholas I*, 215 (emphasis added). For other statements by Russian leaders asserting that Britain was a lesser ideological threat than France, see Ingle, *Nesselrode and the Russian Rapprochement with Britain*, 14, 147; Lincoln, *Nicholas I*, 215; Martin Malia, *Russia under Western Eyes* (Cambridge, Mass.: Harvard University Press, 1999), 156, 158. The fact that Britain was a smaller ideological threat to Russia than France after the July Revolution is important because it means that Nicholas's willingness to align with Britain to isolate France is not a significant violation of my predictions. In this instance, Nicholas wanted to ally with a lesser ideological threat in order to balance a greater one.

Realist theories predict that the domestic changes in France and Britain in the early 1830s would have very little effect on the powers' policies toward one another. Because the capabilities of these states remained virtually the same, neither the western powers' international decisions nor the policies of the other states toward them should have changed to a significant degree. Similar analysis applies to arguments that examine the effects of the specific policy prescriptions of different ideologies since the content of Russian leaders' ideological beliefs remained constant in this period.

The evidence does not support these hypotheses. The increasing ideological gap dividing Russian and French decision makers created by the July Revolution pushed Nicholas to view Louis-Philippe as an inherently untrustworthy individual whose regime represented a subversive threat to the tsar's domestic power. Because Louis-Philippe owed his crown to the support of revolutionary forces in France, Nicholas labeled the French king a "vile usurper" of monarchical authority.[36] This view pushed the tsar to have a "pathological hatred" of Louis-Philippe's regime.[37]

Nicholas's ideological animosity to the July Monarchy was so great that one of his central foreign policy objectives throughout the Concert period was to isolate France from great power alliances, even if this meant that Russia had to unite with its greatest strategic rival: Britain. "It was France," as the historian Barbara Jelavich explains, "with its revolutionary past and its sponsorship of subversion abroad that bore the chief weight of [Nicholas's] disapproval. Throughout his reign . . . the tsar sought to solve the successive eastern crises, if possible, by agreement with Britain . . . to the exclusion of France."[38] The tsar continued to hold these alliance preferences despite the fact that strategic concerns were pushing Russia and France together. Changing ideological distances among the powers due to objective domestic developments in France were to Nicholas and his conservative advisors a greater determinant of which state posed the greatest threat to Russia's interests than was the distribution of power.

This analysis explains one of the central puzzles that Russia's foreign policies in this period pose for realist theories: why Russia's leaders were willing to resolve the Second Egyptian Crisis in 1840 by renouncing the strategic advantages Russia had gained in the 1833 Treaty of Unkiar-Skelessi. Nicholas agreed to unite with Britain and sign the Convention of

36. In Lincoln, *Nicholas I*, 132.
37. Bourne, *Foreign Policy of Victorian England*, 39. See also Anderson, "Russia and the Eastern Question," 87, 89, 90; Roger Bullen, "France and Europe, 1815–1848," in *Europe's Balance of Power*, ed. Sked, 136; Lincoln, *Nicholas I*, 214.
38. Barbara Jelavich, *A Century of Russian Foreign Policy, 1814–1914* (New York: J. B. Lippincott, 1964), 90. See also Sir Charles Webster, *The Foreign Policy of Palmerston, 1830–1841: Britain, the Liberal Movement, and the Eastern Question* (New York: Humanities Press, 1969), 2:671, 661, 773; Herbert Bell, *Lord Palmerston* (Hamden, Conn.: Archon Books, 1966), 1:298; Gillard, *Struggle for Asia*, 60, 63, 64; Anderson, *Eastern Question*, 98.

1840 because isolating the French ideological threat was worth a geopolitical sacrifice. Nicholas and Nesselrode, according to the historian Matthew Smith Anderson, "realized that by negotiating with Britain alone they might be able to break the Anglo-French [liberal] entente which, though often severely strained, had been a leading factor in European politics during the 1830s. . . . *To destroy it would be a great victory for the cause of conservatism in Europe. For such a victory Nicholas was willing to pay a considerable price.*"[39]

Ideological variables also played a critical role in shaping Russia's relations with the other absolutist powers: Austria and Prussia. Despite the fact that these states had been fierce competitors for geopolitical influence in eastern Europe in the eighteenth century, after the French Revolution and the Napoleonic Wars these states to an important degree laid aside their differences and formed largely cooperative relationships that were to last almost a century.

Nearly identical principles of political legitimacy and mutual ideological animosity to all revolutionary groups in the system explain this transformation.[40] As the argument predicts, leaders in the three eastern monarchies believed that their common ideological objectives both made their domestic interests highly interdependent (thus revolution in one of the three would make revolution in the other two more likely), and gave them the same international enemies (liberal and revolutionary actors). Nicholas explicitly recognized the interdependence of the eastern monarchies' domestic and international interests in an 1835 letter to Emperor Ferdinand in which he promised "to consider . . . the conservation and the internal tranquillity of the two Empires, as well as their external security, a question of mutual interest."[41]

The most important formal expression of the eastern powers' common domestic and security interests resulted from a series of meetings between the Austrian, Prussian, and Russian monarchs and their ministers that took place almost immediately after the treaty of Unkiar-Skelessi with Turkey was signed. At Munchengratz in September 1833, Russia and Austria agreed (and Prussia would do so the following month) to maintain the Ottoman Empire, to oppose any further advances by Mehemet Ali, and to act cooperatively if Turkey collapsed despite their best efforts to

39. Anderson, *Eastern Question,* 98 (emphasis added).
40. Schroeder, *Transformation of European Politics,* 559; Harold Temperley, *The Foreign Policy of Canning, 1822–1827* (London: G. Bell and Sons, 1925), 322–23; Kissinger, *World Restored,* 296, 298; H. G. Schenk, *The Aftermath of the Napoleonic Wars: The Concert of Europe—An Experiment* (New York: Howard Fertig, 1967), 211; Cowles, "Failure to Restrain Russia," 692, 700, 719; Schroeder, "Containment Nineteenth-Century Style," 7, 9, 10.
41. In Lincoln, *Nicholas I,* 226. Or as Nicholas commented to the Comte de Ficquelmont, the Austrian ambassador to St. Petersburg: "The union and the steadfastness of the three allies will always serve as the sole fulcrum of the social order and as the last anchor of safety for the monarchical cause" (in Lincoln, *Nicholas I,* 225).

prevent this outcome. Most important, the leaders in each state both pledged to come to the others' aid if their regimes were threatened by revolution,[42] and committed themselves to defending a region of territory against liberal-revolutionary regimes: Austria in Italy, Switzerland, Spain, and Portugal; Prussia in northern Germany and Holland; and Russia in Poland, Hungary, and the Balkans.[43] Leaders in these great powers therefore wanted the others to expand their influence even in some areas that were of traditional interest and security to their own state (e.g., Austria sacrificed some of its influence in the Balkans and both Austria and Prussia did so in Poland). This outcome was acceptable and even desirable to the key decision makers in the eastern powers because efforts to help maintain one another's regime were worth some geopolitical sacrifice.

The preceding analysis that reveals the centrality of ideological distances to Russia's most important international policies throughout the Concert of Europe is corroborated by the fact that Russian leaders' foreign policy preferences varied to an important extent by ideological beliefs. Conservative politicians—those decision makers who were dedicated to the preservation of Russia's autocratic system of government—for the most part recommended that Russia adopt very moderate foreign policy choices. Conservatives, including Alexander, Nicholas, Nesselrode, and Constantine, worried that aggressive policies might undermine monarchical authority in other states, which might have adverse effects for Russia's system of governance.

In contrast, more liberal Russian leaders who desired to bring about constitutional reform in Russia and other states pushed for Russia to adopt more expansionary policies. More liberal politicians favored Russian expansion because the two states that were most likely to suffer by such a policy, Austria and the Ottoman Empire, were widely regarded among Russian liberal circles as two of the most reactionary states in the system.[44]

42. Nicholas would make good on this promise in 1849 when the Austrian Emperor Francis Joseph invited a Russian invasion into his territory to put down a revolt in Hungary. Nicholas both complied with the request and ordered the Russian army to leave when the task was completed.

43. Lincoln, *Nicholas I*, 225–26. Austria's and Prussia's behavior in this period is especially puzzling to realism. Despite the facts that Russia's army was over twice as large as the combined strength of the German powers and that they bordered on Russian territory, Austria and Prussia not only made no significant efforts to ally with either Britain or France (the only powers capable of balancing Russia), but formed a very close alliance with their greatest power-political threat (Wolf, "How Partners Become Rivals," 15; Kennedy, *Rise and Fall of the Great Powers*, 197).

44. Of the seven conservative officials who helped to decide Russia's policies in the Russo-Turkish War of 1828–29, five advocated moderate goals, one expansionary ones, and one wavered between the two. Conservatives were more divided over whether or not to intervene in the Greek crisis (though, as discussed, the three most important conservative leaders, Alexander, Nesselrode, and Constantine, were opposed to intervention). Those conservatives who favored intervention in the Greek rebellion usually justified their recommendations not by power-political considerations, but in terms of helping Russia's co-religionists or fear

The historian Patricia Kennedy Grimsted describes the policy differences between Russian liberals and conservatives by examining the preferences of the most important liberal and conservative advisors to Alexander: Ionnes Capodistrias and Count Nesselrode. According to Grimsted, "Divergent in . . . basic political ideology [Capodistrias and Nesselrode] were diametrically opposed in their approaches to foreign policy. . . . While Capodistrias advocated moderate liberal reform, self-determination of national entities, and gradual extensions of republican and constitutional government, Nesselrode favored strict repression of progressive elements, preservation of legitimate monarchical authority, and the dynastic and territorial integrity of the great powers."[45] Capodistrias favored war with Turkey over Greece and desired a close relationship with constitutional France in order to thwart the conservative policies of Austria's foreign minister, Prince Klemens von Metternich. Nesselrode advocated the exact opposite choices.[46] If international power distributions, and not ideological distances among leaders, were the key determinant of Russian decision makers' perceptions of threat and consequent foreign policy preferences, we would not expect different ideological groups from the same state to advocate such radically different international strategies, including choices of international allies and enemies.

BRITAIN'S FOREIGN POLICIES

An analysis of Britain's foreign policies in the Concert era potentially allows for an easier test of my hypotheses than do Russia's foreign policies in the same period. Britain not only had much more established political parties than Russia, but halfway through the Concert the Whigs replaced the Tories as the dominant group in Parliament. The ideological differences dividing these two groups were important. According to one scholar: "The Tory party . . . declared its respect for the rights of the Crown and the Church of England, and consequently defended the royal prerogative against Parliament. Having led the fight against the French Revolution and Napoleon, it was regarded as a bulwark of political and social conservatism in the face of the Jacobin peril. . . . The Whig party . . . stood

---

that Turkey's brutality during the rebellion, if not stopped, would increase the chances of revolution spreading throughout the Balkans. All four of the more liberal advisors during either the Russo-Turkish War or the Greek crisis favored expansionary war-fighting goals or unilateral intervention by Russia, respectively (Rendall, "Russia, the Concert of Europe, and Greece," 68–79).

45. Patricia Kennedy Grimsted, *The Foreign Ministers of Alexander I: Political Attitudes and the Conduct of Russian Diplomacy, 1801–1825* (Berkeley: University of California Press, 1969), 269–270.

46. Ibid., 239–244, 251, 269, 277.

for the individual and Parliamentary 'liberties.' It was fond of invoking the Calvinist tradition and the 1688 Revolution, and drew its support from the Non-conformist sects."[47] These different ideological beliefs had critical effects on Tories' and Whigs' perceptions of international threats and consequent foreign policies. The Whigs' ascension to power in 1830 therefore marked a watershed year for Britain's foreign policies.

Although Britain after Napoleon's defeat was most likely subject to revolutionary movements to a lesser extent than any of the other great powers, it, too, suffered from substantial levels of left-wing unrest in this period. As British Home Secretary Lord Sidmouth explained in a private letter in November 1817: "We must expect a trying winter, and it will be fortunate if the military establishment which was pronounced to be too large for the constitution of the country shall be sufficient to preserve its internal tranquillity."[48]

As I develop in detail below, an important strategy for Tories in dealing with this threat to their domestic interests was to try to protect monarchical interests throughout Europe against revolutionary forces. "The House of Hanover," as the historian Charles Webster expresses the reasoning underlying this strategy, "shared to the fullest extent in [the] good fortune" that the "legitimacy of thrones was better recognized than that of republics" after the end of the Napoleonic Wars.[49]

Tories' interest in the preservation of monarchical power on the continent went beyond domestic considerations, however. Many of these politicians believed that revolutionary regimes were a great danger to the peace of Europe. Consequently, to Tories a world of monarchies, whether constitutional or autocratic, was likely to be less threatening to Britain's security than when one of the great powers was a republic. Tories, just as with most conservative leaders of the continental powers, thus confronted both domestic and international-security incentives to help preserve the existing ideological arrangement established throughout Europe after Napoleon's demise.[50]

---

47. Jacques Droz, *Europe between Revolutions, 1815–1848* (New York: Harper and Row, 1967), 129. See also Peter Mandler, *Aristocratic Government in the Age of Reform: Whigs and Liberals, 1830–1852* (Oxford: Clarendon Press, 1990), 2–3.

48. In Edward Royle, *Revolutionary Britannia? Reflections on the Threat of Revolution in Britain, 1789–1848* (Manchester: Manchester University Press, 2000), 42.

49. Charles Webster, *The Foreign Policy of Castlereagh, 1815–1822: Britain and the European Alliance* (London: G. Bell and Sons, 1963), 4; see also 9, 55, 515, 520.

50. In a circular to the British Missions in 1816, Foreign Secretary Castlereagh referred to both the domestic and international ramifications of the ideological community that existed among the great powers after Napoleon's defeat: "The immediate object to be kept in view is . . . to make [the great powers] feel that the existing concert is their only perfect security against the revolutionary embers more or less existing in every State of Europe; and that their true wisdom is to keep down the petty contentions of ordinary times, and to stand together in support of the established principles of social order" (in Schenk, *Aftermath of the Napoleonic Wars*, 120).

Tories' belief that supporting monarchical interests on the continent would benefit both their domestic interests and Britain's security explains some of their most important foreign policies made during the first half of the Concert period. For example, this analysis helps us understand why British statesmen were such consistent champions of a non-putative peace against France after both the penultimate and ultimate defeats of Napoleon in 1814 and 1815, respectively.

British leaders' desire for a very lenient peace is sometimes described in terms of an interest in keeping France strong so it could continue to be an important support in the European balance of power, especially as a counterweight to Russia. This analysis misses a more fundamental determinant of British policies, however. According to their own accounts, key British leaders were lenient toward France because they considered this strategy the most likely way of supporting the restored Bourbon regime, the stabilization of which they viewed as critical to both international peace and domestic stability in all the powers.[51] According to Lord Castlereagh (Britain's foreign minister from 1812 to 1822 and the most important foreign policy decision maker in Britain in this period): "The great object is to keep the King [of France] on his Throne. A moderate system [by the allies] is the best chance for doing so."[52] Or as he wrote in a circular dispatch to his subordinates in the Foreign Office: "The conciliatory as well as liberal views which animated the Allied Sovereigns towards Louis the 18th and his kingdom [were implemented to realize] the *first object* of the Alliance [which was], in truth, . . . to save both [the king and his kingdom], and *through them the rest of Europe*, from becoming again a prey to revolutionary anarchy and violence."[53]

The importance of preserving monarchical authority on the continent to Tories' foreign policies is further demonstrated by the fact that many British conservatives were willing to see the other powers engage in counter-revolutionary efforts in neighboring states. Although Castlereagh was unwilling either to commit Britain to a war against revolutionary regimes unless its interests were more immediately involved, or to see the other powers *unite* in counter-revolutionary efforts against a particular

---

51. Schroeder, *Transformation of European Politics*, 592–593; F. R. Bridge, "Allied Diplomacy in Peacetime: The Failure of the Congress 'System,' 1815–1823," in *Europe's Balance of Power*, ed. Sked, 36; Nicolson, *Congress of Vienna*, 100; Kissinger, *World Restored*, 137, 142; Schenk, *Aftermath of the Napoleonic Wars*, 46–47; C. J. Bartlett, *Peace, War, and the European Powers, 1814–1914* (New York: St. Martin's Press, 1996), 10; Paul Schroeder, "Did the Vienna Settlement Rest on a Balance of Power?" *American Historical Review* 97, no. 3 (June 1992), 697; Jervis, "From Balance to Concert," 66–67.

52. In Schenk, *Aftermath of the Napoleonic Wars*, 47.

53. In Webster, *Foreign Policy of Castlereagh*, 510 (emphasis added). Metternich would echo these sentiments in 1817: "Internally tranquil, that power [France] will not disturb any other for a long time; but that tranquillity can only be assured to it with the help of its great neighbors. No displaced rivalry can exist today between Austria and France" (in Schroeder, *Transformation of European Politics*, 593).

state, he was willing to allow and even encourage individual powers to engage in such policies in their own spheres of influence. As Britain's foreign minister wrote to the British missions at the foreign courts in January 1821: "It should be clearly understood that no Government can be more prepared than the British Government is, to uphold the right of any State or States to interfere, where their own immediate security or essential interests are seriously endangered by the *internal* transactions of another State."[54]

In keeping with this set of beliefs, in 1821 Castlereagh encouraged Austria to invade Naples to put down the revolution that had taken place in that region. When Metternich opted for precisely this course of action, this outcome, in Castlereagh's words, "added important additional securities to the European system."[55] Similarly, after Castlereagh's death many British conservatives supported France's invasion of Spain in 1823 for counter-revolutionary purposes. George IV expressed a great interest in the French cause and stated that he saw "with joy the rights of Legitimate royalty" sustained by the French invasion. Marcellus (the French *chargé d'affaires* in London) was told by "several ministers" that a French army ought to go at once to Madrid and that Britain would remain neutral in the conflict. Future prime minister, the Duke of Wellington, advised a rapid march on Madrid.[56] British Whigs, in contrast, were highly opposed to France's intention to invade Spain for counter-revolutionary purposes, and there were even some grumblings among these politicians that Britain should threaten war to deter France from attacking.[57]

Only an argument that asserts that the maintenance of monarchical authority on the continent was an important interest to Tory leaders can explain their enthusiasm for the other powers to regulate, even *expand*, their respective spheres of influence in a manner most conducive to their interests, including by war. Tories' actions were particularly surprising with regard to France's invasion of Spain in 1823. Not only was an independent

---

54. In Rene Albrecht-Carrie, *The Concert of Europe* (New York: Harper and Row, 1968), 51 (emphasis added). When Castlereagh wrote these words was a particularly tumultuous time since Spain, Naples, Greece, and Piedmont all experienced revolutions in this period. Though Britain was the state least threatened by revolutionary contagion, Castlereagh wrote on the subject that "there can be no doubt of the general danger which menaces more or less the stability of all existing Governments from the principles which are afloat" (in Bourne, *Foreign Policy of Victorian England*, 200).

55. In Webster, *Foreign Policy of Castlereagh*, 198. See also 262, 263, 271, 305, 326–327, 499; Kissinger, *World Restored*, 252; Schroeder, *Transformation of European Politics*, 609; Bridge, "Allied Diplomacy in Peacetime," 45; F. R. Bridge, *The Habsburg Monarchy among the Great Powers, 1815–1918* (New York: Berg, 1990), 31.

56. Temperley, *Foreign Policy of Canning*, 82, 88; Wendy Hinde, *George Canning* (London: Collins, 1973), 334. An important exception to Tories' support of France's invasion of Spain was George Canning, who replaced Castlereagh as foreign minister in 1822. Canning's foreign policy choices will be discussed later in this section.

57. Hinde, *George Canning*, 328–331.

Spain an important security interest to Britain, but Britain had spent considerable blood and treasure expelling French armies from Spain less than a decade before France's latest invasion. If maintaining the balance of power on the continent were Britain's primary objective, encouraging war for counter-revolutionary purposes was clearly a threat to this goal. Moreover, if British politicians believed that the foreign policies of other states were simply the product of some material factor (e.g., the distribution of power or geographical position) and not the ideological distances dividing states' leaders, it would not have mattered to Britain if the other powers experienced a change in regime type. Tories encouraged the other powers to engage in counter-revolutionary policies in regions that were of long-standing strategic value to Britain because they recognized the importance of the degree of ideological similarities uniting the great powers' leaders to both their domestic interests and Britain's safety.

Tories' shared commitment with the leaders of the continental powers to the preservation of monarchical authority throughout the system also explains one of the biggest puzzles for realist analyses of Britain's foreign policies during this period: why Britain's most important decision makers for the first half of the Concert consistently adopted a fairly benign view of the threat posed by Russia to British interests.

Although Russia was by far the strongest power on the continent and British leaders were acutely aware that Russia's strength was significantly increasing (repeatedly referred to in their private correspondences, public speeches, and party newspapers),[58] and despite the fact that Russia bordered and had significant interests in two regions of great importance to Britain (the Near East and Central Asia) and that the era was perceived to be offense-dominant, the prevailing attitude among Tories was that Russia was not a terribly potent threat to Britain's interests. According to the historian John Gleason, from 1815 to 1830 "all the evidence afforded by English newspapers, periodicals, private papers, and parliamentary debates suggests that the majority of the nation were not seriously alarmed by the growth of Russian power."[59] This does not mean that British leaders were perfectly trusting of their Russian counterparts' intentions. Most notably, most British decision makers were suspicious that Alexander and Nicholas would use the Greek rebellion to further Russia's influence and power in the Balkans and Middle East. Yet all that

58. John Howes Gleason, *The Genesis of Russophobia in Great Britain* (Cambridge: Harvard University Press, 1950), chaps. 3, 4.
59. Ibid., 104. See also Gillard, *Struggle for Asia*, 27–28; Malia, *Russia under Western Eyes*, 57–102. The fact that the Concert system was close to a bipolar one makes British leaders' sanguine attitude toward Russia all the more puzzling to neo-realist theories' understanding of international threats. To these arguments, bipolar worlds are characterized by "self-dependence of parties, clarity of dangers, [and] certainty about who has to face them" (Kenneth N. Waltz, *Theory of International Politics* [New York: McGraw-Hill, 1979], 171–172).

many British leaders required to allay these suspicions were verbal assurances by the Russians that their intentions vis-à-vis Turkey were limited.[60] Moreover, and as discussed, Britain's politicians' wariness of Russia was not sufficient to prohibit these decision makers from either forming a tacit alliance with Russia in the 1820s or taking actions in the Greek crisis that could only help Russia's relative power position in the region (most notably helping to defeat Turkey's fleet in 1827).

Ideological distances among actors explain most Tories' benign view of Russia's intentions despite the facts that Russia was Britain's greatest power-political rival and that its power was increasing overtime. Although there were substantial ideological differences between Tories and their dedication to constitutional monarchism and Russia's autocratic monarchy, Tories clearly viewed Russia (as well as Prussia and Austria) as a lesser ideological threat than liberal-revolutionary regimes. It is this reasoning that led, for example, both the Duke of Wellington the Earl of Aberdeen (prime minister and foreign secretary, respectively) to declare that had they not been replaced by Whigs in 1830 they would have pursued close cooperation with the eastern monarchies in order to contain "revolutionary France" of the July Monarchy.[61]

Tories' and Russian conservatives' agreement on a greater ideological enemy in liberal-revolutionary regimes pushed these individuals to emphasize their ideological similarities rather than their differences. The resulting membership in a transnational ideological community led Tories to possess a greater degree of trust of Russia's international intentions than we would otherwise expect. For example, Tories believed that because their Russian counterparts had a great interest in preserving the institutional structures of other monarchical states, the Russians would tend to adopt limited foreign policy objectives lest more aggressive policies increase the chances of revolution spreading throughout the system. As Castlereagh told the Austrian ambassador to Britain during the Greek crisis, their hopes that Alexander would not go to war rested on the fact that the aims of Catherine the Great no longer governed Russia. Instead, Castlereagh believed that the status quo in the Balkans would be safeguarded by the fact that "any change in the East threatened . . . the institutions which the Tsar wished to protect."[62] Consistent with these claims, Britain's foreign minister on numerous occasions told his subordinates that despite Russia's great power capacity, leaders in the other powers should not be overly suspicious of it. To Castlereagh, because Russia's statesmen had a preeminent interest in maintaining the institutional

60. Jelavich, *Russia's Balkan Entanglements*, 88.
61. Wolf, "How Partners Become Rivals," 20; Christopher J. Bartlett, "Britain and the European Balance, 1815–1848," in *Europe's Balance of Power*, ed. Sked, 154–155.
62. Webster, *Foreign Policy of Castlereagh*, 361, Webster's paraphrase of Castlereagh's statements.

homogeneity among states that existed throughout Europe in this period, their "true interests," he wrote to the British ambassador in Vienna, "dictate a pacific policy."[63] As a result, Castlereagh believed (as he wrote in a private letter to his brother in November 1818) that "the world has . . . more to hope than to fear from Russia."[64]

Even more liberal Tory leaders like George Canning (foreign minister from 1822 to 1827) recognized that Russian leaders' dedication to the political and ideological union that existed among the great powers after the Napoleonic Wars acted as a brake on the latter's foreign policy ambitions.[65] Consistent with this claim, Canning—despite treaty commitments with Persia—did nothing to prevent or moderate Russia's victory in the Russo-Persian War of 1826. The foreign minister believed Russian leaders' assurances concerning their limited ambitions in the area, and he showed no significant concern for the security of India.[66] Nor did he seem to believe that Russia had overly expansionary aims against the decaying Turkish empire.[67]

The fact that Tories and Russia's key decision makers were both dedicated to the preservation of monarchical authority on the continent pushed British conservatives throughout the Concert period to give their Russian counterparts the benefit of the doubt and attribute limited international ambitions to them. As we shall see in the next section, the more liberal Whigs interpreted virtually the same evidence in the opposite manner, even though power variables remained almost the same.

I conclude this section with additional analysis of the international policies of Foreign Minister Canning. Although Canning concurred with other Tories about Russia's limited international ambitions, he disagreed with other central dimensions of the policies pursued by fellow Tories since the end of the Napoleonic Wars.[68] Unlike Castlereagh, Canning consistently shunned close association with the continental powers. Moreover, a guiding tenet of Canning's foreign policies was strict non-interference in the internal affairs of other states in favor of maintaining Britain's relative power position. This seems to point to the non-ideological nature of Canning's international decisions. Because of the foreign minister's importance to the development of Britain's foreign policies from 1822 to 1827, Canning's choices seem to represent important contradictions to my predictions.

---

63. In Nicolson, *Congress of Vienna*, 253. On the above points, see Webster, *Foreign Policy of Castlereagh*, 66, 68, 76, 100, 104, 107, 360, 361, 374, 386, 394; Gleason, *Genesis of Russophobia in Great Britain*, 36.
64. In Webster, *Foreign Policy of Castlereagh*, 593.
65. Schenk, *Aftermath of the Napoleonic Wars*, 212.
66. Gillard, *Struggle for Asia*, 20; Gleason, *Genesis of Russophobia in Great Britain*, 76–77.
67. Gleason, *Genesis of Russophobia in Great Britain*, 64–65; Temperley, *Foreign Policy of Canning*, 353–354; Jelavich, *Russia's Balkan Entanglements*, 88.
68. For examples of Canning's often fierce foreign policy disagreements with other Tories, see Hinde, *George Canning*, 345, 370; Peter Dixon, *Canning: Politician and Statesman* (London: Weidenfeld and Nicolson, 1976), 234.

Even in Canning's case, however, ideological distances had important international effects. As the foreign minister stated on numerous occasions, in his era there was a struggle in almost all countries between "the principles of monarchy and democracy," and politicians' allegiance to one side or the other was a key determinant of their foreign policy choices.[69] Importantly, Canning did not advocate that Britain stay out of this ideological struggle because he believed that states' domestic interests were not to an important degree interconnected. Instead, he advocated non-interference in the domestic affairs of other countries because he believed that Britain's unique domestic-political system made it to a significant extent immune from the subversive threats created by this worldwide ideological struggle. According to Canning: "[Britain had in its] Constitution enough of democracy to temper monarchy, and enough of monarchy to restrain the caprices of democracy."[70] Britain's unique "compromise and intermeddling of [the] conflicting principles [of monarchy and democracy]" meant that Britain's domestic stability, unlike in other states, was not threatened when one or the other of these principles gained ascendancy in particular countries.[71] Hence Britain could afford to adopt a position of neutrality toward the ideological struggle being waged in both Europe and the Americas. Thus somewhat paradoxically, a particular ideological configuration in Britain (in terms of domestic institutions) allowed Canning to adopt in many ways a non-ideological foreign policy.

In addition to believing that Britain's unique constitution to a great extent immunized it from domestic developments in other states, he also believed that Britain's domestic system granted it opportunities for international influence that the other states, because of their regime types, did not have. To Canning, as long as the world was divided into republics and monarchies, states in each group were likely to look to Britain as either the bridge or the swing state between the two ideological camps.[72] Britain would thus be in an influential position in relation to both groups. As a result of this view, Canning was firmly dedicated not only to maintaining the material balance of power among the key actors in the system, but the ideological balance of power as well. As Canning explained in his self-proclaimed "political testament," Britain's foreign policy should be based on the pursuit of "a middle course between Jacobinism and Ultraism," while attempting "to hold the balance between the conflicting principles of democracy and despotism."[73] This explains, for example, why the foreign

---

69. In Dixon, *Canning*, 212; Temperley, *Foreign Policy of Canning*, 49.

70. In Temperley, *Foreign Policy of Canning*, 47.

71. In Dixon, *Canning*, 212. See also Hinde, *George Canning*, 324, 357.

72. Temperley, *Foreign Policy of Canning*, 458.

73. Ibid., 458, 471. Referring to the ideological struggles between republicanism and autocracy and Britain's interest in not letting one become too powerful, Canning wrote that Britain was treading "a plank which lay across a roaring stream. Attempts might be made to bear us down on one side or the other" (49).

minister was "firmly, almost obsessively convinced" that some of the South American states emerging from the decaying Spanish empire should remain monarchies.[74] Because Britain's influence would be maximized when a multiplicity of regime types existed in a system, it was better for Britain not to have the entire western hemisphere be comprised of republican states. Notice that this view is necessarily founded on the belief that states' foreign policies are to an important extent shaped by the degree of ideological differences dividing their leaders. Thus ideological variables were important even to the decision maker in Britain who is often described as the most "realistic" of politicians in this period.

Probably the most important factor pointing to the centrality of ideological distances to Britain's foreign policies throughout the Concert era is the fact that these policies underwent a dramatic transformation in the wake of domestic changes in Britain and France in the early 1830s. In this period, both France and Britain underwent a liberalizing process. In 1830 the Whigs came to power in Britain, and France experienced the July Revolution that placed Louis-Philippe on the throne and established a much more genuine constitutional monarchy in France. In 1832, Britain's lawmakers passed the Reform Bill, which widened Britain's electoral base and linked representation in Parliament more closely to a district's population than had been done previously.

These domestic changes had a significant impact on the degree of ideological differences separating Britain's leading decision makers from their counterparts in the other great powers. These changes clearly reduced the ideological distance separating British and French leaders, and substantially increased the ideological differences dividing Britain's decision makers from those in the autocratic powers.[75]

These changes led to a significant transformation in Britain's attitudes and policies toward the key actors in the system. To begin with, whereas Whig leaders had been condemnatory of France's domestic institutions and suspicious of France's international intentions during the increasingly autocratic rule of Charles X, these attitudes were largely reversed after 1830. Instead of condemning France's domestic institutions, Whigs after the July Revolution both praised France's new regime as a moral advance for French citizens and, more important for our purposes, claimed that developments in France would help Whigs further their own domestic interests.[76] Many

74. Hinde, *George Canning*, 381, 354.
75. Foreign Secretary Palmerston, for example, wrote that the July Revolution "is decisive of the ascendancy of Liberal Principles throughout Europe; the evil spirit [of autocracy] has been put down and will be trodden under foot. The reign of Metternich is over" (in Roger Bullen, *Palmerston, Guizot, and the Collapse of the Entente Cordiale* (London: Athlone Press, 1974), 5; for similar quotations, see 4).
76. C. K. Webster, "Palmerston and the Liberal Movement, 1830–1841," *Politica* 3, no. 14 (December 1938): 303.

Whigs asserted that the domestic changes in France in 1830 were critical to the passage of the Reform Bill in Britain in 1832 because the former demonstrated that revolutions could be both peaceful and stable. Moreover, once the bill passed, there were many politicians in both Britain and France who believed that the preservation of liberalism in the other state would further their domestic interests since the other's success helped to demonstrate the viability of the liberal cause.[77] These developments conform with the predictions of the demonstration-effects causal mechanism: once the ideological distance separating French leaders from British Whigs had narrowed, the latter came to see France as an important catalyst and support to their own domestic interests instead of a threat to them.

An analogous transformation occurred with regard to most Whigs' views of France's international intentions. Although most Whigs had been suspicious of France's ambitions during the first half of the Concert (with some even recommending threatening war if France invaded Spain in 1823), after 1832 many Whigs, led by Lord Palmerston (who became Britain's foreign minister in 1830), now actively encouraged the augmentation of French influence and power in neighboring states. For example, although before 1832 Whig leaders, including Palmerston, had been highly suspicious of French ambitions in Belgium and Italy, after this period they were supportive of the use of French troops in both states in order to thwart the aims of the autocratic powers.[78] Most important, Palmerston and the Whigs from 1833 to 1837 actively lobbied for a French invasion of Spain in support of the liberal cause in the Iberian Peninsula (Tories went through the reverse transformation).[79] As the ideological differences dividing British Whigs from French leaders diminished, the former came to view the latter as much more trustworthy individuals whose international interests were complementary to Britain's. As a consequence of this change, British Whigs were not nearly as worried about increases in France's relative power as they had been just a few years earlier.

Britain's changing policies toward France after 1832 are linked to another sea change in Britain's foreign policies in this period. After this

77. Bell, *Lord Palmerston*, 192–193; Bullen, "France and Europe," 131; Douglas Johnson, *Guizot: Aspects of French History, 1787–1874* (London: Routledge and Kegan Paul, 1963), 202, 286, 312; Collingham, *July Monarchy*, 191.

78. Bell, *Lord Palmerston*, 161–164; Webster, *Foreign Policy of Palmerston*, 1:139, 169–170; Collingham, *July Monarchy*, 192–193.

79. Webster, *Foreign Policy of Palmerston*, 1:241; Roger Bullen, "Party Politics and Foreign Policy: Whigs, Tories, and Iberian Affairs, 1830–6," *Bulletin of the Institute of Historical Research* 51, no. 123 (May 1978): 48, 57 (this latter study provides an excellent analysis of Whigs' and Tories' foreign policy differences on key issues after 1830). Although British Tories and the king had largely supported France's invasion of Spain in 1823 for the cause of conservatism, they now fought against a French invasion of Spain when fought for liberalism. King William IV said he "would rather lay down his Crown than fight on the side of France in such a cause" (Webster, "Palmerston and the Liberal Movement," 315). For other examples of Tories' opposition to Palmerston's foreign policies, see 308, 310, 319.

year, Britain's leaders to an important degree abandoned the moderate European foreign policy choices that they had adhered to since the end of the Napoleonic Wars in favor of policies that were much more aggressive and expansionary. Most important, during Palmerston's time as foreign minister Britain actively supported the cause of liberalism in domestic struggles in states throughout the continent, including in Portugal, Spain, Belgium, Italy, and Greece. In other words, one of the reasons why 1832 was such a watershed year for British foreign policy was because about this time Britain's leaders "began to include in [their definition of Britain's interests] the extension of constitutionalism to parts of Europe with which Britain had not hitherto concerned herself."[80]

Ideological differences between Whigs and Tories explain this change in Britain's policies. Unlike Tories, Whigs tended to believe that long-run international stability would best be achieved on the continent via the spread of representative institutions. Given this belief, it was in Britain's security interests both to ally with constitutional France and to support the cause of liberalism throughout Europe.

Britain's policies toward the eastern monarchies of Austria, Prussia, and Russia could hardly have been more different than its relations with France in this period. As discussed, in the first half of the Concert, Castlereagh, Canning, and other leading Tories recognized the tremendous power of Russia, but they for the most part believed it to be a satiated and status quo state. They therefore were willing to recognize the legitimacy of Russia's sphere of interest in the Near East and Central Asia.

Palmerston's and the Whigs' policies were significantly different than their predecessors.' These changes were the result of the "ideological abyss which, following the liberal Reform Act [and the Whigs' ascension to power,] began to separate Britain from an increasingly reactionary Russia."[81] Despite the fact that Russia's leaders continued to exhibit clear demonstrations of their limited foreign policy aims, nothing could shake Palmerston from his belief that Russia was bent on significantly expanding its power in both the Near East and Central Asia.[82] In the Near East, Palmerston was convinced that Nicholas (along with Metternich) desired the partition of the Ottoman Empire and the incorporation of the straits

80. Webster, *Foreign Policy of Palmerston*, 1:179. See also 303, 322.
81. Wolf, "How Partners Become Rivals," 12.
82. According to Palmerston: "No reasonable doubt can be entertained that the Russian [government] is intently engaged in the prosecution of those schemes of aggrandizement towards the South, which ever since the reign of Catherine have formed a prominent feature of Russian policy" (in Bell, *Lord Palmerston*, 185). Palmerston attributed Russian aggression to its autocratic regime type, stating that "the military organization of Russia's political fabric renders encroachment upon her neighbors almost a necessary condition of her existence" (in F. R. Bridge and Roger Bullen, *The Great Powers and the European State System, 1815–1914* [New York: Longman, 1980], 57); see also Lincoln, *Nicholas I*, 210–211; Webster, *Foreign Policy of Palmerston*, 1:235).

under Russian control. Similarly, Palmerston (unlike Canning) believed that Russian military actions in Persia were not defensive, but offensive in nature. They were seen as the first step in a plan meant to threaten India.[83] Given Whigs' suspicions of Russia's international objectives, it is not puzzling that a central foreign policy objective of Palmerston's government was to contain, and even roll back, the power of the three autocratic powers, especially Russia's.[84] The huge ideological differences dividing liberal from autocratic leaders pushed British Whigs to behave aggressively in order to address perceived threats to their security.

Palmerston and fellow Whigs repeatedly claimed that the root cause of their mistrust and animosity toward Russia was due to their large ideological differences with this state. Whereas the similar legitimating principles of Britain and France gave the two states very similar interests to the point where they made, as Palmerston put it, "natural allies,"[85] the autocratic governments of the eastern powers made these states to Whig leaders inherently untrustworthy and aggressive.[86] The division of the great powers in the 1830s into two hostile ideological alliances, with the constitutional monarchies on one side and the autocratic powers on the other, was the result of this thinking. As Palmerston wrote in a private letter in 1836: "The division of Europe into two camps . . . is the consequence of the French Revolution of July. The three powers fancy their interests lie in a direction opposite to that in which we and France conceive ours to be placed. . . . The three and the two think differently, and therefore they act differently, whether it be as to Belgium or Portugal or Spain."[87] Realist theories have great difficulty explaining why there was such a marked transformation in Britain's foreign policies that occurred during the years 1830–32 since there was no significant alteration in the international distribution of power in this period.[88] What had substantially changed were

83. Gillard, *Struggle for Asia*, 35–37; Webster, *Foreign Policy of Palmerston*, 2:741–742. Consistent with the predictions of the communications mechanism, Nicholas could not communicate his benign foreign policy intentions to Palmerston and fellow Whigs despite the use of "costly signals" (for details, see Chapter 1).

84. As Palmerston explained in a private letter written in 1834: "The great object of our policy ought now to be to form a Western confederacy of free states as a counterpoise to the Eastern league of arbitrary governments. England, France, Spain, and Portugal united as they now must be, will form a political and moral power in Europe which must hold Metternich and Nicholas in check. We shall be on the advance, they on the decline; and all the smaller planets of Europe will have a natural tendency to gravitate towards our system" (in Webster, *Foreign Policy of Palmerston*, 1:390).

85. In Bell, *Lord Palmerston*, 103. According to the British foreign minister: "The Western Confederation may now be looked upon as firmly established; Spain and Portugal are irrevocably constitutional Powers, and *necessarily allied, therefore* to England and France" (in Webster, *Foreign Policy of Palmerston*, 1:406 [emphasis added]; see also 193, 390, 397).

86. Bridge and Bullen, *Great Powers and the European State System*, 57; Lincoln, *Nicholas I*, 210–211; Webster, *Foreign Policy of Palmerston*, 1:235.

87. In Bell, *Lord Palmerston*, 209.

88. Russia did put down a rebellion in Poland in 1830, thereby achieving more solid control

the ideological distances dividing the great powers' leaders as a result of objective domestic shifts in Britain and France.

Although ideological variables played a central role in shaping Britain's key foreign policy decisions for most of the 1830s, this relationship was not as pronounced after 1837, at least with regard to Anglo-French relations. Two sets of factors worked to weaken and eventually to destroy the liberal entente between Britain and France by the end of the Concert period. First, throughout the 1840s France and Britain were one another's principal competitors for colonies and influence in the Mediterranean, Africa, and the Pacific. This competition placed a significant strain on Anglo-French relations as conflicts of interest between the two states became more prominent toward the end of the Concert.[89] This outcome is consistent with realist predictions and not my own.

Second, after 1837 France became a primary object of Palmerston's animosity. As a result, by the late 1830s he sought not only to prevent French expansion, but to roll back France's power and influence in key regions around the globe. For example, Palmerston signed the previously discussed Convention of 1840, which constituted a tacit alliance between Britain and Russia as a means to settle the Second Egyptian Crisis, knowing full well that the effects of the accord would retard the growth of French influence in the Near East (since this outcome represented a defeat for Mehemet Ali, who was sympathetic to France), and that France's original exclusion from the signing of the accord would humiliate its leaders.[90] This tacit alliance between Britain and Russia clearly violates my predictions. By any objective criteria, France under Louis-Philippe's rule was ideologically closer to Palmerston's Whigs than was Russia.

Two factors, however, mitigate the damage done to an ideological interpretation of international threats created by Palmerston's hostility to France. To begin with, this animosity was not representative of most British leaders' policies. Palmerston's willingness to isolate liberal France in favor of a tacit alliance with autocratic Russia as a means of ending the Second Egyptian Crisis outraged many British politicians, especially Whigs. Indeed, the anger produced by Palmerston's double violation of a foreign policy based on ideological distances was the principal reason why Palmerston's government fell just six months after it signed the convention that

---

over one of the territories of its empire. Many in Britain, however, noted that Russia looked weaker after this event than before because the Russian army performed so poorly in the mission (Gleason, *Genesis of Russophobia in Great Britain*, 168, 171, 172–173; Palmer, *Chancelleries of Europe*, 54).

89. Christopher Layne, "Lord Palmerston and the Triumph of Realism: Anglo-French Relations, 1830–48," in *Paths to Peace: Is Democracy the Answer?* ed. Miriam Fendius Elman (Cambridge: MIT Press, 1997), 61–100.

90. France was later included as a signatory power despite Palmerston's objections.

ended the Egyptian crisis.[91] Thus although the degree of ideological similarities among actors may not have been central to Palmerston's foreign policy choices in the last decade of the Concert, this variable was very important to many other British politicians to the point where they were willing to withdraw their support from Palmerston's cabinet for not subscribing to this position.[92]

Moreover, the conditions under which Palmerston switched from being a vocal champion of the liberal entente to a staunch opponent of France are worth closer examination. Palmerston started to harbor feelings of intense resentment for the French when Louis-Philippe refused to *increase* France's power and influence. As stated, Palmerston wanted France to invade Spain in order to support the cause of liberalism throughout the Iberian Peninsula. But Louis-Philippe, though highly fearful of the negative repercussions in France resulting from a Carlist (the autocratic party) victory in Spain, refused to invade his neighbor. The king of France feared the effects of war on his state, the possibility of counter-revolutionary ideas spreading to his army, and the reaction of the three eastern powers to this act (particularly an attack on the Rhine). Palmerston never forgave Louis-Philippe for his caution, and he wrongfully attributed the king's reticence to his support of the Carlist cause in particular and autocracy in general.[93] It was only after Palmerston came to doubt Louis-Philippe's liberal credentials that he started to view the French king as an untrustworthy actor whose interests were in conflict with Britain's. Without Palmerston's change of view of Louis-Philippe's ideological beliefs, it is uncertain that he would have adopted the hostile policies he did toward France in the late 1830s. According to Charles Webster, who is the leading authority of Palmerston's foreign policies, "It may be doubted whether [Palmerston] would or could have carried through his policy [of isolating France and aligning with Russia during the Second Egyptian Crisis] . . . if France had not herself first abandoned the liberal cause in Europe."[94]

Although Palmerston redefined the nature of the ideological relationship between British and French leaders by the latter's behavior and not by institutional or party changes in France (an outcome that violates my

91. Webster, *Foreign Policy of Palmerston*, 2:713, 717, 718; Bell, *Lord Palmerston*, 306, 308, 312; Ingle, *Nesselrode and the Russian Rapprochement with Britain*, 116, 145; Gleason, *Genesis of Russophobia in Great Britain*, 254; Anderson, *Eastern Question*, 99, 102.

92. Consistent with this analysis, when Palmerston was out of office from 1841 to 1846, there was a rapprochement between British and French leaders, and the liberal entente was to an important extent restored. See Webster, *Foreign Policy of Palmerston*, 2:776; Schroeder, *Transformation of European Politics*, 774; Johnson, *Guizot*, 202; Collingham, *July Monarchy*, 322; David McLean, "The Greek Revolution and the Anglo-French Entente 1843–44," *English Historical Review* 96, no. 378 (January 1981): 118, 121.

93. Webster, *Foreign Policy of Palmerston*, 1:445, 448, 2:788; Bell, *Lord Palmerston*, 216–217; Bullen, *Palmerston, Guizot, and the Collapse of the Entente Cordiale*, 14–17.

94. Webster, "Palmerston and the Liberal Movement," 322.

argument), it is significant that this redefinition occurred at a time when Palmerston believed that French and British interests were sufficiently synergistic that he was pushing for an extension of France's power in areas of considerable strategic value to Britain (e.g., in Spain, Italy, and the western Mediterranean). If politicians' understandings of the ideological distances among states is epiphenomenal of power-political concerns, as some scholars assert, we would have expected Palmerston to adopt a more favorable view of Louis-Philippe at this time instead of the reverse. It is more plausible that Palmerston simply came to believe that the French king was not as committed to liberalism as the foreign minister had previously assumed. This genuine change in belief pushed Palmerston to adopt much more hostile policies toward France than he had since 1830. Without this change, it is likely that the division of the European great powers into two hostile ideological alliances that was created by the domestic changes in Britain and France in the early 1830s would have continued throughout the remainder of the Concert period.

[4]

The 1930s and the Origins of
the Second World War

Many of the most important dimensions of the policies adopted by the great powers in the 1930s that were instrumental in bringing about the Second World War are virtually universally agreed upon among scholars. Germany under Adolf Hitler's rule is described by almost all as a state driven by hegemonic ambitions, and British, French, and Soviet leaders are blamed for facilitating Germany's war plans by acts of omission and commission. British and French statesmen are faulted for not balancing against Germany to the full extent of their states' capabilities and for engaging in policies of appeasement rather than deterrence. Soviet statesmen contributed to the realization of Hitler's ambitions by signing the Nazi-Soviet Pact of August 1939, which both alleviated German leaders' worries about having to fight a two-front war and provided vital raw materials for Germany's war-fighting efforts.

Although the most important policies adopted by the great powers that led to World War II are generally agreed upon, significant disagreement remains concerning the motives behind these choices. Were Germany's leaders primarily driven to war for traditional security reasons or by the implications generated by Nazi beliefs? What impact did Marxism-Leninism have on Soviet policies in this period and on the other powers' views of the Soviet Union? Did the key decision makers in the Western democracies try to appease Germany primarily as a strategy designed to gain time to rearm, because they had an inflated understanding of their states' safety due to their belief in the superiority of the defense, or because they were loath to adopt policies that would necessitate an alliance with communist Russia? This chapter answers questions such as these.

THE FOREIGN POLICIES OF NAZI GERMANY, 1933–41

At first glance, it might appear that demonstrating the importance of ideological variables to Nazi Germany's foreign policies is a relatively easy exercise. Knowing what we do about Germany's horrific policies during the war, how else can we explain the Nazis' demonic conduct except by referring to their ideological beliefs?

In recent years, however, several influential books operating within the realist tradition have challenged the centrality of ideological variables to Germany's foreign policies in the 1930s. Most notably, Dale Copeland and John Mearsheimer claim that Nazi ideology was neither a necessary nor a sufficient condition for Germany to wage hegemonic war.[1] To these authors, power variables created very strong incentives that were pushing Germany to war regardless of its leaders' ideological beliefs. Because of its population advantages vis-à-vis the Western powers and its industrial and technological superiority in comparison to the Soviet Union, Germany in the 1930s had the potential to become the hegemon of the system. Copeland and Mearsheimer thus argue that Germany's leaders confronted incentives to wage major war in order to maximize their state's security. Moreover, these incentives were especially strong in the 1930s because the Soviet Union's industrial, and hence military, capacity was increasing at a fantastic rate.[2] When this fact is coupled with the USSR's resource advantages and huge population, it was highly likely that the Soviet Union in the near future would surpass Germany to become the dominant power on the continent. German leaders' decision to wage a major war when they did was therefore a preventive action against a rising power for the purpose of best ensuring Germany's position of dominance and thus its safety.

Although an analysis of power distributions and trends provides the best explanation for the timing of the Nazis' decision to initiate major war (i.e., while Germany was still substantially stronger than the Soviet Union), these variables fail to adequately explain Germany's motive for conflict: the belief that the other powers, particularly the USSR, were mortal enemies that needed to be defeated before they became too powerful. The mere *possibility* that states will use their power superiority to subjugate others in the future should not be a sufficient reason to impel leaders to engage in a preventive war in the present. Rational decision

1. Dale C. Copeland, *The Origins of Major War: Hegemonic Rivalry and the Fear of Decline* (Ithaca: Cornell University Press, 2000), chap. 5; John J. Mearsheimer, *The Tragedy of Great Power Politics* (New York: W. W. Norton, 2001), chaps. 6, 8. See also Randall L. Schweller, *Deadly Imbalances: Tripolarity and Hitler's Strategy of World Conquest* (New York: Columbia University Press, 1998).

2. Paul Kennedy, *The Rise and Fall of the Great Powers: Economic Change and Military Conflict from 1500 to 2000* (New York: Random House, 1987), 323, 299, 330; Copeland, *Origins of Major War*, chap. 5.

makers should base their actions, especially such risky and costly policies as preventive war, on the *probability* of particular outcomes occurring, not just their potentiality to occur. In terms of the 1930s, it is significant that Hitler and his supporters described a future conflict with the Soviet Union not as a mere possibility, but as a virtual inevitability.[3] Ideological—and not power—variables explain why the Nazis were so certain about the future course of German-Soviet relations.

Nazi leaders' ideological beliefs consisted of two primary organizing concepts: fierce anti-communism and dogmatic racism. The Nazis greatly amplified the aggressive effects of the latter beliefs by wedding them to a crude social Darwinist ethic. Life to Hitler, as he would repeat again and again, was a merciless struggle for existence among different "racial" (i.e., ethnic) groups. "In struggle," he asserted, "I see the destiny of all human beings; no one can escape the struggle if he does not want to be defeated."[4] Or as he stated in his book, *Mein Kampf*: "Those who want to live, let them fight, and those who do not want to fight in this world of eternal struggle do not deserve to live."[5] Jews were the primary, though by no means the only, object of the Nazis' racial enmity.

Hitler's ideological beliefs are often described as a domestic-level pathology that pushed him to aggress regardless of external considerations. There is obviously some truth to this description. However, because of the inherently relational dimension of Nazism's defining components (i.e., racism makes sense only by defining one's own race in relation to others, and anti-communism calls for a focus on communist beliefs and believers), this ideology should not be considered in strictly domestic-level terms. Instead, Hitler and his supporters repeatedly asserted that the ideological and "racial" distances separating states, and thus the nature of *other* regimes, were central to their policies. The greater the ideological and racial differences separating Hitler's Nazi "Aryans" from other groups, the more he feared and loathed them, and the reverse. Hence Hitler's undying enmity for "Jewish," Bolshevik Russia, and his obvious sympathy for fascist Italy. Looking only at the content of Nazi beliefs and not their impact on the ideological distances among regimes obscures these important differences.

3. Cf. Jeremy Noakes and Geoffrey Pridham, eds., *Nazism, 1919–1945: A History in Documents and Eyewitness Accounts*, vol. 2, *Foreign Policy, War and Racial Extermination* (New York: Schocken Books, 1988), doc. 185, p. 281; doc. 186, p. 288.

4. In William Carr, *Arms, Autarky, and Aggression: A Study in German Foreign Policy, 1933–1939* (London: Edward Arnold, 1972), 11.

5. Adolf Hitler, *Mein Kampf* (Boston: Houghton Mifflin, 1971), 289. These are themes that Hitler would repeat throughout his public and private writings, his speeches, and his private talks. For example, as Hitler explained to his senior army commanders in May 1939, Germany's relations with the other powers were not "a question of right or wrong but of to be or not to be for 80,000,000 people" (in Noakes and Pridham, *Nazism*, doc. 539, p. 738). See also doc. 541, p. 741; doc. 185, p. 181; P. M. H. Bell, *The Origins of the Second World War in Europe* (London: Longman, 1986), 81; Hitler, *Mein Kampf*, vol. 1, chap. 11.

Examining the relational dimensions of Nazism thus allows us to better understand why the Nazis adopted the foreign policies they did while at no time excusing the pathological dimensions of their conduct.

The key question the remainder of this section seeks to answer is: How important was Nazism in pushing Germany's leaders to war? Or, to put it another way, in the absence of the impact of Nazi ideology on German leaders' perceptions of threat and consequent international choices, how different would Germany's foreign policies in the 1930s have been? I answer these questions primarily by examining the reasons for Germany's attack on the Soviet Union in 1941, which was an objective that remained the centerpiece of Hitler's foreign policies throughout the 1930s. Hitler was clear that any deviations from enmity with the USSR—most notably the Nazi-Soviet Pact of August 1939—were tactical decisions only that facilitated the realization of his ultimate goal: the destruction of the Soviet Union. As the Führer told Carl Burkhardt (the League of Nations commissioner in Danzig) in August 1939: "Everything I undertake is directed against the Russians; if the West is too stupid and blind to grasp this, then I shall be compelled to come to an agreement with the Russians, beat the West, and then after their defeat turn against the Soviet Union with all my forces."[6]

Although Germany and the Soviet Union shared similar totalitarian political institutions, on other key ideological issues the two states were polar opposites. Most notably, the Nazis' fierce hatred of communism and intense animosity to many of the prominent ethic groups in the USSR clearly overwhelmed any institutional affinity between the two regimes. It is for this reason that both politicians and scholars of the day referred to Germany and the Soviet Union as dictatorships of the "right" and "left," respectively. Despite institutional similarities, the two states were at opposite ends of the ideological spectrum.

Hitler's statements repeatedly reflected this position. From the 1920s until the 1940s, both when he was in power and out, Hitler was clear that Germany's unavoidable conflict with the Soviet Union was primarily a product of the two states' huge ideological and racial differences. For example, in a February 1939 speech to the German army's field commanders, Hitler stated that the next war would be "purely a war of *Weltanschauungen*, that is, totally a people's war, a racial war."[7] Three

6. In Noakes and Pridham, *Nazism*, doc. 540, p. 739. Hitler expressed these points in a more emotional manner when he wrote to Benito Mussolini on the eve of Germany's attack on the Soviet Union: "[The "partnership" with the Soviet Union from 1939 to 1941 was] often very irksome to me, for in some way or other it seemed to me to be a break with my whole origin, my concepts and my former obligations. I am happy now to be relieved of these mental agonies" (in William L. Shirer, *The Rise and Fall of the Third Reich: A History of Nazi Germany* [New York: Simon and Schuster, 1960], 851).

7. In Jürgen Förster, "New Wine in Old Skins? The Wehrmacht and the War of 'Weltanschauungen,' 1941," in *The German Military in the Age of Total War*, ed. Wilhelm Deist (Dover, N. H.: Berg, 1985), 305; see also 306.

months before Germany's attack on the Soviet Union, he told the Wehrmacht generals that the origins, objectives, and means of fighting the upcoming war were rooted in ideological differences between the two powers. According to the Führer: "This struggle is one of ideologies and racial differences and will have to be conducted with unprecedented, unmerciful, and relenting harshness. . . . The commissars are the bearers of ideologies directly opposed to National Socialism. Therefore the commissars will be liquidated."[8] In fact, the "main theme" of Hitler's reasoning for waging war on the Soviet Union, according to the Chief of the Armed Forces High Command, Wilhelm Keitel, was to engage "the decisive battle between two ideologies."[9] The Nazis believed that Germany's relations with a "Jewish," communist regime could only be a state of war. This view made the incentives for preventive hostilities against the USSR while Germany still had military superiority very powerful.

Supporting the claim that the huge ideological distance dividing Nazi Germany from communist Russia was critical to the Nazis' enmity toward this state is the fact that Hitler believed that the ideological differences dividing the Western democracies and the USSR would decrease the likelihood of these states coalescing into an effective alliance in time to prevent Germany's aggressive foreign policy aims. It is most likely this belief that pushed Hitler to try to establish in Western leaders' minds Germany's role as a "bulwark against communism."[10] Such a perception, the Führer obviously believed, would invariably lead to a confused understanding of his true aims by the Western democracies. This belief allowed Hitler to pursue his aggressive goals with more confidence in their success. The fact that Hitler and the Nazis believed that the ideological distances dividing states' leaders would play a significant role in shaping the foreign policies of Britain and France lends credence to the claim that this variable shaped Germany's foreign policies as well.

8. In Shirer, *Rise and Fall of the Third Reich*, 830. See also Schweller, *Deadly Imbalances*, 99; Jürgen Förster, "Barbarossa Revisited: Strategy and Ideology in the East," *Jewish Social Studies* 50, nos. 1, 2 (Winter–Spring 1988/92): 21. No doubt the *content* of Nazi ideology, especially the Social-Darwinist tenet that life is a brutal struggle for survival among ethnic groups, substantially contributed to the Nazis' animosity toward the other powers, including the USSR. Nevertheless, as evidenced by Hitler's explicit emphasis on ideological and racial differences to his choices, ideological distance remained central to the Nazis' acute perceptions of threat and aggressive international policies, especially toward the USSR.

9. In Shirer, *Rise and Fall of the Third Reich*, 846. The quotation is a summary of a "comprehensive political speech" by Hitler to his generals in June 1941.

10. Gerhard Weinberg, *The Foreign Policy of Hitler's Germany*, vol. 1: *Diplomatic Revolution in Europe, 1933–1936* (Chicago: University of Chicago Press, 1970), 310 (hereafter, *Foreign Policy of Hitler's Germany, 1933–1936*); Michael Jabara Carley, "'A Fearful Concatenation of Circumstances': The Anglo Soviet Rapprochement, 1934–6," *Contemporary European History* 5, no. 1 (March 1996): 44, 45.

Ideological variables not only shaped Nazi leaders' estimates of other states' international intentions, but also their fears of domestic subversion, as the demonstration-effects mechanism predicts. The Nazis' conception of subversion was, however, different in emphasis from the way in which this fear manifested itself in other systems. Instead of being predominantly fearful, for example, of a particular regime type spreading throughout the system, Hitler and the Nazis were primarily terrified of *racial* subversion.[11] A foundational tenet of Hitler's political beliefs was that the superior Aryan race was destined to win the interracial struggle for existence that defined history. There was, however, an important caveat to this belief. To Hitler, the Aryans were destined for victory *only as long as they maintained their racial purity.*[12] Hitler believed that a policy of personal and political miscegenation (in which "inferior" races were allowed to possess political influence) had greatly weakened potentially powerful states in the past.[13] He was determined not to let this happen to Germany, though he recognized it as a distinct possibility.[14]

This understanding of threats to Germany's security had a direct impact on the Nazis' foreign policy choices. The desire to maintain the racial purity of the German nation necessitated a policy of racial purification at home—in which individuals of "inferior" races were either expelled from Germany or put in concentration camps—and a policy of racial extermination abroad. If "sub-human" peoples were exterminated or permanently subjugated, the possibility of German blood and political institutions being bastardized would be significantly mitigated, if not eliminated. With this understanding of the threats to Germany, both Hitler's need for war and his horrific policies during it are made more clear. The Führer feared the subversion of the German master race to the point where a war of annihilation against "inferior" races was the "logical" solution to this danger.[15] According to Keitel in a directive on behalf of Hitler on the eve of war with the USSR: "special tasks" (i.e., the murder

11. The Nazis were also fearful of institutional subversion by those Aryan "traitors" who supported either liberalism or communism, but racial subversion is what obsessed Hitler.
12. Hitler, *Mein Kampf*, 285, 286, 289, 296, 297, 327, 328, 688.
13. This is clearly what Hitler believed had happened with Russia, the United States, and to some degree England (Hitler, *Mein Kampf*, esp. vol. 1, chap. 11; Gerhard Weinberg, "Hitler's Image of the United States," *American Historical Review* 69, no. 4 [July 1974]: 1010–1011; and Andreas Hillgruber, "England's Place in Hitler's Plans for World Domination," *Journal of Contemporary History* 9, no. 1 [January 1974]: 10, 21).
14. As Hitler put it in *Mein Kampf*: "The danger to which Russia succumbed [i.e., of "racial poisoning"] is always present for Germany" (661).
15. The differences between ideological content and ideological distance get somewhat blurry in this instance. The specific behavioral prescriptions of Nazism (ideological content) pushed its adherents to extreme forms of racism, but notions of racial and ideological differences (ideological distance) caused the Nazis to target for annihilation some groups and some states more than others.

of racial and ideological enemies) during the war would "result from the struggle which has to be carried out between two opposing political systems."[16] Realist theories cannot explain Germany's leaders' decision to wage a war of annihilation, especially when one considers its costliness in terms of both draining Germany's resources and alienating millions of potential sympathizers in eastern Europe who originally welcomed the German army as a liberating force from the Soviet Union.

Ideological differences among the great powers' leaders also contributed to the war by inhibiting effective understanding among them. Throughout the 1930s, many Western leaders assumed that Hitler had legitimate and limited aims, and that taking a strong deterrent stand against him would only provoke an unnecessary conflict. As a result of these beliefs, statesmen in France and especially in Britain attempted to placate the Führer by offering him various territorial and political concessions. Hitler, who understood life as an inevitable conflict in which war was both a necessary and ennobling activity, did not interpret British and French offers in the spirit in which they were made. Instead, he continually understood them to result from Western weakness.[17] Consequently, each concession made by Britain and France only solidified his conviction that these powers were decadent and that their leaders would never oppose him until it was too late. Thus, with each concession made to him, Hitler's willingness to risk major war grew. The worldviews of the Nazis and politicians in the Western democracies were simply too different to allow them to understand one another.

A final factor revealing the centrality of the Nazis' ideological beliefs to their foreign policy choices is that there is substantial evidence indicating that Germany's international decisions in the 1930s would have been very different if the Nazis had not been in power. Because officers in the German military continued to possess political influence throughout most of the 1930s, they were the most important group of non-Nazi decision makers in this period. If military leaders advocated similar foreign policies as Hitler and his supporters, *and* if they wanted conflict for traditional geopolitical reasons, then the uniqueness of an analysis based on ideological variables must be called into question.[18] Conversely, significant variation in foreign policy preferences between Nazis and non-Nazis would indicate the importance of ideological beliefs to policy formulation, especially in relation to realist arguments since power variables for all members of a particular state are identical.

16. In Shirer, *Rise and Fall of the Third Reich*, 832.
17. Weinberg, *Foreign Policy of Hitler's Germany, 1933–1936*, 206; Gerhard Weinberg, *The Foreign Policy of Hitler's Germany: Starting World War II, 1937–1939* (Chicago: University of Chicago Press, 1980), 141 (hereafter *Foreign Policy of Hitler's Germany, 1937–1939*).
18. Copeland, *Origins of Major War*, chap. 5.

In support of realist arguments, there was throughout the 1930s substantial foreign policy agreement on various important subjects between the Nazis and the traditional German military. Virtually all military officers concurred with the Nazis that the Versailles system that restricted Germany's sovereignty and power had to be destroyed; that the German-speaking peoples in Austria, Czechoslovakia, Poland, and Lithuania should be incorporated into Germany (by war, if necessary); and that Germany should engage in a massive rearmament program (the military's goals in this last area equaled Hitler's highly ambitious objectives for much of the 1930s).[19]

Beyond these objectives, however, substantial disagreement between the Nazis and many members of the traditional military continued to exist. There were a significant number of high-ranking individuals in the military and other security agencies who opposed core elements of Hitler's foreign policies to such a degree that these individuals became known in the historical literature as the "German resistance." Ideological differences between Nazis and the resisters were central to their foreign policy disagreements.

For representative expressions of the German resistance's foreign policy goals, I concentrate largely on the views of General Ludwig Beck, the Army Chief of Staff around whom, according to virtually all his contemporaries and scholars alike, the primary domestic opposition to Hitler focused. Other key military members of the resistance included Colonel Hans Oster (Chief of Staff and head of the Central Division of Abwehr, Germany's armed forces intelligence), Admiral Wilhelm Canaris (head of Abwehr), Colonel General Baron Werner von Fritsch (Army Commander-in-Chief), Lieutenant Colonel Helmuth Groscurth (Chief of an Abwehr division), Colonel General Erwin von Witzleben (Commander of the Berlin military district), and General Karl von Stülpnagel (Deputy Chief and Quartermaster General). The power of the German resistance centered around Beck is perhaps best revealed by the fact that Hitler in the late 1930s felt compelled to engage in deep purges of recalcitrant officers in order to realize his most ambitious international objectives.

Probably the most important foreign policy difference between the Nazis and the Beck group is that many of the latter opposed Germany going to war with France and especially Britain.[20] Not only did the resisters' support for a coup against Hitler reach its apogee in the months

19. Klaus-Jürgen Müller, *The Army, Politics, and Society in Germany, 1933–45* (Manchester: Manchester University Press, 1987); Copeland, *Origins of Major War*, chap. 5; Wilhelm Deist, *The Wehrmacht and German Rearmament* (Toronto: University of Toronto Press, 1981), esp. 91, 95, 108.

20. Robert O'Neill, "Fritsch, Beck, and the Führer," 33, and Klaus-Jürgen Müller, "Witzleben, Stülpnagel, and Speidel," 51–52, both in *Hitler's Generals*, ed. Correlli Barnett (London: Weidenfeld and Nicolson, 1989); Nicholas Reynolds, *Treason Was No Crime: Ludwig Beck, Chief of the German General Staff* (London: William Kimber, 1976), 113–115, 169, 177.

leading up to Germany's attack on France,[21] but some resisters engaged in treasonous correspondence with Britain and France to inform them of Hitler's battlefield plans in an attempt to prevent war with these states. These communications most powerfully illustrate the substantive (as opposed to merely tactical) nature of the differences between the Beck group and the Nazis.

The effects of ideological distances were central to the resisters' opposition to war with the Western democracies. Beck and most of his supporters viewed Britain and France as Germany's ideological allies against the greatest ideological threat in the system: the Soviet Union. Consequently, the Beck group believed that war among Germany, Britain, and France was a grave error because it would only weaken these states to the ultimate benefit of their primary enemy, the USSR.[22]

By claiming that most German resisters viewed Britain and France as ideological allies against the Soviet Union, I do not mean to imply that Beck, his supporters, and the key leaders in the Western democracies were dedicated to identical ideological objectives. Most members of the German resistance, especially in the military, were not liberals, but conservative nationalists. They remained committed to authoritarian political institutions, and believed that domestic order and respect for the armed forces should be of the highest social values.[23]

Despite these ideological differences with the Western democracies, the key point is that virtually all members of the German resistance viewed communism as a much greater ideological danger than liberalism. Beck and his allies therefore saw themselves as much closer ideologically to Western leaders (especially Western conservatives) than they were to Soviet elites.

Although the Nazis agreed with the Beck group that communism was a greater ideological danger than liberalism, this distinction was much more blurred for the Nazis than for the resisters. Beck and his allies repeatedly emphasized that Britain, France, and Germany were united by a "common European identity" that was based not only on mutual opposition to communism, but a common philosophical and moral heritage.[24] The German resisters to Hitler, as Klemons von Klemperer explains, were

---

21. Müller, "Witzleben, Stülpnagel, and Speidel," 51–54.
22. Reynolds, *Treason Was No Crime*, 113–115; Harold C. Deutsch, *The Conspiracy against Hitler in the Twilight War* (Minneapolis: University of Minnesota Press, 1968), 205–207.
23. Klemons von Klemperer, *German Resistance against Hitler: The Search for Allies Abroad, 1938–1945* (Oxford: Clarendon Press, 1992), 10, 19, 23, 25; Reynolds, *Treason Was No Crime*, 33–34. Despite many military resisters' general commitment to authoritarianism, there was agreement among them that in the wake of a successful coup against Hitler, they would replace the Nazi regime with a conservative democracy (Shirer, *Rise and Fall of the Third Reich*, 375; von Klemperer, *German Resistance against Hitler*, 105–106). This preference provides additional evidence of ideological affinity between resisters and the Western democracies.
24. Reynolds, *Treason Was No Crime*, 200.

motivated by a vision of "the West" in which "law and humanity were to prevail."[25] This was a view that was absent from the fascists' ideology. To the Nazis, the Soviet Union was evil incarnate, but the Western powers were not far behind in terms of the Nazis' contempt for other political forms. As Hitler explained in *Mein Kampf*, "Democracy as practiced in Western Europe today is the forerunner of Marxism. In fact, the latter would not be conceivable without the former. Democracy is the breeding-ground in which the bacilli of the Marxist world pest can grow and spread. By the introduction of parliamentarianism, democracy produced an 'abortion of filth.'"[26]

The claims that Germany, Britain, and France should be allies against communist Russia, and thus that war among the former states would be deleterious to German interests, are themes that Beck and his allies would reiterate on a number of occasions, both publicly and privately. For example, in a 1937 meeting in Paris with the Chief of the French General Staff, General Maurice Gamelin, Beck told his French counterpart: "We do not wish to fight a war against France. You are convinced that you would emerge victorious. We think that we would be the victors. . . . But the real conclusion would be the destruction of Europe and our common civilization. The Bolsheviks would profit."[27] The historian Nicholas Reynolds sums up Beck's views on this subject: "Beck obviously feared that Hitler's [aggressive policies] would ultimately lead to a second world war with disastrous consequences for Germany and Europe. . . . [No] matter who won . . . it would offer unparalleled opportunities to Bolshevism. That was the lesson of 1918, and it obsessed Beck. For him it would be terrible if any European nation succumbed to communism. . . . Therefore Germany should try to achieve her goals without plunging Europe into another [great power] war," especially one between Germany, Britain, and France.[28]

In October 1939, Erich Kordt (head of the Foreign Office Ministerial Bureau) and Legation Counselor Hasso von Etzdorf formed a group

---

25. von Klemperer, *German Resistance against Hitler*, 29. See also 8, 9, 193, 196, 434, 437; Müller, *Army, Politics, and Society in Germany*, 80; Deutsch, *Conspiracy against Hitler in the Twilight War*, 206–207; Reynolds, *Treason Was No Crime*, 113.
26. In Werner Maser, *Hitler's Mein Kampf: An Analysis*, trans. R. H. Barry (London: Faber and Faber, 1970), 179. See also Weinberg, *Foreign Policy of Hitler's Germany, 1933–1936*, 4, 15–21; Carr, *Arms, Autarky, and Aggression*, 13. Despite Hitler's contempt for Britain's political system, he remained more sympathetic to this state than others due to perceptions of racial affinity between Anglo-Saxons and German "Aryans." Until almost the end of the war, Hitler believed that racial affinity and mutual antipathy to communism would push Britain to ally with Germany against the Soviet Union (Hillgruber, "England's Place in Hitler's Plans," 18–21; Schweller, *Deadly Imbalances*).
27. In Reynolds, *Treason Was No Crime*, 113.
28. Ibid., 115, 192. Consistent with these views, Beck and his allies were opposed to the Nazi-Soviet Pact (183, 189; see also Müller, *Army, Politics, and Society in Germany*, 119). The agreement not only increased the relative power of the Soviet Union, but made war between Germany and the Western powers more likely.

advocating a coup against Hitler if the Führer ordered Germany to attack France. According to a memorandum written by this group, "Germany had never been closer to chaos and Bolshevism," and war between Germany and France would lead to further "expansionism of Bolshevism in Europe."[29] This document was warmly received by Beck and General Franz Halder (Chief of the General Staff), and it was subsequently shown as a basis for action against Hitler to General Walther von Brauchitsch (Commander-in-Chief of the Army), General Stülpnagel, Colonel Groscurth, and other members of the resistance.[30]

Beck explicitly expressed his opposition to Hitler's aggressive policies that were putting Germany on a collision course with France and Britain when he wrote in a memorandum in September 1939 after Germany's invasion of Poland: "We all want a large, strong, unified Germany with . . . many independent and varied resources. . . . *This goal was to a large extent attained before the war began.* The material life of the German people was by and large adequate, if in need of some improvement. By no means does it necessitate a struggle for existence."[31] According to the historian Klaus-Jürgen Müller, Beck's rejection of Nazi ideology created an "abyss" separating his primary foreign policy objectives from Hitler's. Whereas Hitler felt compelled to conquer the continent, "[Beck's] notion [of foreign policy expansion] was more that of an extension of German power in Central Europe by virtue of a position of influence and supremacy, not of annexations that went beyond the union with areas of German-speaking population."[32]

Because General Beck and his supporters believed Germany, Britain, and France to be ideological allies against the Soviet Union, the German resisters expected the Western powers to allow the creation of a strong German state so that it could be a more effective ally against the USSR.[33] These views are consistent with the predictions of the conflict-probability causal mechanism. The Beck group believed that disputes with the Western powers involving the Rhineland and the incorporation into Germany of Austria and the Sudetenland of Czechoslovakia would "sooner or later have been solved in Germany's favor" without the use of Hitler's aggressive tactics.[34] These were not unrealistic beliefs. Many French and especially British conservatives were willing to allow Germany to expand substantially its sphere of influence in eastern Europe in order to be a more effective "bulwark against com-

---

29. In Deutsch, *Conspiracy against Hitler in the Twilight War,* 206, Deutsch's summary of the memorandum.

30. Ibid., 207–208.

31. In Reynolds, *Treason Was No Crime,* 189–190 (emphasis added). See also 83–84; Deutsch, *Conspiracy against Hitler in the Twilight War,* 97–108.

32. Müller, *Army, Politics, and Society in Germany,* 79.

33. Reynolds, *Treason Was No Crime,* 119, 120, 192, 201, 202.

34. Ibid., 110. See also 108, 110, 150; Harold C. Deutsch, *Hitler and His Generals: The Hidden Crisis, January–June 1938* (Minneapolis: University of Minnesota Press, 1974), 37, 72; Deutsch, *Conspiracy against Hitler in the Twilight War,* 207, 353.

munism," as long as this expansion was done peacefully and in a manner that was consistent with the principle of national self-determination.

One might argue that the Beck group's opposition to Hitler's most aggressive foreign policies was tactical only, that because Germany (in the resisters' minds) had not yet reached its greatest relative power advantage over its adversaries, it was rational to delay attack until that time. In support of this hypothesis is the fact that resisters frequently framed their opposition to Hitler's policies in terms of expediency and timing.[35]

Fear that Germany was not strong enough to win another world war no doubt contributed to military resisters' opposition to Hitler's core international objectives from 1938 through 1940. However, the depth of this opposition indicates that issues of timing were not the principal motivating factor of the Beck group.

In the first place, the fact that Hitler felt compelled both to purge extensively non-Nazis from the military and to eliminate the military's ability to affect policy suggests that the conflict between the Nazis and the military resisters went much deeper than issues of timing, but were instead a product of substantive policy differences. The greatest of Hitler's purges of the military occurred in February 1938 on the heels of the infamous Blomberg-Fritsch crisis (Field Marshal Werner von Blomberg was War Minister and Colonel General Baron Werner von Fritsch was Commander-in-Chief of the Army). Both these individuals were forced from their respective offices for scandalous reasons—Blomberg for marrying a former prostitute, Fritsch on trumped-up charges of homosexuality. Hitler used these scandals and the subsequent demoralization of the army to diminish significantly the power and influence of the military in favor of increased Nazi control.[36]

In the wake of the Blomberg-Fritsch crisis, sixteen (mostly senior) generals hostile to Nazism were forced to retire, and forty-six more were reassigned.[37] The independently minded ambassadors to Rome, Vienna, Beijing, and Tokyo were recalled. The obstinate Constantin von Neurath was replaced as foreign minister by the sycophantic Joachim von Ribbentrop. Hitler demanded that the army move closer to the National Socialist state in its ideology, that Beck be forced to resign in the near future, that new command structures for the military be implemented (including placing Hitler at the head of the armed forces), and that a clean sweep of the Army Personnel Office be made to better facilitate the placement of

35. Copeland, *Origins of Major War*, chap. 5.
36. General Alfred Jodl, a Nazi sympathizer, wrote in his diary at the time of the crisis that Hitler was planning major changes in both military organization and personnel in order to "at last bring the military to heel" (Shirer, *Rise and Fall of the Third Reich*, 316, Shirer's summary of Jodl's diary entry).
37. Matthew Cooper, *The German Army, 1933–1945: Its Political and Military Failure* (London: MacDonald and Jones, 1978), 77–78; Shirer, *Rise and Fall of the Third Reich*, 318–319.

Nazi adherents.[38] These personnel and institutional changes not only removed from positions of power key opponents of Hitler's foreign policies, but no doubt coerced into silence many who retained their positions.

When all was said and done, the events of February 1938 marked the culmination of "Hitler's total success in gradually eliminating the army as a politically relevant factor, in eventually suppressing it completely and finally making it a simple, though thoroughly effective, instrument of his policies."[39] Although it is possible that Hitler felt the need to purge the army because of disagreements over the best time to engage in military hostilities as opposed to more substantive differences in foreign policy objectives, the extent of Hitler's purges and organizational changes belies such an interpretation.

The second, even more powerful, set of evidence that reveals the depths of non-Nazi resisters' substantive opposition to Hitler's foreign policies is that members of the Beck group, including military officers, engaged in a multitude of covert messages to Britain and France that were designed to thwart Hitler's most ambitious international goals. In these messages, the resisters informed British and French representatives of Germany's short- and long-run intentions, and even the details of military plans of attack in Czechoslovakia and the west.[40] The Beck group also pleaded with Britain and France in these messages to make a determined stand against Hitler in order to give Germany a foreign policy defeat that would provide significant aid to their coup plans (many resisters were even *discouraged* by Hitler's' victory at Munich and the defeat of France in 1940 because these outcomes reduced the chances of forcing Hitler from power).[41]

38. Deutsch, *Hitler and His Generals*, 223–225. In addition to Hitler appointing himself as the head of the newly created Supreme Command of the Armed Forces (known by its German acronym, OKW), other structural changes initiated at this time included the end of the Army Commander-in-Chief's authority to direct all fighting services and the significant curtailment of access by military leaders to civilian authorities (see Cooper, *German Army*, 84–86, 190, 192, 248).

39. Müller, *Army, Politics, and Society in Germany*, 34, also 10, 34–37; Deutsch, *Hitler and His Generals*, 230, 267; Donald Cameron Watt, *How War Came: The Immediate Origins of the Second World War, 1938–1939* (New York: Pantheon Books, 1989), 24–25. In his attempt to show that the resisters' opposition to Hitler's foreign policies involved issues of timing only and not substantive aims, Copeland ignores the number of generals and other personnel either forced into retirement or reassigned in the wake of the Fritsch-Blomberg crisis, as well as the important institutional changes made at this time. Nor is there any mention in Copeland's analysis of the resisters' attempts to sabotage Hitler's policies through treasonous communications with the Western powers.

40. For example, in August 1939 Beck passed on to the Western powers minutes from a meeting between Hitler and his generals that detailed the Führer's plans for attack in Poland and his intentions to exterminate "undesirables" in this state. In 1940, Beck and other resisters told the Western powers that Hitler intended to violate the neutrality of Belgium and Holland in order to attack France. See Reynolds, *Treason Was No Crime*, 183–184, 206; Shirer, *Rise and Fall of the Third Reich*, 380–382.

41. Deutsch, *Conspiracy against Hitler in the Twilight War*, 106, 354; von Klemperer, *German Resistance against Hitler*, 89, 97, 109, 112, 219, 220; Reynolds, *Treason Was No Crime*, 211.

That some of Germany's highest-ranking officials would engage in such treasonous correspondence for primarily reasons of expediency (i.e., that Germany had not yet reached its greatest power-political advantage over its rivals) seems very unlikely. It is an illogical position to assert that these individuals both conspired to have Germany suffer international defeat and risked plunging it into domestic turmoil in order to avoid these very pitfalls because Germany's relative military power had not yet peaked. Moreover, the nature of the resisters' treasonous correspondences with Britain and France reveal a level of trust (e.g., that these states would not take advantage of Germany's vulnerability during and after a coup) and a community of interests that cannot be explained with reference to expediency. Instead, these beliefs were a product of ideological affinities between the resisters and the Western democracies. It would have been unthinkable, for example, for the Beck group to send similar treasonous messages to Russia as long as it was a communist regime.

After Germany's defeat of France in 1940, however, there was a clear weakening of the German military's resistance to Hitler's foreign policies. After Hitler's seemingly endless string of foreign policy successes, there was a noticeable bandwagon effect in which former resisters, including such notables as the Chief of the General Staff, General Franz Halder, abandoned their opposition to the Nazis' international objectives. In fact, most officers supported Hitler's decision to wage a war of extermination against the Soviet Union. Because members of the traditional military once again seemed to agree with Hitler's international goals, some have argued that this demonstrates the centrality of geopolitical concerns to Germany's foreign policies. Regardless of the ideological differences dividing Nazis and the traditional German military, most agreed with Hitler's campaign against the USSR.[42]

This argument has some merit, but it also has two significant weaknesses. First, although many in the military were willing to support Hitler's campaign against Russia *in 1941*, it is highly unlikely that without Hitler's constant pressure throughout the 1930s, including both substantial purges of the military and institutional reorganizations that limited the political power of the armed forces, Germany would have been in the situation it was in this year. The Nazis' particular vision of international relations, and especially their willingness to wage war against the Western democracies over the objections of the Beck group, were necessary preconditions for Germany to be in the position in 1941 to attack the USSR without the hazards of a two-front war. The incentives created by Germany's relative position in the international distribution of power were far from sufficient to arrive at this point.

---

42. See especially Copeland, *Origins of Major War*, chap. 5.

Second, the evidence is clear that the German military leaders' fears and hostility toward the USSR, just as for the Nazis, were primarily a product of ideological variables. As indicated in the previous analysis, most members of the military, including those in the resistance, were fervently anti-communist. This ideological antipathy not only pushed German military leaders to view the Soviet Union as both a large subversive and power-political threat, but was, according to Müller, of "utmost importance" to these individuals' support of Hitler's eastern campaign. Bolshevism, to Germany's military officers, was "the very negation, the antithesis of all their political, social and moral values. Therefore, it had to be totally exterminated."[43]

Many leaders in the German military both described their motives for war with the Soviet Union as a result of the huge ideological differences dividing the two states, and supported the Nazis' policies during the war of exterminating undesirables based on ideological/racial criteria. The content of senior commanders' addresses, deployment directives, and battlefield orders supports this assertion.[44] For example, in May 1941 the High Command of the Wehrmacht issued a directive to its troops that stated that Bolshevism is the "deadly enemy of the National Socialist German nation. It is against this destructive ideology and its adherents that Germany is waging war."[45] In the same month, General Erich Hoepner, who was a resister to Hitler killed for his part in the coup of July 1944, wrote that Germany's war against the USSR was "the defense of European culture against . . . Jewish Bolshevism. The objective of this battle must be the destruction of present-day Russia and it must therefore be conducted with unprecedented severity. Every military action must be guided in planning and execution by an iron will to exterminate the enemy mercilessly and totally. In particular, no adherents of the present Russian-Bolshevik system are to be spared."[46]

Consistent with these ideological objectives, from the beginning of the war the army leadership actively aided the SS in murdering hundreds of thousands of people based solely on ideological and racial criteria.[47] The Army High Command adopted these policies even though they proved

43. Klaus-Jürgen Müller, "The Military, Politics, and Society in France and Germany," in *The Military in Politics and Society in France and Germany in the Twentieth Century*, ed. Klaus-Jürgen Müller (Oxford: Berg Publishers, 1995), 18–19; see also Förster, "Barbarossa Revisited."
44. Förster, "Barbarossa Revisited," 23.
45. In Jürgen Förster, "The German Army and the Ideological War against the Soviet Union," in *The Policies of Genocide: Jews and Soviet Prisoners of War in Nazi Germany*, ed. Gerhard Hirschfeld (London: Allen and Unwin, 1986), 20.
46. In Förster, "Barbarossa Revisited," 23.
47. Hirschfeld, ed., *Policies of Genocide*, esp. chaps. 1, 2, 5; Förster, "Barbarossa Revisited"; Peter Longerich, "From Mass Murder to the 'Final Solution': The Shooting of Jewish Civilians During the First Months of the Eastern Campaign within the Context of Nazi Jewish Genocide," in *From Peace to War: Germany, Soviet Russia, and the World, 1939–1941*, ed. Bernd Wegner (Oxford: Berghahn Books, 1997), 253–275.

to be militarily costly since Germany's brutality stiffened Russian soldiers' resistance to the German attack.[48]

This analysis indicates that it is likely that Nazis and non-Nazis in the military advocated similar policies toward the Soviet Union in 1941 not because geopolitical concerns impelled these decision makers to adopt certain policies regardless of ideological beliefs, but because these groups of leaders, regardless of other ideological differences, shared an important ideological conviction: hatred of communism. Put another way, although the contents of the ideological beliefs espoused by Nazis and members of the traditional German military were very different, the ideological distances dividing both groups' beliefs from Soviet principles were extremely large. To both Nazis and non-Nazis in the military, these ideological distances remained key determinants of their foreign policies throughout the 1930s and 1940s.

THE FOREIGN POLICIES OF BRITAIN AND FRANCE, 1933–39

Any analysis of British and French foreign policies in the 1930s must at the outset acknowledge the centrality of relative power concerns to these choices.[49] Most important, there can be no doubt that Germany's large-scale rearmament policies in the 1930s significantly increased British and French leaders' anxieties concerning their states' security. As early as 1934, Britain's Defense Requirements Committee (DRC) labeled Germany in a policy paper as Britain's "ultimate potential enemy."[50] The report was approved by Britain's cabinet, and its claims concerning the potential threat posed by Germany were widely accepted throughout the British establishment for the remainder of the decade. Because of their state's closer proximity to Germany, French leaders were even more concerned about increases in Germany's military capabilities in the 1930s than were their counterparts in Britain. In response to Germany's rearmament efforts in the 1930s, both British and French leaders increased substantially their state's military expenditures and sought to increase their ties with other great powers in the system.

Although realist theories explain important dimensions of British and French foreign policies in the 1930s, significant puzzles for these arguments

---

48. Förster, "Barbarossa Revisited," 27.

49. For a similar examination of the argument of this section that more formally compares the effects of ideological distances on British and French balancing policies to realist, balance-of-threat, and buck-passing theories, see Mark L. Haas, "Ideology and Alliances: British and French External Balancing Decisions in the 1930s," *Security Studies* 12, no. 4 (Summer 2003): 34–79.

50. In Gaines Post, Jr., *Dilemmas of Appeasement: British Deterrence and Defense, 1934–1937* (Ithaca: Cornell University Press, 1993), 25.

remain. Within the context of some degree of internal and external balancing against Germany throughout the 1930s, there was substantial variation in British and French leaders' perceptions of threat and consequent balancing policies toward Germany that to a great extent corresponded with these individuals' party affiliation. Most notable for our purposes, the majority of British and French conservatives desired alignment with Italy as an aid against possible German aggression, but for the bulk of the decade refused association with the Soviet Union. In fact, some British and French conservatives' antipathy to the USSR was so great that they advocated aligning with Nazi Germany against communist Russia. Conversely, the majority of members from parties from the British and French left pushed hard for an alliance with the Soviet Union against Germany, but shunned alignment with Italy. Furthermore, although virtually all Western decision makers viewed Germany in the 1930s as a serious potential threat to their states' security, most British and French conservatives were much less pessimistic than socialists that Germany would actually become an enemy. Hence the widespread belief among conservatives, but not socialists, that the appeasement of Germany would be successful in avoiding great power conflict.

These different preferences and perceptions between the left and right were the key variables responsible for Britain's and France's failure to form alliances with the other great powers against Germany. In France, political power was closely divided between conservatives and socialists throughout the 1930s. Even when not the majority party, each group continued to possess considerable power (the socialists were the majority party in the Popular Front government from 1936 to 1938; the right and/or center-right governed for all but a few months of the remaining years from 1933 to 1940). Both socialists and conservatives were therefore able to prevent significant moves toward the other's preferred ally. As the historian Robert Young explains, "confronted by diplomatic advice to consolidate the alliance with Soviet Russia, and by equally authoritative advice to forge a bond with Fascist Italy, [the French] governments of the 1930s hesitated. . . . They could predict the divisiveness which a decision [for Italy or the Soviet Union] would cause . . . from the benches on the left or from those on the right."[51]

In Britain, conservatives possessed a decisive majority in Parliament for most of the 1930s; there was as a consequence little chance of Britain allying with the USSR. Despite Labour's minority position, they were, however, able to do significant damage to prospects of an Anglo-Italian détente. Although most Tories did not want to initiate sanctions against Italy for invading Ethiopia in October 1935, they were forced to do so

51. Robert J. Young, *France and the Origins of the Second World War* (London: Macmillan, 1996), 96.

because of pressure from both Labour and public opinion (the most concrete expression of the latter was the so-called "Peace Ballot" of June 1935, which overwhelmingly supported the idea of using the League of Nations to sanction aggressors). These sanctions were central both to destroying the Stresa Front that recommitted Britain, France, and Italy to maintain the post-1919 borders of France, Belgium, and Germany, and to retarding Anglo-Italian cooperation for much of the rest of the decade.[52]

In the following, I demonstrate how substantial variation in the ideological distances dividing the great powers' leaders accounts for these partisan differences in perceptions of threat and consequent balancing policies. Because most members of the British and French right considered the Soviet Union to be a greater ideological danger than Nazi Germany, these individuals tended to inflate the perceived threat posed by the USSR to British and French interests, to the point where the perceived costs of an alliance with this state became prohibitive. At the same time, the British and French right tended to deflate the perceived threat posed by Germany, to the point where the appeasement of Germany appeared to most Western conservatives to be both desirable and workable.[53] Nazi Germany was a lesser ideological threat to Western conservatives than the USSR because although most of these politicians opposed Germany's totalitarian institutional structures (just as they did with regards to the Soviet Union), they sympathized with the German fascists' stark anti-communism.

Because of their different ideological beliefs than Western conservatives, British and French socialists viewed the fascist powers as significantly greater ideological dangers than the Soviet Union. Their balancing policies were, as a result, the mirror images of conservatives' views. (Western socialists viewed the Soviet Union as a lesser ideological threat than Germany and Italy because even though all three of the latter were totalitarian states, British and French socialists and Soviet leaders were dedicated to similar socioeconomic goals).[54] Since relative power variables are constant for all members of the same state, conservatives' and socialists' very different views of the ideological relationships with the other powers cannot be viewed as epiphenomenal of power distributions,

52. Richard Lamb, *Mussolini and the British* (London: Jolin Murray, 1997), 78, 87, 125–128, chap. 9.
53. This pattern was clearly noticeable despite the opposition of important, though relatively weak, conservative voices, such as Winston Churchill and Robert Vansittart.
54. The Labour paper, *The Daily Herald*, editorialized in October 1927 in a front-page article: "There is a world of difference between bolshevism and fascism. . . . [Bolshevism, for all its faults, was] based on a theory not of capitalism, private property, competition, but of Communism and cooperation." Or, as one leading Labour politician described the Soviet Union in 1924: "[It is] a great experiment of socialism; and that is not a fact to be forgotten, however we may rightly deplore the want of liberty." This is a point on which "nearly all in the Labour Party were in accord" throughout much of the interwar period. Andrew J. Williams, *Labour and Russia: The Attitude of the Labour Party to the USSR, 1924–1934* (New York: Manchester University Press, 1989), 71, 75.

Table 2. British and French Politicians' Foreign Policy Preferences in the 1930s by Party Affiliation

	Dominant Preferences Toward:		
	USSR	Germany	Italy
Socialists	Ally With	Balance Against	Balance Against
Conservatives[*]	Strategically Isolate/ Balance Against	Appease	Ally With

[*] These preferences apply to French conservatives primarily during the period after the Popular Front's electoral victory in 1936.

nor can realist theories explain these groups' substantial differences in balancing policies, especially given Germany's potential hegemonic status.[55] For a summary of British and French foreign policy preferences by party affiliation, see Table 2.

Conservatives' Balancing Policies

There can be no doubt that the large ideological divide separating the British and French right from Soviet leaders had a profound impact on most conservatives' perceptions of threat and consequent policies toward the USSR. As the demonstration-effects mechanism predicts, throughout the interwar period most British and French conservatives were very fearful of the subversive effects created by close, sustained association in peace or war with any representatives of the Soviet regime.[56] This fear created

55. British and French intelligence reports indicated that in 1937 Germany had substantially *surpassed the combined* army strengths of the Western democracies (in both quantitative and qualitative indices), and that the German army was supported by an air force that was superior to both Britain's and France's (Robert J. Young, *In Command of France: French Foreign Policy and Military Planning, 1933–1940* (Cambridge, Mass.: Harvard University Press, 1978), 163–164; Wesley K. Wark, *The Ultimate Enemy: British Intelligence and Nazi Germany, 1933–1939* (Ithaca: Cornell University Press, 1985), 93–102; Kennedy, *Rise and Fall of the Great Powers,* 317; Peter Jackson, *France and the Nazi Menace: Intelligence and Policy Making, 1933–1939* (Oxford: Oxford University Press, 2000), 103, 112, 207; Mearsheimer, *Tragedy of Great Power Politics,* 318. 56. For example, Pierre Laval (France's foreign minister) resisted an alliance with the Soviet Union, according to notes from a cabinet meeting, because "at heart . . . he dreads the eventual [subversive] effect of [the] Bolshevik army on the French army" (in William Scott, *Alliance against Hitler: The Origins of the Franco-Soviet Pact* [Durham, N.C.: Duke University Press, 1962], 239–240). For examples of British and French conservatives' fears of domestic subversion created by the presence and policies of the Soviet Union, see Martin S. Alexander, *The Republic in Danger: General Maurice Gamelin and the Politics of French Defense, 1933–1940* (New York: Cambridge University Press, 1993), 295–296; Nicole Jordan, *The Popular Front and Central Europe: The Dilemmas of French Impotence, 1918–1940* (New York: Cambridge University Press, 1992), 228; Michael Jabara Carley, *1939: The Alliance That Never Was and the Coming of World War II* (Chicago: Ivan R. Dee, 1999), 16; Carley, "Fearful Concatenation," 50, 51, 56, 59, 63.

substantial barriers to the formation of an alliance with the USSR since any effective coalition between the Western democracies and the Soviet Union required close coordination between the militaries of these states. As Patrice Buffotot explains with regard to the French Army High Command, which was a bastion of conservatism: "[This body] was uneasy about the consequences of a military pact with the USSR. It feared subversive action by the Communist Party, under orders from the Soviet Union, within its own forces. . . . The French High Command rejected a military alliance with the Soviet Union . . . [because of] ideological aversion."[57]

The possibility of ideological subversion resulting from direct contact with Soviet representatives was not the only way in which conservatives' fears of ideological contagion to communist principles affected their foreign policies. Perhaps more important, in the minds of many members of the British and French right there was a tight link between war and the spread of communist regimes. Just as the social, economic, and political disruptions created by the First World War had played a key role in allowing the communists to come to power in Russia, many Western conservatives feared similar results in other states in Europe if great power conflict developed once again.

The belief that there was a direct, almost inevitable, connection between war and revolution was one that was expressed by almost every important British and French statesmen of the right and center-right in the 1930s. For example, in September 1938 French prime minister and Radical leader Eduard Daladier pleaded with the German *chargé d'affaires* in Paris that following great power conflict, "revolution, irrespective of victors or vanquished, was as certain in France as in Germany and Italy. Soviet Russia would not let the opportunity pass of bringing world revolution to our lands." Later in the same month Daladier lamented to the American ambassador in Paris that if Germany and the Western powers went to war, "Cossacks will rule Europe."[58] Similar statements were made by, among others, French foreign ministers Georges Bonnet and Pierre Laval, British prime ministers Stanley Baldwin and Neville Chamberlain, British ambassador to Germany and later France Eric Phipps, and assistant undersecretary of state in the British Foreign Office Orme Sargent.[59]

---

57. Patrice Buffotot, "The French High Command and the Franco-Soviet Alliance, 1933–1939," *Journal of Strategic Studies* 5, no. 4 (December 1983), 556–557.

58. Both in Carley, *1939*, 48. The Radicals were the center party in France in the 1930s, and Daladier was a conservative member of this group.

59. French Foreign Minister Bonnet, for example, told the German ambassador in Paris that in a war between the great powers "all Europe would perish, and both victor and vanquished would fall victims to world Communism" (in Andrew Rothstein, *The Munich Conspiracy* [London: Lawrence and Wishart, 1958], 256). See also Post, *Dilemmas of Appeasement*, 204; Carley, *1939*, 16, 17, 22; William D. Irvine, *French Conservatism in Crisis: The Republican Federation of France in the 1930s* (Baton Rouge: Louisiana State University Press, 1979),

Conservatives' fears of ideological subversion resulting from either close association with the Soviet Union or as a by-product of great power conflict increased the incentives pushing for the appeasement of Germany. Because of the ideological impediments to an effective alliance with the USSR, the balancing options available to British and French conservatives were more limited than they would have been under different ideological conditions. This made a deterrent stand against Germany more difficult to achieve, and as a result made arguments for the appeasement of Germany more persuasive. Maurice Hankey (the Committee on Imperial Defense [CID] Secretary) and Admiral Ernle Chatfield (First Sea Lord, 1933–38, and British Minister for Coordination of Defense, 1939–40), for example, asserted that "concessions to the Axis powers were a logical response" to Soviet communism and French unreliability when led by Socialists.[60] Similarly, the Chief of the French General Staff, General Maurice Gamelin, asserted that the "dangers of contamination" caused by association with the Soviet Union "justified" various policies adopted by the other great powers, including the Munich agreement, which was the apogee of the appeasement of Germany.[61]

Conservatives' fears that military hostilities would lead to the spread of communist regimes throughout Europe had similar effects. If war led to revolution, then the British and French right confronted powerful incentives to eschew all policies, including those designed to form balancing alliances against Germany, which increased the likelihood of great power conflict. Policies of appeasement that were designed to avoid hostilities with Germany therefore became more attractive to conservatives than they would have been under different circumstances. As Phipps told the American ambassador to Paris in January 1939: "Since war would mean the triumph of the forces of Bolshevism on the Continent, any sacrifice necessary to avoid war must be made."[62]

In addition to creating widespread fears about the possibility of ideological subversion to communist principles, the huge ideological differences dividing members of the British and French right from Soviet leaders also played a central role in creating a profound sense of distrust among Western

---

165–166, 170–172, 196; R. J. Q. Adams, *British Politics and Foreign Policy in the Age of Appeasement, 1935–1939* (London: Macmillan, 1993), 68.

60. Martin Thomas, *Britain, France, and Appeasement: Anglo-French Relations in the Popular Front Era* (New York: Berg, 1996), 179, Thomas's summary of the quotation.

61. In Alexander, *Republic in Danger*, 295. Leon Blum, Socialist leader and prime minister from 1936 to 1938, instructed in November 1936 the French ambassador to the Soviet Union, Robert Coulondre, to inform the Soviets the thinking behind French conservatives' decision to appease Germany: "A psychosis is being created according to which the Soviet entente leads to Communism; this fear tends to neutralize that which is inspired by the German threat and to paralyze cooperation among the pacific powers at the very time when this current ought to intensify" (in Jordan, *Popular Front and Central Europe*, 228).

62. In Carley, *1939*, 84–85.

conservatives of Soviet intentions. Time and again, key conservative leaders in Britain and France asserted that Soviet politicians' dedication to communist ideals made these individuals inherently untrustworthy people who were virtually incapable of playing any constructive role in European politics. The most frequent charge that many Western conservatives leveled against the Soviets was that the latter were trying to provoke a war between Britain, France, and Germany in order to facilitate communist revolutions in these states. As Prime Minister Neville Chamberlain wrote in a private letter to his sister Ida in March 1939: "I must confess to the most profound distrust of Russia. . . . I distrust her motives which seem to me to have little connection with ideas of liberty and to be concerned only with getting every one else by the ears."[63] Others, including Foreign Ministers Anthony Eden and Georges Bonnet, expressed nearly identical views.[64]

Demonstrating that British and French conservatives' profound ideological differences with the Soviet Union increased the incentives for these individuals to eschew a balancing alliance against Germany that included the USSR as a member is only half my argument. The fact that most members of the British and French right viewed communist Russia as a greater ideological rival than Germany not only significantly increased their understanding of the danger posed by the Soviet Union, but lowered their perceptions of the threat posed by Germany to a point well below what an analysis based solely on the international distribution of power indicated.

In the first place, Western conservatives' ideological agreement with the Nazis on the subject of anti-communism impelled many of the former individuals to view the fascists' control of Germany as an important support of their domestic interests. Many of these politicians were of the opinion that by crushing communist interests in Germany, Hitler had helped to prevent the spread of this ideology in other states, including potentially their own. It is largely for this reason that many members of the British and French right frequently referred to Hitler with admiration as a "bulwark against communism."[65]

---

63. Ibid., 108; see also 39.
64. Young, *In Command of France*, 234; Young, *France and the Origins of the Second World War*, 67; Michael Jabara Carley, "Prelude to Defeat: Franco-Soviet Relations, 1919–1939," *Historical Reflections* 22, no. 1 (Winter 1996): 184; Carley, *1939*, 14, 43. At another time Chamberlain asserted that he believed that the USSR was "stealthily and cunningly pulling all the strings behind the scenes to get us involved in a war with Germany" (in Raymond Sontag, *A Broken World, 1919–1939* [New York: Harper and Row, 1971], 339). Sir Alexander Cadogan, the Permanent Undersecretary in the British Foreign Office, stated in the minutes from a cabinet meeting in the spring of 1938: "The Russian object is to precipitate confusion and war in Europe: they will not participate usefully themselves; they will hope for the world revolution as a result (and a very likely one too)" (in Keith Middlemas, *Diplomacy of Illusion: The British Government and Germany, 1937–1939* [London: Weidenfeld and Nicolson, 1972], 200).
65. Charles Micaud, *The French Right and Nazi Germany, 1933–1939* (New York: Octagon Books, 1943), 99; Margaret George, *The Warped Vision: British Foreign Policy, 1933–1939* (Pittsburgh: University of Pittsburgh Press, 1965), 88.

Because many conservatives understood their domestic interests to be to some degree interconnected with the continuation of Hitler's regime, coercive or deterrent policies that might weaken the Nazis' hold on power were made more costly to conservatives than they would have been in the absence of this consideration. The appeasement of Germany therefore became more attractive. As one scholar expresses this point with respect to British Tories: "It was primarily to arrest the spread of [the subversive acts of communist agents] that the appeasers looked to such militant anti-Communist leaders as Mussolini, [Francisco] Franco, and especially Hitler, whose depredations in other directions they were reportedly willing to overlook or forgive."[66]

Western conservatives' and the Nazis' mutual antipathy to communist principles impelled the former to appease Germany for reasons other than fear of increasing the power of the left in Germany and thus potentially Britain and France. There was also a sense held by many members of the British and French right that this ideological agreement would help make appeasement successful. As explained, most British and French conservatives viewed war among the great powers as especially deleterious because of their widespread belief in a tight connection between war and the spread of communist regimes. Because many Western conservatives felt that Hitler also believed in this relationship, the former were of the opinion that the Führer shared their interest in avoiding military hostilities. As Hankey, for example, put it in a CID meeting in December 1936: in a war between Britain and Germany, both countries would be "so exhausted by the end that we should probably become a prey to Bolshevism—the very thing Hitler most fears."[67] To this view, Hitler's anti-communism not only benefited British and French conservatives' domestic interests (because it helped to inhibit the spread of communist influence throughout Europe), but would also incline him both to possess limited international ambitions and to resolve peacefully disputes with the Western powers lest conflict result to the advantage of these groups' shared ideological enemy: the Soviet Union.[68]

---

66. Donald Lammers, *Explaining Munich: The Search for Motive in British Policy* (Stanford: Hoover Institution, 1966), 10.
67. In Post, *Dilemmas of Appeasement*, 255. See also Lamb, *Mussolini and the British*, 173; Adams, *British Politics and Foreign Policy*, 97; Jonathan Haslam, *The Soviet Union and the Struggle for Collective Security in Europe, 1933–39* (New York: St. Martin's Press, 1984), 182.
68. On British and French conservatives' tendency to believe that Hitler's international ambitions would be limited to ones consistent with the principle of national self-determination, see Middlemas, *Diplomacy of Illusion*, 189, 191, 347, 375, 376; R. A. C. Parker, *Chamberlain and Appeasement: British Policy and the Coming of the Second World War* (London: Macmillan, 1993), 29, 162; Micaud, *French Right and Nazi Germany*, 206; Peter Jackson, "Intelligence and the End of Appeasement," in *French Foreign and Defense Policy, 1918–1940*, ed. Robert Boyce (London: Routledge, 1998), 244.

The fact that Nazi Germany was a lesser ideological danger than the Soviet Union from the perspective of the British and French right was so important that some prominent Western conservatives even implied that a strong Germany could be a useful ally for the containment of the USSR. For example, Thomas Jones (a close friend and advisor to Prime Minister Baldwin) wrote in a private letter in 1936 that Britain had "to choose between Russia and Germany. . . . [Hitler] is asking for an alliance with us to form a bulwark against the spread of Communism. [Baldwin] is not indisposed to attempt this as a final effort before he resigns."[69] Other prominent conservatives in Britain and France, including Neville Chamberlain, Nevile Henderson, Pierre Laval, Xavier Vallat, Jacques Poitou-Duplessy, Octave Lavalette, and Philippe Henriot, held similar views.[70] Realist arguments cannot explain this interest in aligning with the strongest power in the system against the greatest ideological threat.

Just as with relations with Germany in the 1930s, British and French conservatives' attitudes and policies toward Italy in this period were affected in critical ways by both power and ideological variables. Although the majority of members of the British and French right believed that Hitler possessed limited international ambitions, they could not be completely certain of this fact. Germany's massive rearmament efforts in the 1930s, coupled with the problem of uncertainty about Hitler's intentions, demanded that the Western powers balance against Germany to some degree lest their beliefs about the limited nature of Nazi ambitions turn out to be in error.

Aligning with Italy was central to Western conservatives' security policies in the 1930s. Although most British and French conservatives' first preference with regard to Italy was the creation of a four-power pact between Britain, France, Italy, and Germany that would strategically isolate the Soviet Union from the affairs of Europe,[71] an alliance with Italy as a balancing partner against potential German aggression was the next best alternative. Conservatives throughout the 1930s consistently wooed Mussolini toward these ends.[72]

---

69. In George, *Warped Vision*, 88.

70. Middlemas, *Diplomacy of Illusion*, 73–74; George, *Warped Vision*, 220; Irvine, *French Conservatism in Crisis*, 194; Anthony Adamthwaite, *Grandeur and Misery: France's Bid for Power in Europe, 1914–1940* (London: Arnold, 1995), 195; Maurice Vaïsse, "Against Appeasement: French Advocates of Firmness, 1933–8," in *The Fascist Challenge and the Policy of Appeasement*, ed. Wolfgang J. Mommsen and Lothar Kettenacker (London: George Allen and Unwin, 1983), 233.

71. As Young puts it, Chamberlain hoped to create a new security edifice in Europe that would be "built within an anti-Communist quadrangle linking Berlin, Rome, Paris, and London" (Young, *In Command of France*, 199). See also Thomas, *Britain, France, and Appeasement*, 98–99; George, *Warped Vision*, 180–181; Adamthwaite, *Grandeur and Misery*, 195, 197.

72. These efforts bore some fruit, though they were eventually undercut by socialists' policies. For details, see Robert J. Young, "French Military Intelligence and the Franco-Italian Alliance, 1933–1939," *Historical Journal* 28, no. 1 (March 1985): 143–168; Lamb, *Mussolini and the British*, chap. 8 and 174–175, 210–211.

Although relative power concerns played an important role in shaping Western conservatives' policies toward Italy, these policies cannot be adequately understood outside the context of the ideological distances among the great powers' leaders. Ideological agreement between Western conservatives and Italian fascists on the subject of anti-communism meant that the ideological impediments to an alliance with Italy were not nearly as large as they were with the Soviet Union.[73] This fact, in combination with the power-political incentives created by a need to prepare for possible German aggression, explains why British and French conservatives were relatively quick to forgive Mussolini's often serious transgressions (most notably his decision to attack Ethiopia in 1935 and his active support of Franco's army throughout the Spanish Civil War) in the hopes that the Western democracies and Italy could draw closer together.[74] This tendency stands in clear contrast to Western conservatives' views of Soviet leaders, who could do no right in conservatives' eyes.

The previous analysis applies most straightforwardly to the perceptions of threat and consequent foreign policy choices made by the majority of British Conservatives. Throughout the 1930s, Tories' greater ideological hostility to the Soviet Union than toward Nazi Germany both created substantial barriers to an alliance with the USSR and obscured the German threat in the minds of most of these individuals, to the point where the appeasement of Germany was believed to be the best strategy for protecting Britain's security.

A similar dynamic occurred for most members of the French right, but only in the wake of particular domestic-ideological developments in France. For roughly the first two years of Hitler's time in power, the large majority of French conservatives responded to Germany's power-political rise with policies that are highly consistent with realist balance-of-power theory. To these individuals, Germany's relative power advantages made it the principal threat to France's security. In order to address this danger, members of the French right advocated that France both increase its military spending and form alliances with all the other great powers in the system regardless of ideological considerations, even with the Soviet Union. Conservative politicians were instrumental in negotiating the Franco-Soviet Pact of Mutual Assistance, which was signed (though not ratified) in 1935.

73. On Western conservatives' praise of Mussolini's anti-communism, see George, *Warped Vision*, 26, 181; Post, *Dilemmas of Appeasement*, 121.
74. Arnold Wolfers, *Britain and France between Two Wars* (New York: W. W. Norton, 1966), 313–315; Arthur H. Furnia, *The Diplomacy of Appeasement: Anglo-French Relations and the Prelude to World War II, 1931–1938* (Washington, D.C.: University Press of Washington, D.C., 1960), 239–240.

Most French conservatives' adherence to realist balance-of-power theory with regard to relations with the Soviet Union would last, however, only until the end of 1935. After this year, most members of the French right became adamantly opposed to close association with the USSR. In fact, by 1936 "most of the Center and the Right rejected the [Mutual Assistance] Pact," and many conservatives in the legislature either voted against or abstained from supporting the ratification of the very agreement they had engineered.[75] Although members of the French right were unable to prevent the ratification of the pact that they were instrumental in negotiating, conservatives—including most members of the French High Command—were able to prevent the conclusion of the far more important military convention with the Soviet Union, without which the Franco-Soviet Pact had little operational meaning or effect. Conservatives after 1935 rejected a military alliance with the USSR even though France's relative power position in relation to Germany continued to deteriorate.[76]

Ideological variables and domestic developments in France in the mid-1930s explain this radical shift in international policies advocated by most members of the French right. Specifically, with the growing electoral strength of the Popular Front coalition of Socialists and Communists, culminating in this coalition's electoral victory in May 1936, French conservatives became more worried about the subversive threat created by associating with their chief ideological enemy, the Soviet Union, than they were about the power-political danger posed by Germany. "The domestic bitterness of the summer of 1936," as the historian Anthony Adamthwaite explains, "extinguished any hope of an effective Franco-Soviet alliance. . . . The traditional Germanophobia of the right was dissolved by Blum's Popular Front and the Spanish war. Stalin, not Hitler, was the enemy."[77] By refusing to ally with the Soviet Union, the French right abandoned perhaps the most effective means of forming a balancing coalition against Germany. Fear of communism in this period simply clouded in most French conservatives' minds the dangers posed by Germany. As General Gamelin expressed after the war: "[The Popular Front's victory] made many of us lose sight of the dangers of Hitlerism and fascism at our doorstep because behind the 'Popular Front' one saw the specter of Bolshevism. Therein lies the origin of the slogans that disfigured the soul of the nation: 'Better Hitler than Stalin' and 'Why die for Danzig?'"[78]

---

75. Scott, *Alliance against Hitler*, 264.
76. Young, *In Command of France*, 93; Alexander, *Republic in Danger*, 292; Jordan, *Popular Front and Central Europe*, 107; Thomas, *Britain, France, and Appeasement*, 194–195.
77. Adamthwaite, *Grandeur and Misery*, 207. For similar analyses, see Scott, *Alliance against Hitler*, 265; Micaud, *French Right and Nazi Germany*, 81; Jackson, *France and the Nazi Menace*, 245.
78. In Joel Colton, *Leon Blum, Humanist in Politics* (Cambridge: MIT Press, 1966), 199. Gamelin could have added to this list of slogans another sentiment popular among the French right: "Better Hitler than Blum" (Leon Blum was the leader of the French Socialists).

Socialists' Balancing Policies

British and French socialists' understandings of the threats posed by the other powers in the system were to a great extent the mirror images of those possessed by their conservative counterparts. On no international subject were the differences between most Western socialists and conservatives more pronounced than with regard to their respective attitudes and policies toward the USSR. To begin with, unlike Western conservatives, most British and French socialists did not view the mere existence of the Soviet Union as a subversive threat to their domestic interests. Quite the opposite: many socialists in the Western powers viewed the establishment of a socialist state as a likely support to their domestic objectives. Because Soviet leaders declared allegiance to similar socioeconomic principles as did British and French socialists, the majority of the latter individuals wanted central dimensions of the Soviet experiment to succeed so as to provide a boost to their own domestic position. For example, socialists in the Western democracies, especially after the onset of the Great Depression, asserted that Britain and France could learn much from the USSR's economic policies, and the phrase "economic planning" after the Soviet model became increasingly popular in socialists' vocabularies.[79] Many socialists reasoned that if the Soviet Union succeeded in solving the economic problems of the day using economic methods similar to ones socialists advocated, the salability of these policies to Western audiences would most likely increase. The perceived interdependence of the domestic fortunes of Western socialists with the success of the Soviet Union's economic policies goes far in explaining why British and French socialists were consistent champions of aiding the Soviet Union throughout the interwar period by such policies as political recognition, guaranteed loans, and favorable trade agreements. As one scholar explains with regard to British Labourites: "[Labour] felt that if its own cause at home was henceforth to be salvaged, it had to champion the Soviet cause as well."[80]

French and especially British socialists also exhibited a much greater tendency than Western conservatives to give Soviet leaders the benefit of the doubt and to interpret Soviet foreign policies and intentions in a largely favorable manner, as the conflict-probability mechanism predicts. Perhaps of greatest importance, most Labourites, in clear contrast to most Western conservatives, took Soviet overtures toward creating a collective security system against the fascist states at face value.[81] As a result, the

79. Williams, *Labour and Russia*, 135–141, 157; F. S. Northedge and Audrey Wells, *Britain and Soviet Communism: The Impact of a Revolution* (London: Macmillan, 1982), 186.
80. Michael R. Gordon, *Conflict and Consensus in Labour's Foreign Policy, 1914–1965* (Stanford: Stanford University Press, 1969), 28, 27; Bill Jones, *The Russia Complex: The British Labour Party and the Soviet Union* (Manchester: Manchester University Press, 1977), 6, 16, 22.
81. Williams, *Labour and Russia*, 54, 66, 214, 225; William Rayburn Tucker, *The Attitude of the*

majority of British socialists in the 1930s viewed the Soviet Union as a support for European peace, and they consistently lobbied for an alliance with it either within the structure of the League of Nations or a more traditional multilateral alliance. As one scholar explains with reference to the majority of representatives of the Labour Party: "There was no question upon which Labour opinion was more united than the necessity of an [alliance] agreement with the Soviet Union."[82] Labour leaders argued as early as 1934 that the Soviet Union lacked "aggressive designs towards other states," thus making it "a natural ally of the forces of peace."[83]

Socialists in France exhibited similar tendencies toward the Soviet Union as did most Labourites, although with less consensus than their British counterparts. Throughout the 1930s, a significant number of French Socialists, led by Paul Faure and Marceau Pivert, remained committed to pacifism. They therefore rejected all international alliances, including with the USSR, lest these coalitions either provoke or draw France into war.

Although the combined support of Faure and Pivert remained substantial throughout the 1930s, a clear majority of French Socialists rejected their pacifistic policies in the dangerous international environment of this decade. Guided by Leon Blum, the party's most important leader, and Jean Zyromski, who controlled much of the powerful left wing of the party, most French Socialists advocated that France adopt active balancing policies against the perceived threats posed by the fascist states. Central to these policies were attempts to form a tight alliance with the Soviet Union. During his time as prime minister, Blum pushed over conservatives' objections for closer military ties with the USSR in order to strengthen the Franco-Soviet Pact, and due to his efforts, secret staff talks with the Soviet Union began in November 1936.[84]

With regard to the fascist states, power and ideological variables worked in tandem to create in most Western socialists' minds very high

---

British Labour Party Towards European and Collective Security Problems, 1920–1939 (Genève: Imprimerie du Journal Genève, 1950), 249; Gottfried Niedhart, "British Attitudes and Policies Towards the Soviet Union and International Communism, 1933–9," in *Fascist Challenge and the Policy of Appeasement*, ed. Mommsen and Kettenacker, 289.

82. Tucker, *Attitude of the British Labour Party*, 232. See also Jones, *Russia Complex*, 28; John F. Naylor, *Labour's International Policy: The Labour Party in the 1930s* (London: Weidenfeld and Nicolson, 1969), 225, 278, 293. On similar tendencies in France, see Nathanael Greene, *Crisis and Decline: The French Socialist Party in the Popular Front Era* (Ithaca: Cornell University Press, 1969), 51, 52, 189, 273; Colton, *Leon Blum*, 210, 318, 320, 329.

83. Tucker, *Attitude of the British Labour Party*, 233; Gordon, *Conflict and Consensus in Labour's Foreign Policy*, 31; Jones, *Russia Complex*, 29.

84. Alexander, *Republic in Danger*, 298–299; Jordan, *Popular Front and Central Europe*, 269; Buffotot, "French High Command and the Franco-Soviet Alliance," 551; Michael Jabara Carley, "End of the 'Low, Dishonest Decade': Failure of the Anglo-Franco-Soviet Alliance in 1939," *Europe-Asia Studies* 45, no. 2 (1993): 307.

levels of threat that these powers posed to British and French security. Although socialists in the Western democracies had been the most consistent champions throughout the interwar period of lenient policies toward Germany based on substantial revisions of the Versailles Treaty, within a year of Hitler's ascension to power most socialists' attitudes toward Germany underwent a "remarkable change."[85] By 1934, most socialists in Britain and France had come to view Germany as a significant danger to the peace of Europe. A majority of these politicians therefore rejected appeasement and advocated far more forceful policies against Germany than did most Western conservatives with regard to Germany's absorption of Austria, the Munich crisis, and the Spanish Civil War.[86] For example, the Blum government provided surreptitious aid to the Spanish Republicans during the Spanish Civil War, and during the Munich crisis Blum "unequivocally demanded that the government honor its obligations under the country's mutual assistance pact with Czechoslovakia."[87] Labourites wanted Britain to take similar actions.[88]

There can be no doubt that Germany's power potential and massive rearmament efforts were central to British and French socialists' perceptions of the degree of danger that Germany posed to the security of the Western democracies. In the absence of Germany's relative power advantages, the perceived level of threat posed by Germany would have been much smaller no matter how aggressive Nazi intentions were believed to be.

Yet the large ideological distances dividing British and French socialists from fascists account for key dimensions of the former's very high perceptions of the threat posed by Nazi Germany that power-centered arguments cannot explain. Western socialists were worried that the success of fascism in Germany would be contagious and that the ranks of the right in their state would be swelled with fascist converts.[89] This was an outcome that clearly threatened socialists' domestic interests. Probably even more important, to most members of the British and French left, states governed by politicians dedicated to fascist principles were *by nature* highly aggressive.[90] It is therefore no wonder that most members of the

85. Tucker, *Attitude of the British Labour Party*, 136–137.
86. Ibid., 216–217, 222, 224–225, 227, 229, 249; Jordan, *Popular Front and Central Europe*, 272, 313–314; Colton, *Leon Blum*, 244, 259; Julian Jackson, *The Popular Front in France: Defending Democracy, 1934–38* (New York: Cambridge University Press, 1988), 191. The Spanish Civil War is an excellent example of the importance of ideological distances on leaders' foreign policies, though space constraints prohibit an analysis of its dynamics.
87. Colton, *Leon Blum*, 314, 259.
88. Tucker, *Attitude of the British Labour Party*, 215–230.
89. Naylor, *Labour's International Policy*, 46–48, 81–82; Vaïsse, "Against Appeasement," 232; Ben Pimlott, *Labour and the Left in the 1930s* (London: Cambridge University Press, 1977), 89; Gordon, *Conflict and Consensus in Labour's Foreign Policy*, 73.
90. Colton, *Leon Blum*, 232; Greene, *Crisis and Decline*, 21, 24, 26, 28, 29, 30, 49; Tucker, *Attitude of the British Labour Party*, 136–137, 192–193; Naylor, *Labour's International Policy*, 216; Jones, *Russia Complex*, 24; Sabine Wichert, "The British Left and Appeasement: Political Tactics

British and French left rejected the appeasement of Germany for more forceful deterrent policies.

Socialists' external balancing policies in the 1930s were not, however, as extensive as realist theories would predict given these politicians' understanding of the great threat that Germany posed to the Western democracies. A majority of these politicians refused for most of the 1930s close association with Mussolini's Italy.[91] What makes this decision particularly puzzling for realism is that virtually all analysts (particularly in France) agreed that an alliance with Italy would be extremely valuable from a military perspective in a conflict with Germany.[92]

The effects of socialists' ideological differences with fascist Italy overrode military calculations based on power relationships. As the historian William Shorrock explains with reference to French Socialists: "[The] unrelieved ideological hostility to fascism [by Socialist leaders of the Popular Front government] and [their] tendency to regard the Italian government with contempt . . . blinded [these] leaders to strategic and political reality."[93] Or as Blum himself told a French senator why an alliance with Italy was unacceptable to Socialists: "I am the leader of the Popular Front. . . . For this action, you need another Prime Minister and another majority."[94] Indeed, the same ideological considerations that made Socialists view Germany as an enemy also precluded an alliance with Italy. Blum and his followers were convinced not only that the fascist leaders of Germany and Italy were inherently aggressive and untrustworthy individuals, but that they were bound to form an alliance with one another.[95] Because many French socialists believed that attempts by the Western

---

or Alternative Policies?," in *Fascist Challenge and the Policy of Appeasement*, ed. Mommsen and Kettenacker, 138.

91. This was especially true for British Labourites (Tucker, *Attitude of the British Labour Party,* 128–139, 172, 176–177). From 1933 to 1935, the majority of French Socialists supported, though unenthusiastically, alignment with Italy to deter German aggression (most notably by supporting the Stresa Accords). As soon as Italy invaded Ethiopia, however, the French left's ideological animosity and distrust of Mussolini resurfaced with a vengeance, and they treated fascist Italy as an enemy for the rest of the decade (William I. Shorrock, *From Ally to Enemy: The Enigma of Fascist Italy in French Diplomacy, 1920–1940* [Kent, Ohio: Kent State University Press, 1988], 112, 115, 143, 147, 153, 183, 192, 202, 292, 293; Young, *In Command of France,* 134–136).

92. For details, see Anthony Adamthwaite, *France and the Coming of the Second World War* (London: Frank Cass, 1977), 34; Jackson, "Intelligence and the End of Appeasement," 242; Young, *In Command of France,* 91, 103, 133, 134; Jordan, *Popular Front and Central Europe,* 223–224; Thomas, *Britain, France, and Appeasement,* 43–44.

93. Shorrock, *From Ally to Enemy,* 293; see also Adamthwaite, *France and the Coming of the Second World War,* 57; Thomas, *Britain, France, and Appeasement,* 45. The French embassy counselor in Rome, Jules Blondel, wrote to French foreign minister Yvon Delbos in November 1936 that "ideological factors are currently of maximum importance" to the deterioration of Franco-Italian relations in the Popular Front era (in Shorrock, *From Ally to Enemy,* 202).

94. In Shorrock, *From Ally to Enemy,* 183.

95. Young, *In Command of France,* 135–136; Colton, *Leon Blum,* 219, 312.

democracies to separate Mussolini from Hitler would not succeed, these politicians thought that pursuing an entente with Italy was a waste of vital time and resources. Similar considerations precluded an Anglo-Italian alliance for most Labour politicians.[96]

The preceding analysis of Western conservatives' and socialists' perceptions of threat and resulting policies toward the other powers predominantly applies to the time period from 1933 (when Hitler assumed power) to 1939. After Germany's invasion of "rump" Czechoslovakia in March 1939, the overwhelming majority of the British and French right became convinced that Hitler's international ambitions were neither peaceful nor limited. Conservatives as a result became much more dedicated than they previously had been to balancing against Germany with all the internal and external means that were available to them, including forming an alliance with the USSR (though their attempts to form an alliance with the Soviet Union remained half-hearted throughout 1939).[97] Thus by the end of the 1930s, power-political considerations were becoming of greater importance in relation to ideological variables in affecting conservatives' threat perceptions and consequent foreign policy choices. This statement was even more true for British leaders in the summer of 1941, at which time the Anglo-Soviet alliance was created.

These changes in British and French leaders' policies after March 1939 reveal the limits of ideological distances in shaping states' foreign policies and the corresponding power of realist prescriptions. These developments therefore provide insight into the conditions under which ideological or relative-power variables are likely to weigh more heavily on decision makers' international choices, thereby trumping the incentives created by the other set of variables. I discussed in detail in Chapter 1 these conditions based on the evidence from all the case studies. Consequently, here I simply reiterate a point made earlier: although circumstances demanded that Britain ally with the Soviet Union in 1941, without the effects of ideological distances on British, French, and German foreign policies in the 1930s, Britain would most likely have never been placed in this desperate situation in the first place.

96. Naylor, *Labour's International Policy*, 117, 270, 271; Wolfers, *Britain and France between Two Wars*, 317–318.
97. For details, see Irvine, *French Conservatism in Crisis*, 200; Young, *In Command of France*, 234, 237; Carley, *1939*. Conservatives' ideological antipathy to the Soviet Union was also responsible for the creation of plans to attack the USSR after the Soviets' invasion of Finland in November 1939. Thus in the winter of 1939–40 "the war [was] transformed, under the right's mounting anti-Soviet hostility, from an anti-Fascist into an anti-Communist struggle" (Talbot Imlay, "France and the Phoney War, 1939–1940," in *French Foreign and Defense Policy*, ed. Boyce, 273; see also Patrick R. Osborn, *Operation Pike: Britain Versus the Soviet Union, 1939–1941* [London: Greenwood, 2000], 70, 246–247).

THE FOREIGN POLICIES OF THE SOVIET UNION, 1933–41

Soviet foreign policies from 1933 until 1941 can be categorized into two separate periods. The first lasted from 1933 until the summer of 1939. This was the era of collective security for Soviet leaders. The dominant characteristics of this period included a fairly clear understanding of the German danger to the USSR, a flexibility in alliance choices (the Soviets made a smooth transition from cultivating ties with Germany for most of the interwar period to pursuing alliances with Britain and France after 1933), and above all an interest in forming an overwhelming balancing coalition against Germany. The stark contrast of these policies with central dimensions of British and French foreign policies for most of the 1930s should be clear.[98]

The signing of the Nazi-Soviet Pact in August 1939 indicated a turning point in Soviet international policies. From this point until Germany's attack on the USSR in June 1941, the dominant features of Soviet international decisions during the previous six years were reversed. In these later years, Soviet leaders' foreign policies were characterized by strategies that facilitated the outbreak of war instead of policies designed to deter it, a substantial obscuring of the German threat, and a rigidity in alliance policies when power-political concerns were working for very different outcomes. The similarity of these last two characteristics with defining features of British and French policies in the 1930s is obvious.

Soviet behavior from 1933 to 1941 therefore seems to present puzzles for both realist theories and the argument of this book. From 1933 to 1939, the Soviet Union, which was putatively the most "ideological" state in the system, conformed closely with the predictions of realist theories. Yet after 1939, Soviet leaders largely ignored the dictates of the balance of power even when their state was in imminent danger of attack.

In the following sections, I argue that although realist theories can explain important dimensions of Soviet foreign policies from 1933 to

98. The Soviets did make a number of initiatives to Germany in the 1930s designed to improve relations, including offers of various trade agreements and attempts to reaffirm the Berlin Treaty of 1925 that committed both sides to non-aggression (Jiri Hochman, *The Soviet Union and the Failure of Collective Security, 1934–1938* [Ithaca: Cornell University Press, 1984]). Nevertheless, the dominant tendency in Soviet foreign policies in this period was to develop a collective security system directed against Germany. In response to the Nazi danger, the Soviets joined the League of Nations, pushed for military alliances with Britain and France, and instructed the communist parties in Western states to lobby for increases in defense spending. Soviet officials pushed for a confrontation with Italy over its invasion of Ethiopia, with Germany over the reoccupation of the Rhineland, and with both these powers over their continued aid to Franco's armies in the Spanish Civil War.

1939, the nature of the ideological distances among the great powers' leaders was a key variable that both allowed and impelled Soviet decision makers to act more "realistically" for most of the 1930s than did many of their counterparts in the other powers. When circumstances changed from 1939 to 1941, the incentives created by the nature of the ideological environment in which these politicians operated pushed them to adopt very different policies than they had in the previous six years. Soviet foreign policies in the 1930s therefore provide insight into the ideological conditions under which states' leaders are and are not likely to conform with the predictions of realist arguments.

Realist Theories and Soviet Foreign Policies

Realist theories, especially the power-maximizing variety from offensive-realist arguments, potentially have much to offer in explaining Soviet foreign policies from 1933 to 1941. From 1933 to the early months of 1939, Soviet leaders had very good reasons to want to form an alliance with the Western powers: the strongest power on the continent, Germany, was rearming at breakneck speed; the Nazis were clearly dedicated to offensive aims in Europe; and Germany's most important decision maker, Adolf Hitler, had declared his permanent enmity to the Soviet regime. These facts made a war between Germany and the USSR likely. It is therefore not surprising to realist arguments that for most of the 1930s the Soviets genuinely wanted to form a collective security system against Germany with all available great powers.

In 1939, however, three developments transpired that significantly altered the USSR's security environment. First, in late February or early March, Soviet leaders came to believe that France, and not the USSR, would be Germany's first great power victim. The belief that Germany's armies would attack in the west after defeating Poland resulted from various developments in the six months after Munich: new demands by Hitler for British and French colonies, Germany's denunciation of the Anglo-German naval agreement of 1935, and, most important, information provided by a Soviet spy in Germany's Japanese embassy who had knowledge of Germany's plans of attack.[99]

Second, after Germany's invasion of Prague in March 1939, Britain and France guaranteed the territorial integrity of Poland, Romania, and Greece. The Western powers made these commitments without acquiring

99. Weinberg, *Foreign Policy of Hitler's Germany, 1937–1939*, 534, 551; Watt, *How War Came*, 248; Geoffrey Roberts, *The Unholy Alliance: Stalin's Pact with Hitler* (London: I. B. Tauris, 1989), 112, 114, 118; Ingeborg Fleischhauer, "Soviet Foreign Policy and the Origins of the Hitler-Stalin Pact," in *From Peace to War*, ed. Wegner, 32; Haslam, *Soviet Union and the Struggle for Collective Security in Europe*, 199, 216.

reciprocal guarantees from the Soviet Union. Thus if Germany attacked any of these eastern European states, Britain and France were committed to go to war with the Soviet Union regardless of what the Soviet Union did.[100] Just as important, Soviet leaders believed that British and French public opinion would force the Western powers to honor these military obligations.[101] Thus if Germany attacked Poland, the Soviets had reason to believe that an Anglo-French-German war was likely to follow.

The third major change in 1939 that shaped Soviet leaders' strategic calculations was a newfound willingness by Germany to offer far-reaching concessions to the USSR. With Germany's attack on Poland fast approaching and the Western powers committed to defending this state, Soviet neutrality in a German-Polish conflict, and especially in a war between Germany and the Western democracies, was a strategic imperative for Germany. German representatives as a result became increasingly generous in their offers to the Soviets in order to keep the USSR out of the war.[102] These offers culminated with the Nazi-Soviet Pact that divided eastern Europe into German and Soviet spheres of influence.

These three changes dramatically altered the strategic incentives confronting the Soviet Union.[103] Most important, they offered Soviet decision makers more opportunities to increase substantially their state's relative power than were previously available to them. The beliefs that Germany was headed west after its attack on Poland and that Britain and France were likely to honor their commitments to Poland created the strong possibility that Germany and the Western democracies would conflict while the Soviet Union could stay neutral.[104] The USSR's relative power position

---

100. On the importance of the Western powers' commitment to defend Poland to Soviet policies, see Gabriel Gorodetsky, *Grand Delusion: Stalin and the German Invasion of Russia* (New Haven: Yale University Press, 1999), 4–5; Geoffrey Roberts, *The Soviet Union and the Origins of the Second World War: Russo-German Relations and the Road to War, 1933–1941* (London: Macmillan, 1995), 81; Adam Ulam, *Expansion and Coexistence: Soviet Foreign Policy, 1917–73* (New York: Holt, Rinehart, and Winston, 1974), 267.

101. Roberts, *Unholy Alliance*, 124; Carley, *1939*, 141.

102. Roberts, *Soviet Union and the Origins of the Second World War*, 73; Carley, *1939*, 176, 178, 191.

103. A fourth factor, the breakdown of Anglo-French-Soviet alliance talks, possibly contributed to these changes, though the end of negotiations was at least as much a consequence as a cause of the Nazi-Soviet Pact. From the fall of 1939 to the spring of 1941, the Soviets had ample opportunity to ally with at least one of the Western powers, but chose not to do so.

104. In a March 10, 1939, speech to the Eighteenth Party Congress, Stalin indicated the importance of Germany's likely aggression in the west after defeating Poland. In the speech, Stalin asserted that the Western democracies preferred to appease Germany in the hope that Germany would "embroil herself in a war with the Soviet Union." But the direction of German aggression turned out to be different than British and French leaders anticipated. "Instead of marching farther east, against the Soviet Union . . . [Germany has] turned . . . to the west" (in Roberts, *Unholy Alliance*, 118). In response to this change, Stalin indicated that the USSR would not fight British and French wars for them. This was the meaning of the dictator's famous line in the speech that the Soviet Union would not pull others' "chestnuts out of the fire" for them.

would as a result likely gain substantially while the other powers weak-ened themselves in a war of attrition. Documents from the Soviet archives have revealed that this hoped-for outcome was a dominant motive behind the Soviets' willingness to sign the Nazi-Soviet Pact.[105] German represen-tatives' offers to compensate the Soviet Union with territory in eastern Europe if it remained neutral in a war between Germany, Britain, and France strongly reinforced these hopes.

Soviet behavior from 1933 to August 1939 thus seems to offer substan-tial evidence in support of offensive realism. When Germany appeared to pose an imminent threat to the Soviet Union's security, Soviet leaders laid aside their ideological antipathy to their counterparts in the other powers and pursued alliances with these states. When changing circumstances created an opportunity for Soviet decision makers to increase substan-tially their state's relative power, these leaders abandoned their previous attempts to preserve the balance of power in favor of strategies designed to overturn it to the benefit of the Soviet Union, even if this meant facili-tating the outbreak of war among the other great powers.[106]

There are, however, two key problems with offensive realism's ability to explain Soviet leaders' most important international decisions throughout the 1930s and early 1940s. First, if imminence of a German attack was sufficient for Soviet leaders to lay aside ideological differences with the other powers from 1933 to 1939, why did these same individuals refuse to ally with Britain in 1940 and in the first half of 1941 when the German threat to the USSR was greater than it had been in the previous seven years?

Second, Soviet leaders' conformity with offensive realist predictions from 1933 to 1939 does not necessarily mean that they were motivated by realist logic.[107] The nature of the ideological distances among the great powers' leaders from the perspective of Soviet decision makers was, in fact, central to the latter's power-maximizing policies throughout the 1933–41 period. Although Soviet decision makers perceived the distance separating their legitimating principles from the other powers' leaders to be quite large, they saw no meaningful ideological distinctions among their counterparts in the other great powers. The former perception pushed Soviet leaders to view all the other powers in very threatening

105. Roberts, *Unholy Alliance*, 194; Roberts, *Soviet Union and the Origins of the Second World War*, 98, 122; Gabriel Gorodetsky, "Stalin and Hitler's Attack on the Soviet Union," in *From Peace to War*, ed. Wegner, 347; R. C. Raack, *Stalin's Drive to the West, 1938–1945: The Origins of the Cold War* (Stanford: Stanford University Press, 1995), 52, 195; Robert Tucker, *Stalin in Power: The Revolution from Above, 1928–1941* (New York: W. W. Norton, 1990), 592, 598.

106. The Nazi-Soviet Pact facilitated the outbreak of war both by removing for German decision makers the hazards of a two-front war and by committing the Soviet Union to pro-vide Germany raw materials that were crucial for its war-fighting efforts (for a list of these raw materials, see Tucker, *Stalin in Power*, 607).

107. Even Mearsheimer implies this. Cf. *Tragedy of Great Power Politics*, 192.

terms; the latter view allowed these individuals to make or break alliance commitments to the other powers based largely on power-political considerations. When states are equally threatening in ideological terms, it only makes sense that power variables will become of greater importance in making differentiations among these actors in terms of the level and immediacy of the security threats confronting a particular country. However, once Germany and the Western powers were engaged in battle, Soviet leaders' large ideological differences and consequent mistrust of the Western democracies inhibited these decision makers from either believing British warnings that an attack by Germany was imminent, or allying with Britain before 1941 so that Germany would be confronted with a two-front war. Ideological distances among the powers thus help us understand why Soviet leaders adhered to the prescriptions of offensive realism from 1933 to 1939, but failed to do so from 1940 to 1941.

Ideology and Soviet Foreign Policies

This chapter differs in an important way from most studies that have examined the impact of Marxist-Leninist ideology on Soviet foreign policies. Most of these works explore whether or not Marxism-Leninism shaped Soviet international decisions by giving Soviet leaders unique preferences, such as aiding communist parties throughout the system.

My analysis, with one exception, does not examine the effects of Marxism-Leninism's specific behavioral prescriptions on Soviet leaders' foreign policies. Instead I explore, first, how Marxism-Leninism impacted the ideological distances dividing states leaders' from the perspective of Soviet decision makers, and, second, how these relationships shaped Soviet politicians' perceptions of threat and consequent foreign policy choices.

Marxism-Leninism affects the ideological relationships among states' leaders in two critical ways. First, Marxism-Leninism teaches that the ideological distance separating socialist from non-socialist (i.e., "capitalist") politicians is extremely large. To this system of belief, the legitimating principles of these groups of decision makers are antithetical. Second, to Marxist-Leninist theory, there are no meaningful ideological differences among "capitalist" states and their leaders. Since they are all dedicated to the same system of production, they are in essence ideologically identical.[108]

These understandings of the ideological relationships among states pushed Soviet leaders to view the other great powers in extremely threatening terms for reasons consistent with my argument. In the first place,

---

108. Frederic S. Burin, "The Communist Doctrine of the Inevitability of War," *American Political Science Review* 57, no. 2 (June 1963): 334–354; Sontag, *Broken World*, 160; Bell, *Origins of the Second World War in Europe*, 125.

Soviet decision makers feared that the continued existence in the system of capitalist states would provoke ideological fifth columnists in the Soviet Union. Stalin, for example, "carefully monitored the possible dangerous consequences of Western ideological influence on his regime."[109] These fears of ideological subversion inspired by the capitalist countries fueled Soviet leaders' feelings of enmity toward these states. They also created strong incentives pushing Soviet decision makers to try to convert capitalist regimes to socialist institutions by both the subversive activities of the Comintern and the brute force of the Red Army once the war began.[110]

Ideological differences with the other great powers made Soviet leaders in the 1930s even more fearful for the security of their state than they were about counter-revolution. Time and again, both privately and publicly, Soviet representatives asserted that the ideological nature of the other powers made war between these states and the Soviet Union in the long run inevitable.[111] As Stalin himself asserted: "We live according to Lenin's formula of 'Kto-kogo': either we shall pin them, the capitalists, to the ground and give them, as [Vladimir Ilich] Lenin expressed it, final decisive battle, or they will pin our shoulders to the ground."[112] Or as the Soviet dictator wrote in a private letter to his closest political friend, Vyacheslav Molotov: "We are waging a struggle . . . with the whole capitalist world."[113] This fundamental mistrust of and animosity toward the other powers remained the foundation of Soviet views of international politics throughout the period in question.

The effects of ideological distances on Soviet leaders' perceptions of international threats had direct implications for central elements of Soviet foreign policies from 1933 to 1941. First, Soviet leaders' belief that conflict with the capitalist powers was inevitable pushed them to engage

109. Vladislav Zubok and Constantine Pleshakov, *Inside the Kremlin's Cold War: From Stalin to Khrushchev* (Cambridge: Harvard University Press, 1996), 5, 22, 77. Also Lars T. Lih, Oleg V. Naumov, and Oleg V. Khlevniuk, eds., *Stalin's Letters to Molotov* (New Haven: Yale University Press, 1995), 5, 7, 30, 31, 33, 36.
110. On the Soviet Union's forcible regime exportations during the war, see Roberts, *Unholy Alliance*, 162; Roberts, *Soviet Union and the Origins of the Second World War*, 100, 103, 110–121.
111. On the belief in the inevitability of conflict with the "capitalist" powers as a defining tenet of Soviet leaders' views of international relations, see Burin, "Communist Doctrine of the Inevitability of War"; Robert Tucker, "The Emergence of Stalin's Foreign Policy," *Slavonic Review* 36, no. 4 (December 1977): 565; Roberts, *Unholy Alliance*, 31; Ulam, *Expansion and Coexistence*, 207.
112. In Tucker, *Stalin in Power*, 86; see also 87.
113. In *Stalin's Letters to Molotov*, 178. The Stalin-Molotov letters provide invaluable insight into Stalin's ideological view of the world. According to one of the editors of the volume: "The letters . . . document [Stalin's] unremitting hostility toward and suspicions of the capitalist world even when he was forced to deal with it. He was vigilant lest the foreign policy professionals . . . lose the ability to see the revolutionary aspect of diplomacy. All in all, Stalin comes out of the letters with his revolutionary credentials in good order" (*Stalin's Letters to Molotov*, 36).

consistently in power-maximizing strategies throughout the 1930s (these policies are described throughout this section). Given Soviet officials' understanding of the other powers' intended aggressiveness, any other strategy would have been extremely dangerous to Soviet interests.

The second dimension of Soviet foreign policies that my argument helps explain is why Soviet leaders possessed a more accurate understanding of the German threat for most of the 1930s than did most British and French conservatives. Soviet leaders' ideological relationships with the Nazis differed in a critical way in comparison to British and French conservatives' relations with the German fascists. Unlike most members of the British and French right (who tended to view the USSR as a substantially greater ideological danger than Nazi Germany), Soviet decision makers did not perceive significant ideological distinctions among the other great powers. To Soviet leaders, because all "capitalist" states were based on the same means of production, all were ideologically equidistant from the Soviet regime.[114] Consequently, for Soviet leaders there was no greater ideological threat in the system to mask the strategic danger posed by Germany. The Soviets were therefore more likely than any other group of state leaders to believe Hitler's ambitions as articulated in *Mein Kampf*.[115] This fact pushed the Soviets to adopt more forceful deterrent policies toward the Nazis for most of the 1930s than did most British and French conservatives. A particular ideological configuration among the other great powers from the perspective of Soviet decision makers thus facilitated the adoption of very "realistic" policies toward Germany from 1933 to 1939.

Similar analysis applies to Soviet leaders' ability to be flexible in their alliance policies throughout the 1930s (the Soviets aligned with Germany before 1933, tried to ally with Britain and France against Germany from 1934 to 1939, and formed a tacit alliance with Germany against the Western powers with the signing of the Nazi-Soviet Pact in August 1939). Because Soviet officials viewed all the other powers as ideological enemies with few ideological differences among them, the Soviets were free to change alliances without betraying any ideological loyalties to their former partners.

Third, an ideological understanding of international threats helps to solve an important puzzle for realist explanations of Soviet foreign policies in the interwar period: why Soviet decision makers refused to ally with Britain after Germany's quick victory over France in 1940. France's

114. As future foreign minister Vyacheslav Molotov explained in November 1936, there were two types of states, "Socialist and Capitalist," and Soviet leaders "consider [that] the latter includes the Fascist system" (in Roberts, *Unholy Alliance*, 94). See also Tucker, *Stalin in Power*, 522; Hochman, *Soviet Union and the Failure of Collective Security*, 164.
115. Roberts, *Unholy Alliance*, 57, 58, 67, 100, 103, 106; Roberts, *Soviet Union and the Origins of the Second World War*, 10–12, 14, 19, 21, 29–30, 37, 47, 52, 102, 136, 138; Carley, *1939*, 10.

defeat clearly upset the grand strategy of Soviet leaders.[116] Instead of Germany and the Western powers weakening each other through prolonged conflict, Germany's victory significantly increased the German danger to the Soviet Union. After France's fall, Germany could consolidate its position in the west and then turn on the USSR with more resources than it possessed in 1939 and with a reduced threat of having to fight a two-front war.

France's defeat increased substantially the incentives for Soviet leaders to ally with Britain. If Britain were to be knocked out of the war, not only would British resources be denied to the USSR in a war with Germany, but the possibility of forming a second front, whether it be in western Europe, the Balkans, or the Middle East (where the British fleet still dominated), would be gone.[117] Yet until Germany's attack on the USSR in June 1941, Stalin refused to ally with Britain despite increasing power-political reasons to do so. Realist theories have great difficulty explaining this decision.[118]

A mixture of changing circumstances, the specific prescriptions of Marxism-Leninism, and the effects of the large ideological distances dividing Soviet decision makers from the other powers' leaders explains the former's refusal to obey the dictates of the balance of power in the crucial years of 1940 and 1941. A defining tenet of Marxist-Leninist thought in the interwar period was that war among "capitalist" states was critical to both the survival of the Soviet Union and the spread of socialist regimes. Lenin stated in 1920 that "the basic rule for us until the final victory of Socialism in the whole world . . . [is] that one must exploit the antitheses and contradictions between two capitalist powers, between two systems of capitalist states, and incite them against one another."[119] Stalin made similar statements. In 1925, he asserted that "if the two main coalitions of capitalist countries during the imperialist war in 1917 had not been engaged in mortal combat against one another, if they had . . . not been preoccupied and lacking in time to enter a contest with the Soviet regime, the Soviet regime would hardly have survived then. Struggle, conflicts and wars between

116. As one Soviet official stated after the war: "We . . . thought that if Germany attacked Britain and France, it would bog down there for a long time. Who could have known that France would collapse in two weeks?" (in Tucker, *Stalin in Power*, 592).

117. Gorodetsky, *Grand Delusion*, 58–59.

118. Realists admit that Stalin should have allied with Britain after France's defeat. Their attempts to explain why the Soviet leader chose not to do so, however, are frequently ad hoc. Mearsheimer attributes this decision to Stalin's bad judgment and psychological paralysis brought on by Germany's quick defeat of France (Mearsheimer, *Tragedy of Great Power Politics*, 321, 197). Randall Schweller attributes this choice to Stalin's probable misperception of the balance of power. According to Schweller's account, Stalin likely mistakenly believed that Germany and Italy in 1940 were stronger than the combined might of Britain and the Soviet Union. Britain was therefore doomed to defeat with or without the Soviet Union's help (Schweller, *Deadly Imbalances*, 168).

119. In James McSherry, *Stalin, Hitler, and Europe: The Origins of World War II, 1933–1939* (New York: World Publishing, 1968), 1:2.

our enemies are, I repeat, our greatest ally." He also called intra-capitalist wars "the greatest support of our regime and our revolution."[120]

Implicit in these views is the belief that there are two types of wars: intra-capitalist and capitalist-socialist. A war is unlikely to be a mixture of both. This helps to explain Stalin's conviction revealed by the Soviet archives that as long as Germany was fighting Britain, it would not attack the USSR.[121] The Soviet Union would therefore be safe until the "intra-capitalist" conflict ended. These beliefs reduced the incentives pushing Soviet leaders to ally with Great Britain even after France's defeat.

The effects of the large ideological differences dividing Soviet from British decision makers reinforced the Soviets' aversion to an alliance with Britain. To begin with, the ideological gulf dividing British and Soviet leaders clearly inhibited effective communication between them, as the communications mechanism predicts. In the spring of 1941, Britain possessed accurate intelligence concerning the timing and plans of Germany's attack on the USSR.[122] Despite several attempts to convey this information to the Soviets, British leaders were unable to convince their Soviet counterparts of the veracity of their reports. Stalin and his associates dismissed Prime Minister Churchill's warnings as nothing more than desperate attempts to embroil the Soviet Union and Germany in a conflict. The Soviet ambassador to Britain, Ivan Maisky, even told Foreign Secretary Anthony Eden that British warnings to the Soviet Union about Germany's plans of attack "would not be understood in Moscow and would be resented there."[123]

Soviet leaders' inability to understand the accuracy of Britain's warnings led to ironic outcomes. Instead of heightening Stalin's suspicions of Germany, Britain's communications diminished the Soviet dictator's fears of Germany because Stalin became convinced that Britain was the principal provocateur in the system at that time. As the historian Gabriel Gorodetsky explains: "Churchill's warning to Stalin of the German deployment [of massive numbers of German troops near the Soviet border] in April [1941], rather than being a landmark in the formation of the Grand Alliance, in fact achieved the opposite. Stalin was diverted from the main danger, suspecting that Churchill was bent on drawing Russia into the hostilities."[124]

Soviet leaders' decision not to ally with Britain before June 1941, however, was more than a product of diplomatic misunderstanding. At the

120. Both in Tucker, *Stalin in Power*, 47; see also 49.
121. Roberts, *Unholy Alliance*, 210; Roberts, *Soviet Union and the Origins of the Second World War*, 138; Gorodetsky, *Grand Delusion*, 135; Gorodetsky, "Stalin and Hitler's Attack on the Soviet Union," 347; Raack, *Stalin's Drive to the West*, 21–22.
122. Gorodetsky, *Grand Delusion*, 303, 308; Shirer, *Rise and Fall of the Third Reich*, 843–844.
123. In Gorodetsky, *Grand Delusion*, 302.
124. Ibid., 321. For other examples of Western politicians' and Soviet leaders' inability to communicate effectively in the 1930s despite the use of "costly signals," see Chapter 1.

heart of this decision was a fundamental mistrust of British intentions. Stalin's fears of abandonment were extraordinarily high. He was convinced that if the Soviet Union abandoned its neutral position in the war in favor of an alliance with Britain, Germany would turn on the USSR. As soon as this happened, Stalin and his associates believed that Britain would renege on any commitments it had made to the Soviet Union, by either declaring its neutrality in the German-Soviet war or, even more likely from the Soviets' point of view, by joining Germany in the offensive. As Maxim Litvinov (foreign minister from 1930 to 1939) recalled a few months after the German attack: "All believed that the British fleet was steaming up the North Sea for a joint attack, with Hitler, on Leningrad and Kronstadt."[125] Stalin, too, was "puzzled by the fact that Britain had not joined in a crusade against Russia."[126] In short, Soviet leaders feared that ideological similarities among the "capitalist" states would push them into an alliance directed at their shared ideological enemy: the USSR. This fear was, in the words of one scholar, a "lasting feature" of Soviet leaders' outlook on international relations in the interwar period.[127]

Ideological distances explain this extremely misguided, paranoid understanding of British intentions. By significantly inflating the threat to the Soviet Union posed by Britain, Soviet leaders' ideological beliefs masked the imminence of the German danger to the USSR, and thereby pushed them to ignore the dictates of the balance of power even though their state was in mortal peril.[128] The huge ideological differences dividing the great powers' leaders thus profoundly affected Soviet foreign policies at a critical time, just as this variable did for British, French, and German international decisions throughout the 1930s.

125. In Gorodetsky, "Stalin and Hitler's Attack on the Soviet Union," 359; see also 358.
126. Gorodetsky, *Grand Delusion*, 313.
127. Gorodetsky, *Grand Delusion*, 5; see also 2–3, 14, 269, 270, 274, 313–314; John Erickson, "Threat Identification and Strategic Appraisal by the Soviet Union, 1930–1941," in *Knowing One's Enemies: Intelligence Assessment Before the Two World Wars*, ed. Ernest R. May (Princeton: Princeton University Press, 1984), 291, 403–404, 406; Fleischhauer, "Soviet Foreign Policy," 37, 44.
128. Gorodetsky, *Grand Delusion*, 274. See also 95, 113; Roberts, *Unholy Alliance*, 208, 215, 217, 225–226; Walter Laqueur, *Stalin: The Glasnost Revelations* (London: Unwin Hyman, 1990), 209; James McSherry, *Stalin, Hitler, and Europe* (New York: World Publishing, 1970), 2:254.

[5]

The Rise and Fall of the Sino-Soviet Alliance, 1949–60

Perhaps the most obvious (apparent) exception to this book's core claims with regard to great power relations over the last two centuries concerns the relationship between the Soviet Union and the Peoples' Republic of China (PRC) in the decades following the PRC's creation in 1949. The ideological similarities uniting these states' leaders were substantial. Both groups of individuals were dedicated to Marxist-Leninist political and economic principles, including state ownership of the means of production, collectivization of agriculture, and the creation of totalitarian political institutions governed by a single party. Although the Soviet Union and China did form a close alliance in the 1950s, after this decade their relationship degenerated into a state of acute enmity. By the end of the 1960s, decision makers in both China and the Soviet Union believed war between their states to be likely.

Scholars have offered various theories to account for the origins and demise of the Sino-Soviet alliance. Realists assert that the coalition originated primarily as a balancing response to America's power and antagonistic behavior in East Asia in the 1940s.[1] By the early 1960s, however, differences in national interests and security concerns that are virtually inevitable among powers that share a common border increasingly dominated Sino-Soviet relations until each state viewed the other as an adversary.[2] In this case, geographical propinquity between the Soviet Union

1. John J. Mearsheimer, *The Tragedy of Great Power Politics* (New York: W. W. Norton, 2001), 201; Stephen M. Walt, *Revolution and War* (Ithaca: Cornell University Press, 1996), 318, 323.
2. Richard Lowenthal, *World Communism: The Disintegration of a Secular Faith* (New York: Oxford University Press, 1969), viii, 256; Joseph Camilleri, *Chinese Foreign Policy: The Maoist Era and Its Aftermath* (Oxford: Martin Robinson, 1980), 10.

and China became a more important determinant of their choices of allies and enemies than the power superiority of the United States.

Other scholars argue that the key cause of the Sino-Soviet split was not security fears that tend to plague virtually all neighboring great powers, but the effects created by the specific properties of Marxism-Leninism. Adherents to perfectionist ideologies, like Marxism-Leninism, tend to be intolerant of different interpretations of the same body of thought. Recognizing the legitimacy of rival interpretations of the same perfectionist belief system is difficult because this admission tends to undermine a core claim of these types of ideologies: the ability to understand perfectly for all times and places the laws of politics. Consequently, relations among groups dedicated to different strains of the same perfectionist ideology tend to degenerate into sectarian battles over ideological "correctness" and "purity." To this logic, there can only be one true interpreter of a perfectionist belief system; the rest are perceived as heretics.[3]

To this analysis, the fact that Soviet and Chinese leaders were dedicated to the same perfectionist ideology was a powerful source of strife between them. Neither group could accept the other's unique interpretation of Marxism-Leninism as legitimate without calling into question their own domestic authority. The existence of the other communist power therefore became a subversive threat to their domestic position.

These effects were compounded by the fact that historically the international communist movement had been led by a single state: the Soviet Union. To the extent that a transnational ideological group looks to a single leader to give it direction, different powers within the same ideological community are likely to see each other as rivals for this position of international leadership.[4] Thus Soviet and Chinese leaders' mutual dedication to Marxism-Leninism not only threatened each other's domestic authority, but their international position as head (or, in the Chinese case, potential head) of the international communist movement.

Although these explanations of Soviet and Chinese foreign policies contain important elements of truth, they miss a more central determinant of the rise and fall of the Sino-Soviet coalition. Not only were ideological similarities between CCP and Soviet leaders critical to the formation of highly cooperative relations from 1949 to 1958, but a key cause of the end of the Sino-Soviet alliance was the substantial ideological changes initiated by Mao Zedong and his followers during the period of Chinese history known as the "Great Leap Forward." Without Mao's ideological radicalization, the Sino-Soviet split might never have occurred.[5] Thus instead of being an

3. Lowenthal, *World Communism*, viii, 162, 228; Hans J. Morgenthau, *A New Foreign Policy for the United States* (New York: Frederick A. Praeger, 1969), 34–43, 53–54; Stephen M. Walt, *The Origins of Alliances* (Ithaca: Cornell University Press, 1987), 35–36.
4. Walt, *Origins of Alliances*, 35–37.
5. Odd Arne Westad, introduction to *Brothers in Arms: The Rise and Fall of the Sino-Soviet*

important exception to my argument, key elements of the origins and demise of the Sino-Soviet alliance from 1949 to 1960 support its hypotheses.

IDEOLOGY AND THE ORIGINS OF THE SINO-SOVIET ALLIANCE OF 1950

Realist explanations of the formation of the Sino-Soviet alliance in February 1950 are to a certain extent correct: to both Soviet and Chinese decision makers, an important objective of the alliance was to balance against American capabilities. From the USSR's perspective, an alliance with China would not only help protect Soviet interests in the Far East from American encroachment, but might force the United States to transfer resources from the European theater, which was the more important one to the Soviets.

From the CCP's perspective, the need for a balancing coalition against the United States was if anything even more urgent. America's leaders were not only helping to rebuild Japan, which was a traditional enemy of China, but were demonstrating increasing sympathy for Taiwanese independence, which was a direct challenge to Chinese territorial integrity. In addition, throughout the Chinese civil war the Americans had supported the Chinese Nationalists led by Jiang Jieshi (Chiang Kai-shek). Thus to the CCP, the United States had already demonstrated its animosity toward Chinese communist interests.

This explanation of Chinese leaders' animosity to the United States, and their consequent interest in allying with the Soviet Union, is not so much wrong as it is greatly incomplete.[6] Recent releases from the Chinese archives reveal that ideological distance played a crucial role in shaping CCP leaders' profound hostility toward the United States.

Probably the most important way in which ideological differences between CCP and American decision makers translated into acute perceptions of threat was by pushing the former to believe that military hostilities between China and the United States were inevitable. In the two decades before the creation of the PRC in 1949, Mao and fellow CCP leaders had adopted an understanding of the nature of international politics based on a bipartite division of states. On one side were the forces of socialism and revolution led by the Soviet Union; on the other were the forces of imperialism led by the British and then the Americans. There

---

Alliance, 1945–1963, ed. Odd Arne Westad (Stanford: Stanford University Press, 1998), 31.

6. I concentrate primarily on Chinese leaders' motives for the Sino-Soviet alliance because the Chinese were the principal provocateurs of the split with the Soviet Union in the late 1950s and early 1960s. To understand why the Chinese abandoned the alliance, it is therefore important to know why they, in particular, wanted to create it.

was no question as to which side the Chinese communists gave their loyalties: the socialist/revolutionary camp led by the USSR.[7]

There was also no question in Mao's mind that armed conflict between the two camps was unavoidable in the long run because of their huge ideological differences.[8] Mao believed that China was particularly likely to be attacked because it was both a socialist power and the revolutionary leader of the increasingly important Third World. As the historian Chen Jian explains, based on an examination of evidence from the Chinese archives:

> From a long-term perspective . . . CCP leaders were firmly convinced that sooner or later revolutionary China had to face a direct military confrontation with the imperialist United States. Because of the growing international influence of the Chinese revolution, as the CCP leaders perceived it, revolutionary movements following the Chinese model would develop in other Asian countries. The United States, as the 'head of the reactionary forces' in the world, would then resort to the most desperate means to prevent revolutionary changes in East Asia. As a result, a showdown between China and the United States would eventually occur.[9]

In addition to the power-political danger, CCP leaders were also very concerned about the subversive effects of America on the Chinese political system. These fears had important policy effects. For example, even though the United States could provide China much more economic aid than the Soviet Union, Mao refused to explore this possibility because of his concern that American economic penetration would weaken communist political control.[10] Chinese leaders' fears of ideological subversion

7. Steven M. Goldstein, "Nationalism and Internationalism: Sino-Soviet Relations," in *Chinese Foreign Policy: Theory and Practice*, ed. Thomas W. Robinson and David Shambaugh (New York: Oxford University Press, 1994), 228; Chen Jian, *China's Road to the Korean War: The Making of the Sino-American Confrontation* (New York: Columbia University Press, 1994), 21, 65; Chen Jian, "The Sino-Soviet Alliance and China's Entry into the Korean War," *Cold War International History Project*, Working Paper No. 1 (1992), 2; Michael Sheng, *Battling Western Imperialism: Mao, Stalin, and the United States* (Princeton: Princeton University Press, 1997), 5, 7, 163, 184.

8. Kathryn Weathersby, "Stalin, Mao, and the End of the Korean War," in *Brothers in Arms*, ed. Westad, 99; Chen Jian and Yang Kuisong, "Chinese Politics and the Collapse of the Sino-Soviet Alliance," in *Brothers in Arms*, ed. Westad, 247; Shu Guang Zhang, *Mao's Military Romanticism: China and the Korean War, 1950–1953* (Lawrence: University of Kansas Press, 1995), 38; Chen, *China's Road to the Korean War*, 15, 16, 20, 39, 40, 43, 93, 128; Yang Kuisong, "The Soviet Factor and the CCP's Policy toward the United States in the 1940s," *Chinese Historians* 5, no. 1 (Spring 1992): 21, 22, 34.

9. Chen, *China's Road to the Korean War*, 93.

10. Yang, "Soviet Factor and the CCP's Policy toward the United States," 32; Sheng, *Battling Western Imperialism*, 163, 184. Because of Mao's ideological antipathy to the United States, the claim that America in the late 1940s and early 1950s missed a golden opportunity to separate China from the Soviet Union is a myth, as Michael Sheng convincingly demonstrates in his book. See also Thomas J. Christensen, *Useful Adversaries: Grand Strategy, Domestic Mobilization, and Sino-American Conflict, 1947–1958* (Princeton: Princeton University Press, 1996), 139–146.

significantly increased their perceptions of threat and enmity toward the United States.[11]

The large ideological divide separating Chinese from American decision makers also contributed to high levels of threat by inhibiting understanding between them, as the communications mechanism predicts. Although American leaders' intentions toward China after the CCP's victory in the civil war were by no means friendly, they were not as hostile as Chinese communists believed them to be. U.S. decision makers had no intention of attacking China or attempting to control "the vast intermediate zone" (Mao's phrase for the Third World) separating the Soviet Union and the United States, as CCP leaders believed. Ideological differences between Chinese and American leaders, however, inhibited an accurate assessment of American objectives in favor of worst-case beliefs. In the late 1940s, as Chen explains, China and America "did not lack channels of communication; they lacked, however, mutually understandable political language and common codes of behavior essential for communication. The Americans stressed the importance of individual liberty, international law and custom. . . . The CCP claimed that 'any struggle on the part of the oppressed . . . was a just one.' Both sides believed that they were correct; neither of them was able to place itself in the other's shoes. Consequently, the more they contacted each other, the greater the conflict became."[12]

In sum, one reason why ideological distance must be considered central to any adequate explanation of the origins of the Sino-Soviet alliance of 1950, especially from the Chinese perspective, is that the huge ideological differences dividing CCP leaders from their U.S. counterparts were largely responsible for the former's perceptions of the very high threat posed by America. A second, perhaps more important, reason for this claim is based on that fact that the Sino-Soviet alliance was never grounded solely on mutual antagonism to the United States. Ideological similarities between Soviet and Chinese leaders created incentives for these states to draw together independently of their conflict with America. Thus instead of being merely a balancing response to American capabilities, the Sino-Soviet alliance was "based on deeply shared, common goals; not just *against* . . . but *for* something more profound than momentary calculations of common interest."[13] This fact represents an even

11. On CCP officials fears of ideological subversion to American principles, see Odd Arne Westad, "The Sino-Soviet Alliance and the United States," in *Brothers in Arms*, ed. Westad, 168, 169; Shu Guang Zhang, "Sino-Soviet Economic Cooperation," in *Brothers in Arms*, ed. Westad, 190; Chen, *China's Road to the Korean War*, 66, 160, 184, 206; Michael H. Hunt, *The Genesis of Chinese Communist Foreign Policy* (New York: Columbia University Press, 1996), 195, 196, 198, 217; Sheng, *Battling Western Imperialism*, 164, 184.

12. Chen, *China's Road to the Korean War*, 62–63.

13. Steven M. Goldstein, "The Sino-Soviet Alliance," in *China's Cooperative Relationships: Partnerships and Alignments in Modern Chinese Foreign Policy*, ed. Harry Harding (Washington,

clearer challenge to realist explanations of the origins of the alliance between the two communist powers.

Ideological similarities between Chinese and Soviet leaders brought the two groups together independently of their mutual enmity toward the United States for reasons consistent with my argument. Although Chinese decision makers recognized that Soviet interests would not always be identical with theirs, these individuals consistently tended both to trust their Soviet counterparts and to believe that their interests would coincide on the most important issues. What makes these beliefs all the more remarkable is that Mao and fellow CCP leaders continued to hold them even after Stalin had refused for much of the 1940s to offer unambiguous support for the CCP in the latter's struggles to gain control of China. Despite Stalin's sometimes lukewarm support for the CCP during China's civil war, ideological affinity with the Soviets pushed the Chinese communists to interpret Soviet behavior in the best possible light and to largely forgive Soviet transgressions when they occurred.[14] "Despite the fact that Soviet policy [in the 1940s] seemed to fit the profile of the unreliable ally," as one scholar of Chinese politics explains, "the unrelenting thrust of Maoist and CCP statements—both public and private—was to argue precisely the opposite. . . . The Soviet Union was presented as China's 'revolutionary comrade' with whom a relationship could be maintained based not on mutual advantage but rather on 'principle.'"[15] In short, "from an overall view . . . the problems that existed between the CCP and the Soviet Union were treated by both sides as no more than differences between comrades following the same ideals."[16]

In addition to creating similar international interests, ideological similarities also pushed the Chinese communists to ally with the Soviet Union in order to advance their domestic objectives. The USSR provided the CCP a working model from which the latter could learn how to build a socialist society. It therefore made sense for the Chinese communists to cleave closely to the Soviets in order to benefit most effectively from Soviet experience and aid (which the Chinese expected to receive because

D.C.: Brookings Institution, 1990), 3. emphasis in original. For similar analysis, see Goldstein, "Nationalism and Internationalism"; Westad, introduction to *Brothers in Arms*, 30; Chen and Yang, "Chinese Politics and the Collapse of the Sino-Soviet Alliance," 246, 276–277; Thomas W. Robinson, "Chinese Foreign Policy from the 1940s to the 1990s," in *Chinese Foreign Policy*, ed. Robinson and Shambaugh, 561; Chen, *China's Road to the Korean War*, x; Westad, introduction to *Brothers in Arms*, 3.

14. Goldstein, "Nationalism and Internationalism," 228–230; Niu Jun, "The Origins of the Sino-Soviet Alliance," in *Brothers in Arms*, ed. Westad, 51, 52, 58; Weathersby, "Stalin, Mao, and the End of the Korean War," 104–105; Chen, *China's Road to the Korean War*, 68; Yang, "Soviet Factor and the CCP's Policy toward the United States," 22–24, 34.

15. Goldstein, "Nationalism and Internationalism," 229.

16. Yang, "Soviet Factor and the CCP's Policy toward the United States," 29; Chen, *China's Road to the Korean War*, 68.

of their ideological similarities with Soviet leaders). A series of CCP internal documents in the late 1940s, for example, stressed that "if the Chinese people hope to win a complete victory in the revolution, they had to pursue a solid brotherly alliance with the Soviet Union."[17]

The Soviets to a great extent reciprocated these sentiments. Although the CCP's more vulnerable domestic and international position in the 1940s made them more anxious than their Soviet comrades to secure an alliance with a socialist great power, ideological similarities between the two groups of decision makers were also pushing the Soviets to align with the PRC. Soviet leaders "knew that the ideological affinity between Chinese and Soviet Communists would provide the Soviets with leverage [in Chinese politics]. . . . In an attempt to create a physical and ideological bridgehead on its East Asian frontiers, the Soviet leadership regarded Mao and the CCP not only as probable allies but also as ideological comrades-in-arms and fellow antagonists of the United States."[18]

Ideological similarities with China's leaders pushed even Stalin, whose highly paranoid and xenophobic personality made him suspicious of any foreign leaders whom he could not control, to have a fairly low perception of the threat posed by China under Mao's rule. Thus by the summer of 1949, at the latest, Stalin had decided that China "would become his number one ally, with a sphere of responsibility of its own."[19] As the Soviet dictator explained to the Soviet emissary he sent to advise the CCP as the Chinese civil war was entering its final stages: "We definitely will render all possible assistance to the new China. If socialism is victorious in China and other countries follow the same road, we can consider the victory of socialism throughout the world to be guaranteed. No unexpected events can threaten us. Because of that, we must not spare any effort or resources in assisting the Chinese communists."[20]

The details of the negotiations between Soviet and Chinese officials that led to the signing of the Sino-Soviet alliance in February 1950 reveal

17. In Chen, *China's Road to the Korean War,* 68; see also Chen and Yang, "Chinese Politics and the Collapse of the Sino-Soviet Alliance," 248, 250; Westad, introduction to *Brothers in Arms,* 9; Goldstein, "Nationalism and Internationalism," 231; Frederick C. Teiwes, "Establishment and Consolidation of the New Regime," in *The Cambridge History of China,* ed. Roderick MacFarquhar and John K. Fairbank (London: Cambridge University Press, 1987), 14: 64–67, 96.

18. Sergei Goncharenko, "Sino-Soviet Military Cooperation," in *Brothers in Arms,* ed. Westad, 143. See also Westad, introduction to *Brothers in Arms,* 10–11, 15; Jun, "Origins of the Sino-Soviet Alliance," 62–63.

19. Sergei N. Goncharov, John W. Lewis, and Xue Litai, *Uncertain Partners: Stalin, Mao, and the Korean War* (Stanford: Stanford University Press, 1993), 64; also 72.

20. Ibid., 31. In support of this pledge made by Stalin, recently released archival materials have revealed that cooperation between the Soviets and the CCP during the Chinese civil war was much more extensive than widely believed. Ideological similarities between these groups was central to the cooperation. See Sheng, *Battling Western Imperialism,* 5, 7, 13, 15, 56, 163, 169–170, 184.

the importance of ideological similarities to their relations. During the alliance negotiations and their preliminary talks, Stalin made a number of concessions which "deeply impressed Mao and his fellow CCP leaders."[21] Perhaps most important, Stalin both apologized for not having provided the CCP with greater aid during the Chinese civil war, and asserted that China should provide the model for revolutionary forces in East Asia. By making this last claim, Stalin acknowledged both the CCP's revolutionary credentials and the synergy of the Soviet Union's and the PRC's interests in Asia due to their common ideological beliefs.[22]

In the alliance agreement of 1950 negotiated by Stalin and Mao, Stalin promised to give China military assistance in case of aggression by Japan or its allies (i.e., America); to provide China a $300 million credit at only 1 percent interest;[23] to return to Chinese control the naval base at Lushan (Port Arthur), the Changchun Railway at the end of 1952, and the port of Dalian on the completion of a peace treaty with Japan;[24] and to restore Chinese sovereignty in Manchuria, which was a must for Mao.[25]

Neither Mao nor Stalin was completely satisfied with the agreement. Contra Mao's wishes, Stalin insisted on the continued independence of Outer Mongolia, and he refused to give the CCP sufficient aid to conquer Taiwan. Conversely, Stalin most likely did not want to have to commit to reducing Soviet influence in key regions in northeast China. To the end, Stalin and Mao possessed different conceptions of what policies would best advance their state's interests.

The fact that both leaders continued to possess different interests is not surprising. The argument I present in this book does not predict that actors from the same ideological community will have harmonious interests, only that their relations will take place within a low-threat environment which allows their interactions to be largely cooperative.

The evidence supports this prediction. Both Mao and Stalin came to the negotiating table with the expectation that their ideological similarities would lead to cooperative policies, especially in relation to their shared ideological and power-political enemy, the United States. As Vojtech Mastny explains:

> There cannot be a doubt that Mao Zedong on his first visit to Moscow treated Stalin as the supreme authority of world communism, with a reverence that was not merely pretended but rooted in a perception of common interests, to which the Chinese leader repeatedly and cogently alluded. The

21. Chen, *China's Road to the Korean War,* 73.
22. Ibid., 72–76.
23. Westad, introduction to *Brothers in Arms,* 11–12.
24. Hunt, *Genesis of Chinese Communist Foreign Policy,* 182; Goncharov et al., *Uncertain Partners,* 119.
25. Camilleri, *Chinese Foreign Policy,* 49.

same perception determined Stalin's uncharacteristically considerate, even generous, attitude toward his junior partner. . . . The Russian documents hardly bear out the self-serving Chinese descriptions of his stinginess and boorishness, an image that Mao himself . . . later tried to disseminate. Of course not everything was sweet and smooth between the two ruthless and devious dictators; still, their ability to dispose of potentially contentious issues was remarkable.[26]

Without the effects of common principles of political legitimacy between Soviet and Chinese leaders, it is doubtful that Stalin's and Mao's negotiations would have been as "substantial, comprehensive, and effective" as they were.[27] On the whole, both Stalin and Mao were satisfied with the outcomes of their negotiations.[28] Sino-Soviet cooperation during the last years of Stalin's life set the stage for the most cooperative years of the alliance, which occurred during the first five years after the Soviet dictator's death, from 1953 to 1958.[29]

Sino-Soviet Relations, 1953–58

The Sino-Soviet alliance from 1953 to 1958 was one of the most dynamic peacetime coalitions in modern history, especially from the Soviet side. During the first five years of Nikita Khrushchev's rule, the USSR engaged in large-scale economic, military, and political cooperation with China that was in important ways unprecedented.

Soviet aid to China in the 1950s was the most extensive in the area of economic and technical assistance. During China's first five-year plan (1953–57), for example, the Soviets helped to build as many as 166 industrial plants in China (or roughly 50 percent of all new plants built in China in this period).[30] The Soviets were also instrumental in securing significant

---

26. Vojtech Mastny, "Talks with Mao Zedong and Zhou Enlai, 1949–1953," *Cold War International History Project Bulletin* 6–7 (Winter 1995/1996), virtual archive, 35. http://wwics.si.edu/index.cfm?topic_id=1409&fuseaction=library.Collection.

27. Chen, "Sino-Soviet Alliance and China's Entry into the Korean War," 34.

28. Zhang, *Mao's Military Romanticism*, 41; Jun, "Origins of the Sino-Soviet Alliance," 73, 74; Hunt, *Genesis of Chinese Communist Foreign Policy*, 180–181; Chen, "Sino-Soviet Alliance and China's Entry into the Korean War," 18. For the most part Mao claimed great disappointment with the treaty only after the Sino-Soviet split began.

29. Space constraints prohibit an examination of the Korean War on the evolution of Sino-Soviet relations. For studies that demonstrate how the war strengthened the alliance, especially by demonstrating to both parties the other's ideological bona fides, see Goncharov et al., *Uncertain Partners*, 199–201; Chen and Yang, "Chinese Politics and the Collapse of the Sino-Soviet Alliance," 253–256; Chen, *China's Road to the Korean War*, 208; Westad, "Sino-Soviet Alliance and the United States," 171; Weathersby, "Stalin, Mao, and the End of the Korean War," 109, 104–105.

30. Goncharenko, "Sino-Soviet Military Cooperation," 160; Zhang, "Sino-Soviet Economic Cooperation," 202.

aid for China from Eastern European states, including East Germany, Poland, Romania, Hungary, and Bulgaria. These states agreed to construct in China sixteen fully equipped industrial plants and eighty-eight partially equipped ones.[31] By 1956, the Soviet Union had delivered industrial equipment to China costing 8.5 billion rubles, and had sent over 5,000 specialists to work in China, including engineers, workers, and foremen (the number of specialists increased to 8,000 by 1960).[32] In January 1958 (which was just months before Sino-Soviet relations took a significant turn for the worse), the two states signed an agreement for joint research on 122 scientific and technical projects over the next five years.[33] All told, Soviet economic support for China in the 1950s constituted, in one scholar's estimation, "the most comprehensive technology transfer in modern industrial history."[34]

Soviet military aid to China was almost as impressive as its economic and technical assistance.[35] This was especially true with regard to the development of China's nuclear capabilities. Between 1955 and 1958, the Soviet Union and China signed six accords related to the development of China's nuclear science, industry, and weapons programs. In these accords, Khrushchev agreed, among other things, to give China an experimental atomic reactor, a cyclotron, and fissionable materials for research, along with pertinent technical assistance for this equipment and materials. The Soviets also agreed to sell China the equipment necessary for the production of enriched uranium.[36]

In October 1957, Khrushchev agreed to share with China nuclear arms and missile technology, including providing in-depth training of Chinese nuclear scientists and delivering large amounts of technical information, "a sample medium-range ballistic missile minus its atomic warhead, a G-class ballistic missile submarine without its missiles, and TU-16 jet fighters."[37] Khrushchev also agreed to provide China with a prototype nuclear weapon and related technical information (though the sample weapon was never delivered, for reasons I discuss below). The Soviet Union's nuclear aid to China surpassed that of America to its allies.[38]

31. Zhang, "Sino-Soviet Economic Cooperation," 202.
32. Goncharenko, "Sino-Soviet Military Cooperation," 155, 160; Zhang, "Sino-Soviet Economic Cooperation," 202.
33. Melvin Gurtov and Byong-Moo Hwang, *China under Threat: The Politics of Strategy and Diplomacy* (Baltimore: Johns Hopkins University Press, 1980), 74.
34. Hans Heymann cited in A. Doak Barnett, *China and the Major Powers of East Asia* (Washington, D.C.: Brookings Institution, 1977), 28.
35. Westad, introduction to *Brothers in Arms*, 16; Goncharenko, "Sino-Soviet Military Cooperation," 141, 148, 152, 155, 156, 160; Chen, *China's Road to the Korean War*, 75–77; John Wilson Lewis and Xue Litai, *China Builds the Bomb* (Stanford: Stanford University Press, 1988), 7.
36. Lewis and Xue, *China Builds the Bomb*, 41, 53, 60–64; Goncharenko, "Sino-Soviet Military Cooperation," 157–159.
37. Constantine Pleshakov, "Nikita Khrushchev and Sino-Soviet Relations," in *Brothers in Arms*, ed. Westad, 233.
38. Goncharenko, "Sino-Soviet Military Cooperation," 159.

Cooperation between the two socialist powers on key foreign policy issues was also substantial during this period. In 1954 Khrushchev relinquished to Chinese control the Lushan Naval Base (Port Arthur) and Soviet shares in the joint companies in Manchuria and Xinjiang, all without compensation.[39] These initiatives were important concessions to Chinese nationalist sentiments.

More significant, Khrushchev was also supportive of China's most important foreign policy objective: the reunification with Taiwan. Before the opening of the Soviet and Chinese archives in the 1990s, one of the most prominent explanations of the Sino-Soviet split examined disagreements over the future of this island. According to this argument, because China was much more interested in liberating Taiwan from Nationalist control than were the Soviets, Soviet leaders were not willing to be sufficiently aggressive on this issue in order to satisfy Chinese demands. Soviet caution during the Taiwan Straits crises between China and the United States in 1954 and 1958 was supposedly a key cause of the schism because it taught the Chinese that they could not rely on the Soviet Union to support their most important international interests.

Recently released archival evidence casts significant doubt on the accuracy of this analysis. Far from deploring Chinese aggressiveness over Taiwan during the 1958 crisis, new evidence shows that Khrushchev "welcomed the news that [the CCP was planning to "bring Taiwan back under China's jurisdiction"] and offered both political and military backing for China's efforts."[40] In the first few weeks of August 1958, Khrushchev sent to China long-range artillery, amphibious equipment, air-to-air missiles, combat aircraft, and military personnel who could both advise and take part in the upcoming operation (the Chinese began to shell Quemoy island on August 23). All this was designed to facilitate a "decisive move against the Jiang Jieshi regime."[41] Although western analysts have often asserted that Khrushchev supported China against the United States only after the Taiwan crisis was winding down, new evidence reveals that this position is inaccurate. While tensions were at their height, Khrushchev "met secretly with the Chinese ambassador, Liu Xiao,

39. Westad, introduction to *Brothers in Arms,* 16. Although Stalin had agreed during his meetings with Mao in 1950 to return the Lushan base to Chinese control in 1952, during the Korean War the Chinese asked the Soviets to keep their forces stationed there, where they remained even after the signing of the Korean armistice (Goncharov et al., *Uncertain Partners,* 119).
40. Mark Kramer, "The Soviet Foreign Ministry Appraisal of Sino-Soviet Relations on the Eve of the Split," *Cold War International History Project Bulletin* 6–7 (Winter 1995/1996), virtual archive, 8–9; Westad, introduction to *Brothers in Arms,* 17–18; Goncharenko, "Sino-Soviet Military Cooperation," 15–151; Vladislav Zubok, "Khrushchev's Nuclear Promise to Beijing during the Crisis," *Cold War International History Project Bulletin* 6–7 (Winter 1995/1996), virtual archive, 2–3. Both virtual archives available at:
http://wwics.si.edu/index.cfm?topic_id=1409&fuseaction=library.Collection.
41. In Kramer, "Soviet Foreign Ministry Appraisal of Sino-Soviet Relations," 9.

and gave every indication that he still expected and hoped that China would proceed with its 'decisive' military action against Taiwan."[42] In short, with regards to the PRC's goal of reacquiring control of Taiwan, Khrushchev went as far as Mao himself was willing to go.

Ideological similarities between Soviet and Chinese decision makers were central to these high levels of Soviet economic and military support. Khrushchev both felt an obligation to provide substantial aid to China in order to ensure the victory of the Chinese socialist revolution, and believed that the CCP could be trusted to use this aid in ways that were supportive of Soviet interests.[43] As Sergei Goncharenko explains with regard to probably Khrushchev's most risky policy, the decision to aid substantially the development of the Chinese nuclear weapons program: "The most obvious reason why the early Khrushchev leadership was willing ["to take the extraordinary risks involved in providing another country with nuclear weapons"] . . . was the enthusiasm for socialist construction and technological achievement in Moscow during the mid-1950s. Khrushchev and his close associates believed in the alliance with China . . . in a way that [they] later regretted bitterly. During these leaders' first enthusiastic years in power, providing China with nuclear weapons may have seemed a small price to pay for an alliance that would lead two continents into socialism."[44] Without Soviet and Chinese leaders' mutual dedication to Marxist-Leninist principles, it is very doubtful that their alliance would have reached the very high levels of cooperation that it did from 1953 to 1958.

Nineteen fifty-eight, however, marked the high point of the Sino-Soviet relationship. After this year, relations between the two communist powers quickly and steeply degenerated. In June 1959, Khrushchev reneged on his commitments to continue aiding the development of China's nuclear weapons program, including his promise to deliver a prototype atomic bomb. In the summer of 1960, Khrushchev withdrew Soviet economic and technical advisors. According to one estimate, this decision led to the withdrawal of 1,400 experts, the violation of hundreds of contracts and agreements, and the breaking of 200 projects of scientific and technical cooperation.[45] These outcomes did substantial damage to the development of China's economy. By the mid-1960s, Soviet and Chinese decision makers were more likely to view one another as probable enemies than reliable allies. What accounts for this rapid, steep deterioration of the Sino-Soviet relationship?

42. Ibid., 10.
43. Westad, introduction to *Brothers in Arms,* 15.
44. Goncharenko, "Sino-Soviet Military Cooperation," 159.
45. Goldstein, "Sino-Soviet Alliance," 34.

The Origins of the Sino-Soviet Split: Alternative Explanations

As explained in the introductory section of this chapter, there are two dominant explanations in the literature examining the origins of the Sino-Soviet split. One group of scholars examines the divisive effects of realist variables such as differences in Chinese and Soviet "national interests" and security fears that plague relations among virtually all neighboring great powers. Thomas Christensen, for example, attributes China's increasing fears of the Soviet Union that led to the schism to increases in Soviet power, especially nuclear capabilities, in the fall of 1957. With the development of the USSR's nuclear-delivery capabilities, revealed most dramatically by new delivery capabilities associated with the launches in 1957 of an ICBM missile in August and the Sputnik satellite in October, China feared both Soviet abandonment and exploitation. Abandonment because the Soviet Union's nuclear arsenal reduced the utility of the Sino-Soviet alliance from Moscow's perspective; exploitation because the USSR's growing power would allow it to treat China like one of its satellites in Eastern Europe.[46] These fears pushed the CCP to break with the Soviet Union in order to protect China's security.

Others explain the split as a result of divisive tendencies created by the perfectionism of Marxism-Leninism and the hierarchical nature of the international communist alliance. The perfectionism of Marxism-Leninism made Sino-Soviet relations ripe for degeneration into sectarian squabbles, and international communism's hierarchical structure created another important area of zero-sum competition between the two communist powers.

Both sets of arguments contain important elements of truth. There is little doubt that Moscow's growing nuclear arsenal and subsequent discussions with the Americans over nuclear test bans (which began in 1957) and non-proliferation provoked fears of abandonment among China's leaders.[47] America's European allies had similar feelings of angst throughout the Cold War. These concerns are inherent to the nature of extended deterrence in the nuclear era. Fears of abandonment, just as they did for Britain and France, created for China substantial incentives to develop a more independent foreign policy from its superpower ally, including creating its own nuclear deterrent.

It is also clear that Marxism-Leninism's perfectionism and the hierarchical nature of international communism contributed to Sino-Soviet enmity. Sino-Soviet relations eventually did degenerate into fierce sectarian

---

46. Christensen, *Useful Adversaries*, chap. 6.
47. Donald S. Zagoria, *The Sino-Soviet Conflict, 1956–1961* (New York: Atheneum, 1964), 291. Khrushchev's interest in détente with the United States did not gain substantial momentum, however, until 1959 (chap. 9).

battles and an intense struggle for leadership of the international communist alliance.

Recognizing that realist variables and the specific properties of Marxism-Leninism *eventually* contributed to growing Sino-Soviet hostility does not, however, mean that these factors were the ultimate source of these states' enmity. Both sets of arguments, in fact, confront a number of empirical puzzles which indicate that these variables were not the root cause of the Sino-Soviet rivalry which began in the spring of 1958.

In the first place, power variables had not sufficiently changed in 1957–58 to explain the revolution in Sino-Soviet relations that occurred in this latter year. The only significant changes in Soviet capabilities that occurred in this period were the ICBM and Sputnik launches, which augured the development of second-strike nuclear capabilities for the USSR. Real Soviet military expenditures from 1951 to 1959 remained "essentially flat." In fact, throughout the 1950s, including 1957–59, Khrushchev both decreased overall spending on weapons procurement and steeply reduced the number of men under arms.[48]

The development of second-strike nuclear capabilities did increase China's fears of abandonment. It is a much more dubious proposition, however, that this development provoked in CCP leaders fears of Soviet exploitation similar to the Soviet Union's relations with its Eastern European satellites. Mao himself doubted the coercive (as opposed to deterrent) power associated with Moscow's growing nuclear arsenal. In private conversations, the Chinese dictator asserted that the Sputnik launch was only a "symbol" of power, not a substantial shift in offensive capabilities.[49]

If anything, power variables, as well as Soviet behavior, were in the spring of 1958 pushing for a strengthening of the Sino-Soviet alliance, not its weakening. Although Soviet power in the Far East was not significantly increasing in the late 1950s, American capabilities were. In 1958, the United States deployed and test-fired tactical nuclear missiles in Taiwan. These actions, according to a CCP spokesman, indicated "a U.S. conspiracy to turn Taiwan into a nuclear base against China."[50] Chinese officials also correctly noted America's increased military activity and capabilities in this period in Korea, Japan, and Southeast Asia as part of the United States' forward defense and containment strategies.[51] These facts should have increased the incentives for China to maintain its close relations with the USSR.

48. Noel E. Firth and James H. Noren, *Soviet Defense Spending: A History of CIA Estimates, 1950–1990* (College Station: Texas A&M Press, 1998), 100, 102–113.

49. Christensen, *Useful Adversaries*, 236, 229.

50. In Shu Guang Zhang, *Deterrence and Strategic Culture: Chinese-American Confrontations, 1949–1958* (Ithaca: Cornell University Press, 1992), 226, 228.

51. Roderick MacFarquhar, *The Great Leap Forward, 1958–1960*, vol. 2 of *The Origins of the Cultural Revolution* (London: Oxford University Press, 1983), 264; Gurtov and Hwang, *China under Threat*, 82, 84.

A similar statement can be made with regards to Soviet behavior. At the same time that Mao's suspicions of the USSR were escalating, "Khrushchev was . . . dealing with China in an extremely generous fashion."[52] In 1958, not only was Khrushchev increasing the USSR's economic and military assistance to China (apparently including in June a new offer to help China acquire nuclear-power submarines), but he was also treating China as a virtual "co-equal" in the international communist movement.[53] In June 1958—the very month that Mao's intense suspicions of the Soviet Union became evident—Mao could even reasonably hope that Khrushchev would continue to grant China substantial assistance in developing its atomic weapons program.[54]

Similarly, with regards to many of the most important foreign policy issues of the period, including Taiwanese independence and "peaceful coexistence" with capitalist states (including America), the commonalties that united the key Soviet and Chinese decision makers were greater than the differences that divided them. As discussed, Khrushchev was supportive of Mao's belligerency during the second Taiwan Straits crisis of 1958, and Mao was generally satisfied with this aid.[55] Similarly, although CCP leaders, most notably Mao, would eventually vehemently denounce the doctrine of "peaceful coexistence" as a viable strategy for dealing with capitalist states, they did not do so for much of the 1950s.[56] In fact, before 1958, Mao adopted a similar stance on this subject as did Khrushchev. In 1955, the Chinese claimed that peaceful coexistence was the correct strategy for all Third World states to follow in their relations with imperialist powers. This position became known as the "Bandung Line" of Chinese foreign policy.[57]

Importantly, Sino-American relations in this period were no exception to the Bandung Line. In January 1956, Mao told the CCP's Central Committee that by following a strategy of peaceful coexistence with America, China could expect at least a dozen years of peace to complete industrialization. At the Eighth Party Congress in September 1956, Liu Shaoqi (a top CCP official) reiterated Khrushchev's praise of "sober-minded people" within "American ruling circles" (a group that included President Dwight

---

52. John W. Garver, "Review Article: Mao's Soviet Policies," *China Quarterly* no. 173 (2003): 207.
53. Ibid., 207–208.
54. Lewis and Xue, *China Builds the Bomb*, 71.
55. Zubok, "Khrushchev's Nuclear Promise to Beijing during the Crisis," 2.
56. The Soviet Union formally adopted the doctrine of peaceful coexistence at the Twentieth Party Congress in 1956. The doctrine asserted that indefinite peaceful relations among the great powers (especially those states possessing nuclear weapons) was both desirable and possible.
57. Mineo Nakajima, "Foreign Relations: From the Korean War to the Bandung Line," in *Cambridge History of China*, ed. MacFarquhar and Fairbank, 14:283.

Eisenhower). The report issued by this congress concluded that "the possibility of lasting world peace has now begun to materialize."[58]

Because Soviet and Chinese decision makers were more likely to agree than disagree over the most important foreign policy issues of the day for most of the 1950s, the end of the Sino-Soviet alliance is difficult to explain by merely appealing to differences in Chinese and Soviet "national interests," as realist theories would have it. In the words of one scholar of Chinese politics, "When serious disagreements began to emerge between Beijing and Moscow in the . . . late 1950s, China and the Soviet Union had more shared 'national interests' than ever."[59]

Khrushchev's policies from 1954 to 1958 also reveal the inadequacies of those arguments that attribute the Sino-Soviet schism to the inevitable tensions between proponents of different strains of the same perfectionist ideology and/or common membership of a hierarchical alliance system. Far from crusading to enforce either ideological orthodoxy or the Soviet Union's sole position as head of the international communist movement, Khrushchev was fairly tolerant of both national communist and polycentric movements that favored China.

Throughout the 1950s, Khrushchev repeatedly admitted that it was legitimate for other states not to imitate precisely the Soviet model for building a socialist society. Instead, as long as leaders of other communist states adhered to certain basic prerequisites, such as a dictatorship of a Marxist-Leninist party dedicated to nationalization of industry and collectivization of agriculture, they were free to adapt their institutions in accord with their idiosyncratic domestic characteristics (a phenomenon known as "national communism").[60] For example, in an attempt to heal the rift between the Soviet Union and Yugoslavia that was created during the Stalin years, Khrushchev agreed to recognize that "questions of internal organization . . . and of different forms of socialist development are solely the concern of individual countries."[61] Or as Khrushchev asserted at the Twentieth Party Congress in 1956, there were "different roads to socialism" that were equally legitimate.[62]

Khrushchev was particularly accepting with regards to Chinese institutional innovations (as was Stalin).[63] The CPSU, for example, "decided to be careful in criticizing the rapid and enforced collectivization of agriculture on which Mao embarked in early 1955 against Soviet advice. The

58. All in Goldstein, "Sino-Soviet Alliance," 18.
59. Chen Jian, *Mao's China and the Cold War* (Chapel Hill: University of North Carolina Press, 2001), 9.
60. Lowenthal, *World Communism*, 38; Zagoria, *Sino-Soviet Conflict*, 59–61.
61. Lowenthal, *World Communism*, 16–17.
62. In Zagoria, *Sino-Soviet Conflict*, 53.
63. Ibid., 90–95, 113–115; Pleshakov, "Nikita Khrushchev and Sino-Soviet Relations," 232; Goldstein, "Nationalism and Internationalism," 235; Goldstein, "Sino-Soviet Alliance," 14, 22.

'excesses' that the Chinese committed [were] interpreted as signs of their eagerness in building socialism, according to Soviet foreign ministry analysts. In an era in which the enthusiasm for socialist construction probably was at its all-time high in the Soviet Union . . . the Chinese ardor was a welcome addition to Khrushchev's ebullience."[64]

Similar analysis applies to Khrushchev's attempts to preserve the Soviet Union's position as undisputed head of the international communist movement. Khrushchev, in fact, renounced "the claim to total subordination of all Communist parties and governments to centralistic Soviet discipline and [instead recognized] their formal 'equality.'"[65] As early as October 1954, the Soviet press referred to the Socialist Bloc "led by the Soviet Union *and* People's China."[66] In 1956, Khrushchev dissolved the Cominform, which was an instrument used by Stalin to discipline the international communist movement. By 1957, "Khrushchev accorded Mao and the CCP a privileged position among foreign communist parties . . . [to the point where] Khrushchev treated the CCP as co-equal with the CPSU" within the international communist movement.[67] Although the Chinese were at times critical of Moscow's "big-power chauvinism" toward other members of the international communist alliance, in 1956 and 1957 they were pleased by the direction that Soviet policies were taking on issues of both national communism and polycentrism, and they continued to assert that the Soviet Union remained the head of international communism.[68]

Thus from 1949 to 1958 mutual dedication to Marxism-Leninism by Soviet and Chinese decision makers was much more of a source of cooperation between the two groups than it was a source of division. Again, I do not deny that the specific properties of Marxism-Leninism, including the hierarchical nature of international communism, and the effects of geography eventually contributed to a substantial worsening of Sino-Soviet relations. These factors, however, were clearly not a sufficient cause of Sino-Soviet hostility. If they were, why the substantial, in some ways unprecedented, cooperation between the Soviet Union and PRC for most of the 1950s? It was only after Mao's domestic radicalization in the late 1950s that the divisive effects of Marxism-Leninism and the effects of geography superseded the forces working for cooperation between the two communist great powers. Domestic-ideological changes in China therefore should be viewed as the root cause of the Sino-Soviet schism.

64. Westad, introduction to *Brothers in Arms,* 17; Pleshakov, "Nikita Khrushchev and Sino-Soviet Relations," 232.
65. Lowenthal, *World Communism,* 45. This devolution of authority within the international communist movement was a tendency known as polycentrism.
66. Ibid., 9.
67. Garver, "Review Article," 208.
68. Chen, *Mao's China and the Cold War,* 70, 151, 153–155, 159.

MAO'S IDEOLOGICAL RADICALIZATION AND THE
ORIGINS OF THE SINO-SOVIET SPLIT

Before 1958, one of the core features that united the leadership of the Communist Party of China was a commitment to applying the Soviet model of socialist development, with some relatively minor changes, to their state.[69] This consensus, however, broke down in the late 1950s due to the effects of the two most important domestic developments in China from 1956 to 1960: the Hundred Flowers campaign of 1956 and the Great Leap Forward of 1958.

The central motivating factor for the Hundred Flowers campaign was Mao's belief that socialism had emerged victorious over capitalism in China. With this victory, the intensity of the class struggle in China was substantially reduced, and thus the CCP's use of highly coercive policies was no longer needed to push China in a socialist direction.[70] Instead persuasion and the contending of different socialist ideas, including criticisms of state policies, were now believed to be the best means for socialist advancement.[71]

The Hundred Flowers program failed miserably from the CCP's perspective. Criticisms of the CCP went well beyond critiques of specific individuals or policies. Instead, the entire socialist system in China came under attack. Organized opposition and student protests against the CCP became increasingly common. The party's hold on power as a result became more insecure.[72]

In order to restore party control and authority in the wake of the Hundred Flowers debacle, the CCP leadership launched in the summer of 1957 an "anti-rightist" campaign. Many individuals who opposed the dictatorship of the CCP were jailed, and many party members who proposed liberalizing policies within the CCP were censured or expelled.[73] The "anti-rightist" campaign was so successful that by the Third Plenum in September-October 1957, party leaders believed that the damage of the Hundred Flowers experiment had been undone and the leading role of the party had been restored.[74]

---

69. Teiwes, "Establishment and Consolidation of the New Regime," 57–58; Chen and Yang, "Chinese Politics and the Collapse of the Sino-Soviet Alliance," 261.

70. Frederick C. Teiwes, *Politics and Purges in China: Rectification and the Decline of Party Norms, 1950–1965* (London: M. E. Sharpe, 1993), 167, 185, 214. Mao did not see the Hundred Flowers campaign as an alternative to the Soviet model of socialist development. Indeed, successful emulation of the USSR was largely responsible for Mao's belief that by 1957 socialism had defeated capitalism in China (167, 182).

71. Merle Goldman, "The Party and Intellectuals," in *Cambridge History of China*, ed. MacFarquhar and Fairbank, 14:243.

72. Ibid., 254.

73. Teiwes, *Politics and Purges in China*, 217, 220, 229, 256, 257.

74. Ibid., 257.

The six months following the Third Plenum marked a critical turning point in Chinese domestic and international politics. In this period, two different visions for the future of Chinese society, that is, two different ideological factions, emerged among the CCP leadership.[75] On one side were those individuals who were largely satisfied with the status quo after the victory of the anti-rightist campaign of 1957. With the restoration of party control by the fall of this year, this faction wanted the further development of a "centralized, highly articulated Party and state bureaucracy and moderate economic policies."[76] This group was initially led by Zhou Enlai and Chen Yun, and eventually by Defense Minister Peng Dehuai.[77]

The other faction, which was a majority group led by Mao, prescribed very different policies. The principal lesson that Mao and his followers drew from the failure of the Hundred Flowers campaign was not that it had been a mistake to decrease the coercive policies of the state, but that it was an error to do so before the Chinese people were sufficiently indoctrinated with the correct ideological beliefs. To this view, the Chinese socialist revolution could still be advanced, but the people would have to be sufficiently radicalized first.

Thus instead of desiring to preserve the status quo created in the wake of the anti-rightist campaign of 1957, Mao wanted to move China in a much more revolutionary direction. Indeed, Mao believed that the CCP *had* to further radicalize Chinese society in order to preserve the socialist revolution. The failure of the Hundred Flowers campaign had taught Mao that the anti-socialist forces in China remained strong. To try to maintain the status quo without eradicating this opposition would be, to Mao, ultimately untenable. Unless Chinese society were further radicalized through strategies of "continuous revolution," socialism in China would eventually be forced to retreat.[78] This thinking marked the first major step toward the policies that became known as the "Great Leap Forward." After beating back those CCP leaders (initially led by Zhou Enlai until his capitulation to Mao's position) who opposed the "rash advance" of China's political and economic policies, the CCP publicly launched the Leap in early May 1958, though this decision was privately decided upon months earlier.[79]

75. Zagoria, *Sino-Soviet Conflict*, 68–69, 85–86.
76. Teiwes, *Politics and Purges in China*, 257.
77. Ibid., 301–302; Kenneth Lieberthal, "The Great Leap Forward and the Split in the Yenan Leadership," in *Cambridge History of China*, ed. MacFarquhar and Fairbank, 14:308; Chen, *Mao's China and the Cold War*, 66.
78. Teiwes, "Establishment and Consolidation of the New Regime," 141–142; Lieberthal, "Great Leap Forward and the Split in the Yenan Leadership," 303–304; Chen, *Mao's China and the Cold War*, 72, 174, 202.
79. In Chen, *Mao's China and the Cold War*, 70; David Bachman, *Bureaucracy, Economy, and Leadership in China: The Institutional Origins of the Great Leap Forward* (New York: Cambridge University Press, 1991), xxi.

The primary goals of the Great Leap Forward were to transform China economically, politically, and ideologically at record speed. Toward these ends, Chinese citizens were divided into "People's Communes," which were a new organizational form that served as both governmental bodies and economic units. The communes were designed to induce massive labor mobilization, income redistribution, the elimination of virtually all remaining forms of private property in favor of economic collectivization, and large-scale ideological indoctrination of the people in order to create more selfless and self-disciplined individuals.[80]

The new goals, political strategies, and organizational methods associated with the Leap came into conflict with the core policy preferences of the Peng Dehuai faction within the CCP. Instead of a "centralized, highly articulated Party and state bureaucracy" determining political and economic policies, the Leap "necessitated organization shorn of bureaucracy that could be linked directly to the people, the motive force of the new strategy. In work methods ad hoc adaptation to rapidly changing circumstances was preferred to careful planning . . . and this could be better provided by local Party cadres . . . than by remote planners in Beijing." Consequently, the Leap resulted in "major decentralization" as "vast administrative powers were ceded by the central government to provincial and lower level authorities" (Beijing, or at least Mao, retained control over general policy and political and economic targets). This change both represented a significant threat to vested party interests, and was substantially different from the Soviet model of development.[81]

At the same time that Mao was initiating the policies of the Great Leap Forward, he was attempting to increase his own authority through the development of a cult of personality.[82] Beginning "early in 1958 . . . Mao was described as a 'great prophet,'" and his leadership was equated with that of the CCP. "By the end of 1959 . . . Mao's ideology was being increasingly equated with Marxism-Leninism and sometimes given priority over it."[83] Mao's increasing power associated with the development of his personality cult violated the CCP's long-standing norm of collective leadership, and pushed a number of CCP officials to offer increasing resistance to Mao as the latter's leadership style more and more resembled that of Stalin.[84]

---

80. Zagoria, *Sino-Soviet Conflict*, 66, 77–78, 85; Teiwes, *Politics and Purges in China*, chap. 8; Lieberthal, "Great Leap Forward and the Split in the Yenan Leadership"; Nicholas R. Lardy, "The Chinese Economy under Stress, 1958–1965," in *Cambridge History of China*, ed. MacFarquhar and Fairbank, 14:360–397.
81. Teiwes, *Politics and Purges in China*, 257, 262, 261.
82. The two outcomes were not unrelated. Opposition within the CCP to the Leap pushed Mao to consolidate his power in 1958 (Chen, *Mao's China and the Cold War*, 66).
83. Zagoria, *Sino-Soviet Conflict*, 103; Teiwes, *Politics and Purges in China*, 319.
84. Teiwes, *Politics and Purges in China*, 319, 342–343; Li Zhisui, *The Private Life of Chairman Mao: The Memoirs of Mao's Personal Physician* (New York: Random House: 1994), 183. Mao

Almost all observers, in China, the Soviet Union, and elsewhere, recognized that Mao's domestic changes associated with the Great Leap Forward and the development of his personality cult were revolutionary changes from previous positions.[85] Chinese journals, for example, claimed that Mao had produced a unique and revolutionary variant of Marxism-Leninism, and CCP officials asserted that the policies of the Leap would allow China to build communism at a record pace.[86] These statements clearly implied that all other variants of Marxism-Leninism were not only very different from, but inferior to, the institutions created by Mao during the Great Leap Forward.

A critical implication of these domestic developments was that they opened an important ideological divide with the Soviet Union that had heretofore not existed. In fact, in the late 1950s Mao was institutionalizing domestic forms that Soviet leaders were explicitly condemning in their state. While the Soviets were developing a highly bureaucratized, centralized system of political and economic development, China was greatly decentralizing policy implementation and basing overall political development on the principles of "continuous revolution." Soviet leaders denounced Mao's theory of permanent revolution as a revival of "Trotskyism," which was a set of ideological beliefs that continued to be anathema in the USSR.[87]

Perhaps even more important, while Khrushchev and other Soviet leaders had staked much of their legitimacy on denouncing and preventing a return to the tyrannical system of governance practiced by Stalin, Mao in the late 1950s was institutionalizing the very type of personality cult that the CPSU continued to repudiate. Consequently, by the end of the 1950s "power in the Soviet state was diverging dramatically from the increasingly personalized control of Mao Zedong in China."[88] By implementing ideological forms in China that Soviet leaders explicitly condemned in their state, Mao "introduced an element of [ideological] discord" into Sino-Soviet relations that had previously not existed.[89]

---

recognized this source of friction within the CCP leadership. At the Lushan Conference in July-August 1959, he stated that CCP officials were claiming that Mao had "reached Stalin's later years," was "despotic and dictatorial," "biased in view and faith," and refused to give the CCP "freedom" and "democracy" (all in Teiwes, *Politics and Purges in China,* 319).

85. Goldstein, "Nationalism and Internationalism," 239–246; Nakajima, "Foreign Relations," 285; Teiwes, *Politics and Purges in China,* 319, 326–328, 342; Li, *Private Life of Chairman Mao,* 115, 119, 181, 281–282; Westad, introduction to *Brothers in Arms,* 23; Gurtov and Hwang, *China under Threat,* 75; Vladislav M. Zubok, "Deng Xiaoping and the Sino-Soviet Split, 1956–1963," *Cold War International History Project Bulletin* 10 (March 1998), virtual archive, 4. http://wwics.si.edu/index.cfm?topic_id=1409&fuseaction=library.Collection.

86. Zagoria, *Sino-Soviet Conflict,* 78, 98.

87. Ibid., 79.

88. Pleshakov, "Nikita Khrushchev and Sino-Soviet Relations," 232.

89. Zagoria, *Sino-Soviet Conflict,* 86; also 78.

This book's argument predicts that the emerging ideological divide between Chinese and Soviet leaders that was created by Mao's domestic radicalization beginning in the spring of 1958 would result in increasing perceptions of threats to these groups' domestic and international interests. The evidence supports this prediction, especially from the Chinese perspective. As discussed, before 1958 Mao viewed the Sino-Soviet alliance as an important support to the CCP's domestic objectives. However, once Mao rejected both the Soviet model of socialist development and Khrushchev's destalinization campaign for the policies of the Great Leap Forward and the development of his own cult of personality, respectively, the Chinese dictator's fears of the subversive effects resulting from close association with the USSR increased substantially. In the wake of Mao's "unfolding plans for China's domestic transformation," as Steven Goldstein explains, the Chinese dictator "came to believe that close alliance with the Soviet Union carried with it [the danger of] . . . the importation of harmful ideas" (i.e., the danger of ideological subversion).[90] Consequently, after 1957 Mao viewed close association with the USSR as a much greater danger to his domestic interests than he had for the previous decades.

Also coincident with Mao's ideological changes in 1958 was a growing mistrust of Soviet international intentions. Until the launch of the Great Leap Forward and the development of Mao's cult of personality, the Chinese dictator tended to view the Soviet Union's international objectives in a largely positive light, and similarly, the Sino-Soviet alliance as an important support of China's security.[91]

These beliefs underwent a dramatic and relatively swift reversal by the late spring of 1958. No instance better illustrates Mao's newfound animosity toward the Soviet Union than an exchange between Mao, Khrushchev, and their representatives in late May and early June 1958. At this time, Khrushchev asked the Chinese permission to build a radio station on Chinese territory that would allow the Soviets to communicate better with their nuclear-powered submarines in the Pacific Ocean. This was not an unreasonable request given the terms of the Sino-Soviet alliance, the great level of military and economic cooperation that existed between China and the Soviet Union for the previous decade, and the two states' mutual enmity to the United States. In November 1957, the two states had even reached an agreement stating that they would closely cooperate in developing air and naval forces in East Asia.[92] According to

---

90. Goldstein, "Nationalism and Internationalism," 240. See also 241, 244, 246; Westad, introduction to *Brothers in Arms*, 23; Gurtov and Hwang, *China under Threat*, 75; Lewis and Xue, *China Builds the Bomb*, 53.
91. Gurtov and Hwang, *China under Threat*, 73–74; Goldstein, "Sino-Soviet Alliance," 17, 24.
92. Chen, *Mao's China and the Cold War*, 73.

Khrushchev's memoirs, Soviet leaders "fully expected the Chinese to cooperate" on this issue.[93]

The Soviets were therefore taken aback by the vehemence with which Mao rejected this request. He described it as an insult to China's sovereignty, and refused even to discuss the issue with the Soviet ambassador to China, Pavel Yudin.[94]

Khrushchev was so concerned by Mao's reaction that he immediately flew to China to try to smooth things over. Throughout Khrushchev's meetings with Mao, the Chinese dictator treated Khrushchev with anger and contempt. When Khrushchev suggested creating a joint naval fleet to counter America's, Mao accused Khrushchev of attempting to compromise China's control of its own territory. Khrushchev responded by making the more modest request of allowing Soviet submarines to refuel and take shore leave at Chinese ports. Once again, Mao reacted angrily to the Soviet leader, and he even compared the Soviets to the imperialist powers: "We don't want you to come to our country. . . . The British, Japanese, and other foreigners who stayed in our country for a long time have already been driven away by us, Comrade Khrushchev. . . . We do not want anyone to use our land to achieve their own purposes anymore."[95]

Mao's ideological radicalization beginning in 1958—and thus the emerging ideological divide between China and the Soviet Union after this year—was the root cause of Mao's intense suspicions of the USSR exhibited in these exchanges. (Ideological distance, not content, was responsible for these changes because Mao's domestic objectives did not necessitate specific foreign policy prescriptions calling for a rupture with the USSR.)[96]

---

93. Nikita Khrushchev, *Khrushchev Remembers: The Last Testament* (Boston: Little, Brown, 1974), 258.
94. MacFarquhar, *Great Leap Forward*, 94–96; William Taubman, "Khrushchev vs. Mao: A Preliminary Sketch of the Role of Personality in the Sino-Soviet Split," *Cold War International History Project Bulletin* 8–9 (Winter 1996/1997), virtual archive, 3–4.
http://wwics.si.edu/index.cfm?topic_id=1409&fuseaction=library.Collection.
95. In Taubman, "Khrushchev vs. Mao," 4. Mao made similar statements in private settings. For example, he told his physician and frequent confidant on this subject that "[the Soviets'] real purpose is to control us" (in Li, *Private Life of Chairman Mao*, 261; also Garver, "Review Article," 205).
96. Some scholars claim that Mao's fears of the Soviet Union led to the Great Leap Forward in order to increase China's relative power position, not the reverse as I claim (cf. Christensen, *Useful Adversaries*, chap. 6). This view is problematic for a number of reasons. In the first place, Mao launched the Leap before his intense suspicions of the Soviet Union became evident. The CCP opted for the Leap early in 1958; Mao's intense suspicions of the USSR did not surface until the late spring. This does not mean that Mao never had negative views of the Soviet Union before this date, only that his attitudes remained more positive than negative. Second, because both Soviet behavior and capabilities were largely constant in 1957–58, these variables cannot adequately explain the revolution in Mao's attitudes toward the USSR in this period. Third, if Mao's primary goal of the Leap was to stimulate China's economy to counter a Soviet power-political threat, it was grossly inefficacious. Not only did the Leap and its consequences lead to a substantial weakening of China's economy as Soviet

Three facts justify this conclusion. First, the timing of the split strongly points to the centrality of ideological changes in China as the key to the deterioration of Sino-Soviet relations. At the time that Mao's views of the Soviet Union were changing in the spring of 1958 from seeing the USSR as an important support of China's domestic and international interests to viewing it as both a subversive and power-political threat, only domestic-ideological variables in China had sufficiently altered to account for this revolutionary shift. In fact, other than domestic developments in China, the forces working for the continuation of very close relations between the PRC and USSR remained quite strong in this period. Not only was Khrushchev "dealing with China in an extremely generous fashion" at this time, but America's power in the Far East was increasing.[97] Power-political variables were therefore pushing for a strengthening of the Sino-Soviet alliance at the very time that Mao was weakening it.

Second, documentary evidence from the Chinese and Soviet archives points squarely at Mao's domestic radicalization starting in 1958 as the root cause of Sino-Soviet tensions. For example, according to a secret report written in 1959 by Mikhail Suslov (a senior member of the Soviet Politburo), the increasing frictions between the Soviet Union and China were "largely explained by the atmosphere of the cult of personality of . . . Mao Zedong."[98] A top secret survey of "The Political, Economic, and International Standing of the PRC" that the Foreign Ministry prepared for Khrushchev in 1959 to analyze the emerging differences between the two communist powers reached similar conclusions. The report "devoted considerable attention to the Sino-Soviet ideological quarrels that began to surface during the Great Leap Forward" as a key cause of the conflict.[99]

Evidence from the Chinese archives points to similar conclusions. Primary source documents indicate that Mao's ideological changes were the key cause of the CCP's decisions both to adopt much more militant foreign policies after 1957 (which resulted in substantial levels of mistrust and hostility toward the USSR), and to challenge the Soviet Union for leadership of the international communist movement.

Until the end of 1957, top CCP officials, including Mao, had followed the Soviet Union's lead and adhered to a strategy of peaceful coexistence with non-socialist states, including America (the Bandung Line of foreign policy). After this year, however, China's key decision makers abandoned

---

economic aid was abruptly withdrawn in response, but these policies helped to make the USSR into an enemy at a time of continuing Sino-American hostility.

97. Garver, "Review Article," 207.

98. In "A New 'Cult of Personality': Suslov's Secret Report on Mao, Khrushchev, and Sino-Soviet Tensions, December 1959," *Cold War International History Project,* virtual archive, 2. http://wwics.si.edu/index.cfm?topic_id=1409&fuseaction=library.Collection.

99. Kramer, "Soviet Foreign Ministry Appraisal of Sino-Soviet Relations," 3.

these positions in favor of much more belligerent international policies that "called for maximum political and military pressure on the West all over the globe."[100] The Taiwan Straits crisis of 1958 and the Sino-Indian border clashes of 1959 were expressions of China's newfound international aggressiveness coincident with the Great Leap Forward, as was Mao's support and encouragement after 1961 of military aggression by communist North Vietnam against the south.

Archival evidence indicates that Mao's domestic move to the left beginning in 1958 was in large part responsible for China's increasing international belligerency.[101] Most important, Mao's ideological radicalization led to a significant increase in his fears for China's safety. The farther China advanced along the road to communism, and thus the greater the ideological distance separating China from rival groups, the more he anticipated efforts to stop this progress by international and domestic enemies of the revolution. On several occasions in early 1958, the chairman asserted: "It is destined that our socialist revolution and reconstruction will not be smooth sailing. We should be prepared to deal with many serious threats facing us both internationally and domestically."[102]

The belief that the increasing ideological distance dividing China from the imperialist powers was making conflict with these states much more likely created incentives for Mao to abandon the more moderate foreign policies of the preceding five years in favor of preventive hostilities that could begin at times and places of China's choosing. Mao, for example, told the Eighth Party Congress in late May 1958 that U.S. leaders "looked down upon us [because] we have not yet completely shown and proven our strength." Thus the best way to protect China's security against the imperialists was to "demonstrate our boldness" by adopting more aggressive international policies.[103]

Mao's increasing international belligerency after 1957 contributed to Sino-Soviet tensions because the Soviet Union in important ways refused to match Mao's aggressiveness (the Taiwan Straits crisis of 1958 was an important exception to this tendency). Unlike Mao, Khrushchev in the late 1950s continued to insist that peaceful coexistence, and even some

---

100. Zagoria, *Sino-Soviet Conflict*, 150.

101. Westad, introduction to *Brothers in Arms*, 31; Chen and Yang, "Chinese Politics and the Collapse of the Sino-Soviet Alliance," 246, 276–277; Goldstein, "Nationalism and Internationalism," 227, 246; Goldstein, "Sino-Soviet Alliance," 25, 38, 42–44; Chen Jian, "China's Involvement in the Vietnam War, 1964–69," *China Quarterly* no. 142 (June 1995): 361.

102. In Chen, *Mao's China and the Cold War*, 174.

103. In Zhang, *Deterrence and Strategic Culture*, 229. See also Chen, *Mao's China and the Cold War*, 173; Zagoria, *Sino-Soviet Conflict*, 154; see also MacFarquhar, *Great Leap Forward*, 73; Garver, "Review Article," 209. A threatening international environment had the additional benefit for Mao of helping to mobilize Chinese society in order to better realize the domestic goals of the Great Leap Forward. See Chen, "China's Involvement in the Vietnam War," 361; Christensen, *Useful Adversaries*, chap. 6; Chen, *Mao's China and the Cold War*, 180, 183.

form of détente with the United States (including a possible nuclear test ban treaty between the superpowers), was both desirable and possible. These important policy disagreements with the Soviet Union led the Chinese dictator to doubt the sincerity of Khrushchev's commitment to socialist ideals at home and abroad, and as a consequence the utility of the Sino-Soviet alliance for China.[104] Thus differences in Chinese and Soviet "national interests" were indeed critical to the origins of the split, but these differences were primarily a product of Mao's ideological shift to the left in 1958. Until this time, the Chinese and Soviets agreed on international objectives more than they disagreed.

Documents from the Chinese archives also indicate that Mao's decision to challenge Khrushchev for leadership of the world communist movement was not a rationalization of an underlying power-political conflict or the byproduct of the triumph of realpolitik over ideological concerns. Instead, China's rivalry with the USSR in this area was at root a product of the emerging ideological gap dividing them. "It is clear [from internal documents]," as one scholar of Chinese politics explains, "that for Mao [ideology] was not some sort of rationalization added on after calculations of power . . . had been made. [Instead, ideology] was the key to history and to successful political action." "The issues that were the substance of the ideological debates between the CCP and the CPSU [in the late 1950s and early 1960s] were debated at length, for days on end, month after month, by [Chinese] Politburo or central leader conferences."[105] It was these ideological differences with the Soviets that pushed Mao to challenge the USSR for leadership of the international communist alliance because after 1957 he greatly disagreed with the Soviets about how best to promote socialist revolutions at home and abroad. Without Mao's ideological shift to the left in 1957–58, it is likely that China would have continued its policies of the previous decade and supported Moscow's leadership of international communism, albeit jointly with the PRC as Khrushchev seemed to be advocating at this time.

The third set of evidence that supports the claim that the domestic-ideological changes associated with the Great Leap Forward were the key source of the origins of the Sino-Soviet conflict is the fact that primarily only those CCP leaders who supported the Leap viewed the Soviet Union in increasingly threatening terms. This variation indicates perhaps most powerfully that neither Chinese leaders' perceptions of threat nor their understandings of their ideological relationships with the Soviet Union were epiphenomenal of the two states' relative power positions.

---

104. Herbert J. Ellison, introduction to *The Sino-Soviet Conflict: A Global Perspective*, ed. Herbert J. Ellison (Seattle: University of Washington Press, 1982), xvi–xvii; Lowenthal, *World Communism*, 149; Zagoria, *Sino-Soviet Conflict*, 299.
105. Garver, "Review Article," 198; Chen, *Mao's China and the Cold War*, 6–9.

Those CCP members whose ideological ties to the Soviet Union remained the strongest tended to continue to push for close strategic and economic cooperation with it.[106] (Mao's principal domestic competitors and Soviet leaders were both committed to centralized political control, high levels of bureaucratization, moderate economic policies, and the rejection of a Stalinist system of governance in favor of collective decision making.) For example, Mao's key domestic opponent, Peng Dehuai, who was openly critical of both the radical policies of the Great Leap Forward and Mao's growing personality cult at the expense of collective leadership, personally apprised Khrushchev about his misgivings concerning Mao's domestic policies (and Khrushchev allegedly encouraged Peng to return to China to oppose Mao).[107] Peng even went so far as to assert repeatedly at a party conference at Lushan in 1959 that if the policies of the Great Leap Forward continued, "a Hungarian incident [will occur] in China and it [will be] necessary to invite Soviet troops in" to restore communism in China.[108]

Peng was not alone in his sympathy to the USSR.[109] Perhaps most surprising, moderates in the Chinese military remained through the first half of 1958 "a virtual carrier of Soviet influence which had maintained intimate links with Moscow and whose strategic vision required dependence on Soviet aid and cooperation."[110] If issues of relative power and differences in national interests were the critical causes of the Sino-Soviet split, we would expect the organization most responsible for China's safety to have been one of the bodies most opposed to close association with the USSR. The opposite, however, was the case.

Mao himself recognized the ideological connection between his opponents within the CCP and the Soviet Union, as well as the dangers this linkage created for his domestic interests. At the Lushan Conference, the

106. Teiwes, *Politics and Purges in China*, 294, 326–327, 334–335; Zagoria, *Sino-Soviet Conflict*, 371; Westad, introduction to *Brothers in Arms*, 24–27; Lieberthal, "Great Leap Forward and the Split in the Yenan Leadership," 308; Zhang, *Deterrence and Strategic Culture*, 231–232; Gurtov and Hwang, *China under Threat*, 71.

107. Teiwes, *Politics and Purges in China*, 311, 314, 328; Lieberthal, "Great Leap Forward and the Split in the Yenan Leadership," 295.

108. In Teiwes, *Politics and Purges in China*, 313. Peng's and his associates' fears of abandonment were also significantly lower than Mao's. The former believed that they could rely on the Soviet Union for an effective nuclear deterrent (Gurtov and Hwang, *China under Threat*, 71).

109. On the high-ranking officials in the CCP who expressed opposition to the Leap, see Parris H. Chang, *Power and Policy in China* (University Park: Penn State University Press, 1979), 77–78, 115–117; Avery Goldstein, *From Bandwagon to Balance-of-Power Politics: Structural Constraints and Politics in China, 1949–1978* (Stanford: Stanford University Press, 1991), 88.

110. Goldstein, "Sino-Soviet Alliance," 25; Chang, *Power and Policy in China*, 113. In a May–July 1958 conference of the Central Military Commission, Mao criticized those military leaders who possessed "blind faith in foreign dogmas and in the Soviet Union" (in Lewis and Xue, *China Builds the Bomb*, 71). Later Mao and other CCP leaders claimed that at Lushan Peng's actions were those of a "Soviet agent" and a "coup attempt supported by [his Soviet] friends" (in Chen, *Mao's China and the Cold War*, 79, 81).

chairman railed against those Chinese "Khrushchevs [who] oppose or are skeptical about . . . people's communes and [the] Great Leap Forward" and who try to take "advantage of a difficult time when the Party is under a double attack both internally and externally." A few months later, Mao denounced those Chinese politicians who would "betray one's fatherland by conspiring with foreign countries [viz., the USSR]. . . . We won't allow Chinese party members to sabotage the Party . . . by encouraging one segment of the people to oppose another segment."[111]

The ideological links between the Soviet Union and Mao's domestic opponents not only increased the incentives for Mao to end China's close strategic relationship with the Soviet Union so as to reduce "Soviet political influence on the domestic political process within China,"[112] but to initiate large-scale purges of his domestic rivals. During the first half of 1958, as many as one million party members were expelled or put on probation. Following the Lushan Conference, upward of twenty percent of cadres were dismissed. High-ranking party officials were not spared in these purges, including, after Lushan, Peng and his key associates, PLA Chief of Staff Huang Kecheng, Vice Minister of Foreign Affairs Zhang Wentian, and Hunan First Secretary Zhou Xiaozhou. Because the ties between China's military and the Soviet Union remained particularly strong, Mao was especially aggressive in bringing the PLA under his control.[113] If one of these rival groups that opposed Mao's domestic radicalization had governed China, it is likely that Sino-Soviet cooperation would have continued, despite potential differences in "national interests" and the potentially divisive qualities of both Marxism-Leninism and international communism.

EPILOGUE

Although the evolution of Sino-Soviet relations after the functional termination of their alliance at the end of the 1950s is beyond the scope of this chapter, a few words on this subject are in order.

Despite the fact that the beginnings of Sino-Soviet hostilities were a product of Mao's ideological radicalization starting in 1958, there are a number of important dimensions of Chinese-Soviet hostilities after this year that my argument cannot explain. Most important, the level of threat

111. Both in Teiwes, *Politics and Purges in China*, 328; Chang, *Power and Policy in China*, 114; Goldstein, *From Bandwagon to Balance-of-Power Politics*, 88.
112. Goldstein, "Nationalism and Internationalism," 240; Gurtov and Hwang, *China under Threat*, 75.
113. On these points, see Teiwes, *Politics and Purges in China*, 267, 274, 302, 343; MacFarquhar, *Great Leap Forward*, 63; Goldstein, "Sino-Soviet Alliance," 25; Chang, *Power and Policy in China*, 78, 120–121.

that developed between the PRC and the Soviet Union in the 1960s was disproportionate to the ideological divide that was created between them. Despite the very important ideological changes associated with the Great Leap Forward and the development of Mao's personality cult, the two states continued to share many important ideological similarities. Most notable, both states remained dictatorships governed by Marxist-Leninist parties that were dedicated to socialist economic and political objectives. These continuing ideological similarities were reinforced by the fact that by any objective indicator, China and the USSR remained ideologically closer to one another than they did to the United States. As a result of these facts, there should have been substantial countervailing ideological pressures that limited the scope of Sino-Soviet tensions despite their increasing ideological differences after 1957.

This was not the case, however. Within a few years of the launching of the Great Leap Forward, Mao came to view the Soviet system as fundamentally degenerate. In his mind, the Soviet Union had switched from a socialist to an imperialist state that was guilty of "revising, emasculating, and betraying" the most important tenets of Marxism-Leninism.[114] This view not only increased Mao's feelings of hostility toward the USSR, but made the Chinese dictator more determined than ever to push forward as rapidly as possible the socialist revolution in China, lest it follow a similar degenerative path.[115] This thinking played an important role in the genesis of the Cultural Revolution, which resulted in a set of policies that only increased the ideological differences—and thus the perceptions of threat—dividing Soviet and Chinese leaders.

The Soviets countered with an ideological attack of their own, accusing the "leadership" of China in 1960 of succumbing to the pathologies of "leftism, sectarianism, and dogmatism," and of losing "their Marxist-Leninist bearings, veering off into Left-wing deviationism."[116]

Paralleling these views of ideological degeneracy were progressively worsening state-to-state relations. Throughout the 1960s, the Sino-Soviet border became increasingly militarized, and the two states fought a number of border skirmishes. By the end of this decade, many key Soviet and especially Chinese leaders came to view one another as a greater danger to their interests than liberal, capitalist America.[117]

114. In Zagoria, *Sino-Soviet Conflict*, 299.
115. Lieberthal, "Great Leap Forward and the Split in the Yenan Leadership," 296, 319, 352–353; Teiwes, *Politics and Purges in China*, 388–389.
116. In Zagoria, *Sino-Soviet Conflict*, 323–324.
117. In support of my argument, however, are the facts of how long it took for the PRC to align with the United States against the Soviet Union and how difficult it was for the former to do so. Even after the USSR's invasion of Czechoslovakia in 1968 and a large-scale Soviet military buildup on China's border in the same period, CCP leaders' ideological animosity to the United States precluded a geopolitical move toward America for another three years. Only with the purging of Chinese radicals in the 1970s was China able to align

To understand the depths to which Sino-Soviet relations sunk, we must look primarily to the particular qualities of Marxism-Leninism and the effects of geography. The perfectionist nature of Marxism-Leninism and the hierarchical nature of the international communist alliance made cooperative relations between the Soviet Union and PRC much more tenuous than among states in other ideological communities. As many scholars have noted, the perfectionism of Marxism-Leninism contributed to the creation of fierce sectarian battles, and international communism's hierarchical structure created another important area of zero-sum competition between the two communist states. Geography added fuel to the fire by creating additional conflicts of interest and exacerbating the effects of the security dilemma. Moreover, the two sets of variables were very likely feeding into one another: the greater the sectarian differences between Chinese and Soviet variants of Marxism-Leninism, the greater the perceived conflicts of interest and threat; the greater the perceived conflicts of interest and threat, the more ideologically degenerate the other communist state appeared to be. All these outcomes are problematic for my argument.

Nevertheless, it is worth reemphasizing that the increasing ideological differences dividing Soviet and Chinese leaders resulting from Mao's substantial domestic changes beginning in 1958 were the key precondition before differences in "national interests" created by geography or the divisive effects of Marxism-Leninism had a substantial negative impact on Sino-Soviet relations. Before the initiation of the Great Leap Forward and the creation of Mao's personality cult, mutual dedication to Marxism-Leninism was a much greater force for cooperation than conflict between the two communist powers. However, once the Sino-Soviet conflict began due to Mao's ideological radicalization, the divisive qualities of Marxism-Leninism and the effects of geography pushed China and the Soviet Union to levels of animosity well beyond what an argument based solely on the degree of ideological differences dividing them can explain. In sum, this book's causal logic explains both the origins of the Sino-Soviet alliance and the beginnings of their rift; realist and other ideological arguments explain the depths to which Sino-Soviet relations eventually deteriorated.

---

with its primary ideological enemy of the previous quarter-century. Westad, introduction to *Brothers in Arms*, 30; Camilleri, *Chinese Foreign Policy*, 142, 164–167, 173–174; Carol Lee Hamrin and Jonathan D. Pollack, "The Sino-American Alignment," in *China's Cooperative Relationships*, ed. Harding, 11–14; Kenneth Lieberthal, "The Background in Chinese Politics," in *Sino-Soviet Conflict*, ed. Ellison, 9–12, 17–22.

[6]

The 1980s and the End of the Cold War

This chapter examines the factors that led to the end of the Cold War between the United States and the Soviet Union in the late 1980s. The transformation of the relationship between these two states, in terms of both the depth of the change and the shortness of time in which it took place, was remarkable. In the early 1980s, leaders in both superpowers believed their counterparts to be highly aggressive and duplicitous. In one particularly vitriolic moment in 1983, President Ronald Reagan described the Soviet Union as an "evil empire" and the "focus of evil in the modern world."[1] Even more alarmingly, several Soviet leaders believed at this time that the United States was preparing a preventive nuclear strike against the Soviet Union.[2]

Within five years, however, this dangerous situation had changed dramatically. By the end of the 1980s, the most important decision makers in both superpowers declared both privately and publicly that they believed one another to be trustworthy people who were dedicated to cooperative international objectives. Moreover, both scholars and policy makers agree that the negotiations involved with ending the central disputes associated with the Cold War rivalry, including the unification of Germany and its membership in NATO, were extremely smooth given the stakes involved with these talks.[3] What accounts for this extraordinary transformation in U.S.-Soviet relations?

1. In Raymond Garthoff, *The Great Transition: American-Soviet Relations and the End of the Cold War* (Washington, D.C.: Brookings Institution, 1994), 98.
2. Ibid., 60–62, 138–139; Anatoly S. Chernyaev, *My Six Years with Gorbachev*, trans. and ed. Robert D. English and Elizabeth Tucker (University Park: Penn State University Press, 2000), 16; Vladislav M. Zubok, "Why Did the Cold War End in 1989? Explanations of 'The Turn,'" in *Reviewing the Cold War: Approaches, Interpretations, Theory*, ed. Odd Arne Westad (London: Frank Cass, 2000), 348, 363.
3. William C. Wohlforth, ed., *Cold War Endgame* (University Park: Penn State University

Soviet Foreign Policies

Probably the most straightforward explanation of the revolution in Soviet foreign policies that occurred in the 1980s examines the effects of the Soviet Union's faltering economy. From 1975 until 1985, the USSR's GNP increased by an average of less than 2 percent a year. In the same period, the GNP of the United States grew over one and one half times as fast. By 1986, Soviet defense expenditures were over 15 percent of GNP, and internal debt was 20 percent of GNP. Compounding these problems was the fact that between 1970 and 1982 the costs associated with the USSR's geopolitical position, both in Eastern Europe and around the globe, had more than doubled.[4]

The Soviet Union's substantial economic troubles revealed by these and other variables created powerful incentives for Soviet leaders to retrench internationally, including by significantly reducing military spending and cutting loose the Soviet Union's empire in Eastern Europe. Many scholars, including those operating within the realist tradition, have adopted this argument to explain the end of the Cold War.[5] Without the USSR's economic decline, claim realists, the Cold War would not have ended.

There is important evidence supporting this explanation of Soviet foreign policies in the 1980s. Many Soviet decision makers in this period were acutely aware that the USSR's slowed rate of economic growth and mounting debt demanded that some changes in the Soviet Union's international policies be made. There was widespread agreement that in order to bring commitments more in line with the Soviet Union's declining capabilities, Soviet leaders needed to reduce the USSR's commitments in the Third World, make substantial cuts in the Soviet Union's stockpile of strategic nuclear weapons, scrap obsolete weapons, and, most important, reduce the amount of money spent on defense.[6]

Press, 2003), 21, 35, 42, 84; Derek H. Chollet and James M. Goldgeier, "Once Burned, Twice Shy? The Pause of 1989," and Andrew O. Bennett, "Trust Bursting Out All Over: The Soviet Side of German Unification," both in *Cold War Endgame*, ed. Wohlforth.

4. On these points, see David M. Kotz and Fred Weir, *Revolution from Above: The Demise of the Soviet System* (New York: Routledge, 1997), 24, 32, 43, 76; Stephen G. Brooks and William C. Wohlforth, "Power, Globalization, and the End of the Cold War: Reevaluating a Landmark Case for Ideas," *International Security* 25, no. 1 (Winter 2000/2001): 20; Stephen G. Brooks and William C. Wohlforth, "Economic Constraints and the End of the Cold War," in *Cold War Endgame*, ed. Wohlforth, 277.

5. John J. Mearsheimer, *The Tragedy of Great Power Politics* (New York: W. W. Norton, 2001), 202; Randall L. Schweller and William C. Wohlforth, "Power Test: Evaluating Realism in Response to the End of the Cold War," *Security Studies* 9, no. 3 (Spring 2000): 60–107; Brooks and Wohlforth, "Power, Globalization, and the End of the Cold War."

6. Stephen M. Meyer, "The Sources and Prospects of Gorbachev's New Political Thinking on Security," *International Security* 13, no. 2 (Fall 1988): 124–163; Brooks and Wohlforth, "Economic Constraints and the End of the Cold War"; Brooks and Wohlforth, "Power, Globalization, and the End of the Cold War"; William E. Odom, *The Collapse of the Soviet Military* (New

In 1986, for example, General Secretary Mikhail Gorbachev asserted that a preeminent foreign policy objective of his administration was to achieve far-reaching arms control agreements with the Americans. If the Soviets were unsuccessful in realizing this goal, Gorbachev told the Politburo that the country would "be pulled into an arms race that is beyond our capabilities, and we will lose it because we are at the limit of our capabilities. . . . If a new round [of the arms race] begins, the pressure on our economy will be unbelievable."[7] Key supporters of Gorbachev, including Anatoly Chernyaev (Gorbachev's personal advisor on foreign affairs), Georgi Shakhnazarov, and Vadim Medvedev (deputy head and head of the Socialist Countries Department of the Central Committee, respectively), among others, expressed similar views.[8]

Soviet decision makers who were dedicated to political and economic liberalization, also known as "New Thinkers," were not the only ones who claimed that the Soviet Union's economic woes necessitated important foreign policy changes. Key conservative leaders (or "old thinkers") who remained committed to Marxist-Leninist principles and the Soviet Union's authoritarian political system expressed similar views. For example, Chief of the General Staff Sergei Akhromeyev, who was critical of both Gorbachev and New Thinking, asserted in 1990 that "all who knew the real situation in our state and economy in [the] 1980s understood that Soviet foreign policy had to be changed. The Soviet Union could no longer continue a policy of military confrontation with the U.S. and NATO after 1985. The economic possibilities for such a policy had been practically exhausted."[9] Similarly, Second Secretary Yegor Ligachev, who was the second most powerful Soviet politician after Gorbachev from 1985 to the fall of 1988, wrote in his memoirs that "after April 1985 we faced the task of curtailing military spending. Without this, large-scale social programs could not have been implemented: the economy could not breathe normally with a military budget that comprised eighteen percent of the national income."[10]

The fact that both old and New Thinkers believed that the Soviet Union's failing economy made some form of international retrenchment a

---

Haven: Yale University Press, 1998), 89, 91–92, 115, 392; Aleksandr' G. Savel'yev and Nikolay N. Detinov, *The Big Five: Arms Control Decision-Making in the Soviet Union* (London: Praeger, 1995),5, 121, 161; Zubok, "Why Did the Cold War End?," 356.

7. In Zubok, "Why Did the Cold War End?," 349.

8. Chernyaev, *My Six Years with Gorbachev*, 46; Michael Ellman and Vladimir Kontorovich, "The Collapse of the Soviet System and the Memoir Literature," *Europe-Asia Studies* 49, no. 2 (March 1997): 261; Brooks and Wohlforth, "Economic Constraints and the End of the Cold War," 43.

9. In Zubok, "Why Did the Cold War End?," 347.

10. In Odom, *Collapse of the Soviet Military*, 92. See also the quotes by Defense Minister Dmitri Yazov in Brooks and Wohlforth, "Economic Constraints and the End of the Cold War," 287.

virtual inevitability shows the importance of power variables to the development of Soviet foreign policies in the 1980s. Regardless of Soviet leaders' ideological objectives, most believed that the USSR's declining relative power meant that the Soviet Union simply could not afford to wage the Cold War with the United States in the manner it had done since the end of the Second World War. The incentives pushing for the end of the Cold War on American terms were therefore very powerful.

Although there are important elements of truth to these claims, they suffer from key limitations. Perhaps most notable, economics-based explanations of Soviet foreign policies in the 1980s make the error of conflating outcomes with policies. Recognizing that economic variables made the end of the Cold War on America's terms the most likely ultimate outcome to the U.S.-Soviet rivalry does not mean that economic considerations were the primary motive for Soviet international policies in the 1980s. We must not assume that the eventual need for the Soviet Union to retrench was the primary motive for Gorbachev doing so in the 1980s.

Ideological variables played a critical role in determining how the Cold War ended when it did. Because Gorbachev and fellow New Thinkers rejected orthodox Marxism-Leninism in favor of legitimating principles much closer in identity to those of the Western powers, these individuals tended to view the United States and its allies as much smaller threats to Soviet interests than did Soviet conservatives. Consequently, the forces working for an early and crisis-free ending to the Cold War were much stronger for New than for old thinkers. To put this analysis another way, although the Soviet Union's economic decline created incentives for all Soviet leaders to retrench internationally, ideological beliefs were critical to how far and how fast these individuals were willing to act on these incentives. Most scholars, as well as Soviet decision makers, are in agreement that despite the USSR's economic problems in the mid-1980s, the Cold War did not have to end in this decade. According to many accounts, the Soviet Union continued to possess sufficient resources to extend the Cold War into the early twenty-first century.[11] If Soviet conservatives had continued to govern, it is very doubtful that the Cold War would have ended as early and as smoothly as it did. Conversely, even in the absence of the Soviet Union's economic decline, New Thinkers' rejection of traditional Marxist-Leninist beliefs would have led to a substantial decrease in U.S.-Soviet tensions.

11. Ellman and Kontorovich, "Collapse of the Soviet System and the Memoir Literature," 259; Boris Yeltsin, *Against the Grain: An Autobiography* (New York: Summit Books, 1990), 139; Frances Fitzgerald, *Way Out There in the Blue: Reagan, Star Wars, and the End of the Cold War* (New York: Simon and Schuster, 2000), 561; Brooks and Wohlforth, "Economic Constraints and the End of the Cold War," 282–283; Robert D. English, "The Road(s) Not Taken: Causality and Contingency in Analysis of the Cold War's End," in *Cold War Endgame*, ed. Wohlforth, 245.

The Ideological Objectives of New and Old Thinkers

There can be no doubt that the ideological objectives of Gorbachev and his principal advisors were both radically different from those of their predecessors and, more important for our purposes, much closer in identity to the legitimating principles of the ruling parties of the Western powers, including the United States. "New Thinking," as one scholar puts it, "did not just posit an end to conflict with the West or the desirability of cooperation with the liberal international community. It argued that the USSR was, or should be, a *member* of that community. Thus . . . New Thinking is best viewed as a watershed in national identity—not in opposition to, but in unity with the West."[12]

In terms of political institutions, Gorbachev and fellow New Thinkers by 1988 were committed to the creation in the USSR of a more democratic political system that shared many of the features of the Western democratic states, including separation of powers, an independent judiciary, and respect for civil liberties.[13] On economic issues, New Thinkers agreed that the Stalinist command system of political economy had to be destroyed and that some degree of marketization and privatization should be institutionalized within Soviet society. Finally, instead of a class-based understanding of politics, New Thinkers asserted that "universal human values" should form the foundation of the Soviet political system. In both the formulation and implementation of these objectives, New Thinkers, including Gorbachev, explicitly looked to Western Europe, America, and Japan as models.[14]

---

12. Robert D. English, *Russia and the Idea of the West: Gorbachev, Intellectuals, and the End of the Cold War* (New York: Columbia University Press, 2000), 5 (emphasis in original). Although the Soviet Union's declining economy no doubt helped Gorbachev become elected, New Thinkers' ideological beliefs should not be considered epiphenomenal of relative power considerations, as is sometimes asserted (cf. Schweller and Wohlforth, "Power Test," 29–30). The ideas that became New Thinking had existed among a group of CPSU members for decades, including when the Soviet Union's relative power position was increasing. Moreover, Gorbachev was not elected general secretary of the CPSU on a New Thinking platform, but a much less ambitious reformist agenda similar to the one Yuri Andropov adopted from 1982 to 1984 when he was general secretary (English, "Road(s) Not Taken," 247–250, 268).

13. I say "by 1988" because it was not until this year that Gorbachev's most revolutionary domestic objectives were made known, especially to foreign observers. I develop this point more fully below.

14. Jerry F. Hough, *Democratization and Revolution in the USSR, 1985–1991* (Washington, D.C.: Brookings Institution Press, 1997), 213; John Gooding, "Gorbachev and Democracy," *Soviet Studies* 42, no. 2 (April 1990): 225; Gregory Freidin, "How Communist Is Gorbachev's Communism?," in *Dilemmas of Transition in the Soviet Union and Eastern Europe*, ed. George W. Breslauer (Berkeley: University of California Press, 1991), 31, 33–34; Stephen F. Cohen, "Introduction: Ligachev and the Tragedy of Soviet Conservatism," in Yegor Ligachev, *Inside Gorbachev's Kremlin: The Memoirs of Yegor Ligachev* (Boulder: Westview Press, 1993), xxiii, xxx; Vladislav M. Zubok, "Gorbachev and the End of the Cold War," in *Cold War Endgame*, ed. Wohlforth, 229.

Soviet conservatives prescribed and defended a very different domestic vision for the USSR than did New Thinkers. This does not mean that old and New Thinkers always disagreed over domestic policies. Almost all Soviet leaders from across the political spectrum supported some of Gorbachev's domestic reforms that were designed to make the Soviet Union's existing political-economic system more efficient. These policies included an anti-alcoholism campaign, initiatives designed to root out corruption, attempts to increase worker discipline and morale, and increased capital investment.[15] These strategies dominated Gorbachev's domestic agenda from 1985 to 1987.

However, once Gorbachev shifted from in-system reforms to policies designed to move the USSR toward a market-based economy and a more democratic regime, significant opposition to the general secretary's policies emerged. Instead of supporting or largely acquiescing to New Thinkers' domestic policies, after 1987 many key Soviet leaders, including Gennady Yanaev (vice president of the USSR), Boris Pugo (minister of internal affairs), Valentin Pavlov (Soviet prime minister), and Vladimir Kryuchkov (chairman of the KGB), wanted to revert to "neo-Stalinist techniques: discipline, coercion, heavy industrial investment, and belt-tightening."[16] These preferences continued virtually to the time of the dissolution of the Soviet Union, and were a driving force behind the attempted coup against Gorbachev in August 1991. No matter how far the Soviet Union's economy declined, most conservatives simply refused to approve economic and political liberalization as acceptable policies to solve the USSR's problems.

Ideology and Old and New Thinkers' Perceptions of Threat

Scholars who attribute the revolution in Soviet foreign policies in the 1980s primarily to the Soviet Union's economic troubles are correct in the core assumption that grounds their analysis: a certain level of relative power is necessary for states to sustain geopolitical conflicts, especially hot and cold wars. Without sufficient capabilities, leaders will not be able to maintain highly antagonistic behavior against even those states that they view as extremely threatening to their security.

---

15. Ellman and Kontorovich, "Collapse of the Soviet System and the Memoir Literature," 261; Coit D. Blacker, *Hostage to Revolution: Gorbachev and Soviet Security Policy, 1985–1991* (New York: Council on Foreign Relations Press, 1993), 152; Meyer, "Sources and Prospects of Gorbachev's New Political Thinking," 148.

16. James Clay Moltz, "Divergent Learning and the Failed Politics of Soviet Economic Reform," *World Politics* 45, no. 2 (January 1993): 319, 317; John B. Dunlop, "Anatomy of a Failed Coup," in *The Soviet System: From Crisis to Collapse*, ed. Alexander Dallin and Gail W. Lapidus (Boulder: Westview Press, 1995), 606, 596.

I do not deny the importance of relative power to leaders' ability to realize their foreign policy objectives. Instead, I demonstrate how the ideological distances dividing states' leaders is central to their understandings of the level of threats posed by the other actors in the system. What policies decision makers will be able to adopt to address these threats will, however, be largely a function of relative power.

Distinguishing between leaders' understandings of the threats posed by the other actors in the system and their ability to adopt highly coercive or effective deterrent policies has important implications for an analysis of Soviet foreign policies in the 1980s. Even if the Soviet Union's declining economy left Soviet leaders very little choice but to end the Cold War on American terms, this does not mean that different groups of Soviet decision makers did not interpret the security implications resulting from this forced retreat in very different ways.

Those individuals who were dedicated to preserving the Soviet Union's totalitarian institutions and class-based foundation of Soviet society tended to view America and its allies as significant dangers to both their domestic and international interests. Consistent with the predictions of the demonstration-effects mechanism, a dominant theme of conservatives' writings and speeches was that close association with the Western powers represented a significant subversive danger to Soviet institutions and beliefs. This threat was much more than a matter of the simple diffusion of particular ideas from the West to the East. Soviet conservatives, led by Second Secretary Yegor Ligachev and KGB chief Viktor Chebrikov, repeatedly accused America and its allies of actively seeking to create ideological fifth columnists in the USSR with the ultimate goals of sowing confusion and dissension in the Soviet Union in the short run and establishing "bourgeois democracy" in the long run. Their public and private statements were replete with such phrases as "ideological sabotage," "inspiring anti-socialist manifestation," and attempts by internal and external "class" enemies to "weaken the influence of the Marxist Leninist ideology" in the Soviet Union.[17]

A key policy implication resulting from old thinkers' fears of subversion was that these individuals opposed Gorbachev's attempts to integrate the Soviet Union into the global capitalist economy. To many Soviet conservatives, the likelihood of ideological contagion resulting from economic interdependence with the Western powers was a greater threat to Soviet interests than was the Soviet Union's failing economy. KGB chief

17. Baruch A. Hazan, *Gorbachev and His Enemies: The Struggle for Perestroika* (Boulder: Westview Press, 1990), 20, 23, 27, 46–47, 63–65; Michael R. Beschloss and Strobe Talbott, *At the Highest Levels: The Inside Story of the End of the Cold War* (Boston: Little, Brown, 1994), 393–394; Anders Åslund, *Gorbachev's Struggle for Economic Reform*, rev. ed. (Ithaca: Cornell University Press, 1991), 52–54; Susanne Sternthal, *Gorbachev's Reforms: De-Stalinization through Demilitarization* (London: Praeger, 1997), 82.

Vladimir Kryuchkov, for example, saw the "grand bargain" (which was a 1991 proposal that promised significant amounts of Western economic aid in exchange for Soviet economic reform) "as part of a sinister American plot to destabilize, 'demilitarize and even occupy' the Soviet Union."[18] Instead of integration with Western economic institutions, Kryuchkov and other key conservatives, including Vice President Yanaev, Minister of Internal Affairs Pugo, and Prime Minister Pavlov, continued to push for both the preservation of more traditional state-led policies at home in order to address the USSR's economic troubles, and continued confrontational policies with America in order to mitigate the likelihood of ideological subversion.

Security concerns weighed even more heavily on old thinkers' perceptions of the threats posed by the United States and its allies than did fears of domestic-ideological subversion. To those individuals who continued to adhere to traditional Soviet ideological beliefs, including a class-based understanding of politics, "the focus on and expectation of conflict" in the international system remained a "central theme."[19] Soviet conservatives were convinced that because of the ideological objectives of the Western powers' leaders, the latter were bound to remain highly aggressive actors who were determined both to roll back Soviet international influence and promote counter-revolution in the Soviet Union.[20]

The Soviet Union's international retrenchment in the 1980s, regardless if this retreat was made all but inevitable by the USSR's ailing economy, only increased old thinkers' sense of vulnerability at the hands of the Western powers. In other words, even if Soviet conservatives agreed that their country's economic woes made all of Gorbachev's retrenchment policies

18. In Leon V. Sigal, *Hang Separately: Cooperative Security Between the United States and Russia, 1985–1994* (New York: Century Foundation Press, 2000), 225. See also Celeste A. Wallander and Jane E. Prokop, "Soviet Security Strategies in Europe: After the Wall, with Their Backs Up to It," in *After the Cold War: International Institutions and State Strategies in Europe, 1989–1991*, ed. Robert O. Keohane, Joseph S. Nye, and Stanley Hoffmann (Cambridge: Harvard University Press, 1993), 69, 86; Gail W. Lapidus, "The Crisis of Perestroika," in *Dilemmas of Transition*, ed. Breslauer, 17; English, *Russia and the Idea of the West*, 164; Garthoff, *Great Transition*, 441, 458–459; Beschloss and Talbott, *At the Highest Levels*, 375–376, 393–394.

19. Allen Lynch, *The Soviet Study of International Relations* (Cambridge: Cambridge University Press, 1987), 147. See also Thomas Nichols and Theodore Karasik, "Civil-Military Relations under Gorbachev: The Struggle over National Security," in *Gorbachev and His Generals: The Reform of Soviet Military Doctrine*, ed. William C. Green and Theodore Karasik (Boulder: Westview Press, 1990), 33–34, 39–40, 47–48.

20. William Curti Wohlforth, *The Elusive Balance: Power and Perceptions During the Cold War* (Ithaca: Cornell University Press, 1993), 42–46, 52–58, 235, 256; Michael MccGwire, *Perestroika and Soviet National Security* (Washington, D.C.: Brookings Institute, 1991), 2, 80, 124–126; Jeffrey Checkel, *Ideas and International Political Change: Soviet/Russian Behavior and the End of the Cold War* (New Haven: Yale University Press, 1997), 19–24; Odom, *Collapse of the Soviet Military*, 389–390; Blacker, *Hostage to Revolution*, 168–169, 178; Hannes Adomeit, *Imperial Overstretch: Germany in Soviet Policy from Stalin to Gorbachev* (Baden-Baden: Nomos Verlagsgesellschaft, 1998), 372.

unavoidable in the short run (which, as we shall see, they did not), bowing to the inevitable did nothing to alleviate their security concerns. The more the Soviet Union's relative power declined in relation to the United States, the more their fears grew. Key conservative civilian and military leaders asserted both publicly and privately that New Thinkers' belief in a benign international environment in the 1980s was a myth. Akhromeyev, for example, asserted in a private conversation with Shakhnazarov that he believed war with the United States to be virtually unavoidable.[21] In a January 1989 interview, he warned that the belief that the Soviet Union did not face a significant military threat was "mistaken." Moreover, in light of the continued dangers posed by "imperialist sources of aggression," designs to cut substantially Soviet armed forces were "naive."[22]

In 1990, the archconservative General Albert Makashov (commander of the Volga-Urals Military District) claimed that only New Thinkers believed that "no one is going to attack us." The commander of the Pacific Fleet, Admiral Gennadi Khvatov, similarly asserted that the Soviet Union's strategic situation in this year was comparable to that of 1939.[23] Defense Minister Yazov stated that it was "obvious" that the dangers of war for the Soviet Union were substantial at the end of the 1980s.[24] A majority of the Committee for Defense and State Security (which consisted of many of the USSR's top military leaders) believed in 1990 that "the West still threatens [the Soviet Union], and that [the USSR] may become a victim of aggression at any time."[25]

These statements should not be dismissed as mere rhetoric or scare tactics. Documents from the Soviet archives and interview data reveal that in 1983 decision makers in the Central Committee and security agencies were extremely concerned that the chances of war with the United States were reaching frighteningly high levels.[26] This war scare was a reflection of Soviet leaders' "pessimistic assessment of the 'correlation of forces' and the ever-widening gap in the USSR's technological lag behind the West."[27] As the Soviet Union's relative power position steadily declined

21. Odom, *Collapse of the Soviet Military*, 105–106.
22. In Sternthal, *Gorbachev's Reforms*, 139.
23. Both in Adomeit, *Imperial Overstretch*, 511–512; also Sternthal, *Gorbachev's Reforms*, 139.
24. In Odom, *Collapse of the Soviet Military*, 170. See also 97, 122, 154, 159, 171, 181–182; Adomeit, *Imperial Overstretch*, 372, 490, 511–512, 536–537; and Chernyaev, *My Six Years with Gorbachev*, 273.
25. In Sternthal, *Gorbachev's Reforms*, 150. The quotation is from a reformist member of the committee who opposed the group's conclusions.
26. Zubok, "Why Did the Cold War End?," 348, 363; Garthoff, *Great Transition*, 60–62, 138–139.
27. Ben B. Fischer, *A Cold War Conundrum: The 1983 Soviet War Scare* (Washington, D.C.: Center for Study of Intelligence, 1997), quoted in Zubok, "Why Did the Cold War End?," 348. Nuclear parity with the United States (which had existed since the early 1970s) did not eliminate conservatives' security fears. The safety afforded by this variable therefore cannot explain the end of the Cold War from the Soviet Union's perspective.

as the 1980s progressed, it should be expected that those same individuals who feared war in 1983 would be similarly inclined in 1990.

Old thinkers' depictions of the high levels of threat to the Soviet Union posed by the United States and its allies also cannot be explained with reference to these individuals' bureaucratic interests, that is, attempts by members of the Soviet military and other security agencies to keep defense spending as high as possible for parochial reasons. Liberals in the military agreed with civilian New Thinkers that the threats to Soviet interests posed by the United States and its allies were fairly low. Those military officers who shared New Thinkers' goals of bringing "the military bureaucracy under strong parliamentary oversight and [making] its operations open to public scrutiny" tended to possess "radically different views of what constituted a threat" than did conservatives in the military.[28] Instead of perceiving an increasingly dangerous international system, military personnel in the Soviet Union who shared New Thinkers' commitment to political liberalization tended to see a "benign international environment."[29] Thus ideological orientation was a more accurate predictor of individuals' perceptions of threat than was institutional affiliation.

Because of their very different ideological beliefs from those of Soviet conservatives, Gorbachev and fellow New Thinkers viewed the United States and its allies as much less threatening than did old thinkers, despite operating within identical relative power environments. Differences in Soviet perceptions and related policies were thus not epiphenomenal of changes in the international distribution of power.

In the first place, because many of the reforms eventually implemented by New Thinkers were modeled on the institutions of the Western powers, Gorbachev and his advisors believed that integration with the West would be an important aid to their goals of domestic liberalization, rather than subversive threats to them as old thinkers believed.[30] According to Chernyaev, in order for New Thinkers to "succeed with a new foreign policy, we had to demolish the myths and dogmas of a confrontational ideology. . . . Our contacts with Western Europe [helped realize this goal of domestic change, while] relations with socialist countries, especially China and Cuba, were holding back de-ideologization."[31] Ideological distances

---

28. Odom, *Collapse of the Soviet Military*, 188–189.
29. Ibid., 189, 168.
30. Carolyn McGiffert Ekedahl and Melvin A. Goodman, *The Wars of Eduard Shevardnadze* (University Park: Pennsylvania State University Press, 1997), 59; Tuomas Forsberg, "Power, Interests, and Trust: Explaining Gorbachev Choices at the End of the Cold War," *Review of International Studies* 25, no. 4 (October 1999): 612–615. Various talks with the Americans supported this hope. President Bush, for example, explained to Gorbachev at the Malta Summit in December 1989 (according to Beschloss's and Talbott's account) that "the more accommodating the USSR was on ideological and humanitarian issues, the more help it could expect from the United States on the economic front" (Beschloss and Talbott, *At the Highest Levels*, 158).
31. Chernyaev, *My Six Years with Gorbachev*, 144, also 148–149.

among actors, in short, determined which groups were supports or threats to New Thinkers' domestic interests. The greater the internal resistance to Gorbachev's domestic policies, the more he felt he had to align with ideological allies in the West to overcome this resistance.[32]

New Thinkers' largely benign view of the Western powers also held with regard to security issues. For example, instead of viewing the continued presence of American forces in Europe as a substantial danger to Soviet interests, New Thinkers came to view American power in the region as a key source of stability and thus as a support to Soviet security.[33] As Gorbachev told President George Bush at the Malta Summit in 1989 in a statement that repudiated core international positions of the Soviets since the end of the Second World War (and ones that old thinkers continued to hold in the 1980s): "We don't consider you an enemy anymore. Things have changed. We want you in Europe. You ought to be in Europe. It's important for the future of the continent that you're there."[34]

Most surprising, Gorbachev and his advisors even asserted that Soviet retrenchment would likely *increase* Soviet security rather than diminish it. New Thinkers repeatedly referred to the "mutuality" and "indivisibility" of the Soviet Union's security with America's, as opposed to the zero-sum view of conservatives.[35] To New Thinkers, if one of the superpowers were made insecure by the other's actions, both would end up more vulnerable. Conversely, if one of the superpowers were made more secure, both would benefit. Hence New Thinkers' claimed that by making the Americans feel safer by not increasing or even reducing Soviet force levels, the Soviet Union's security would also be enhanced. As Gorbachev explained in a speech to the Supreme Soviet in November 1985: "We would not . . . want changes in the strategic balance to our favor. We would not want this because such a situation would heighten suspicion of the other side and increase the instability of the general situation."[36] Old thinkers strongly disagreed with these views.

Old and New Thinkers' very different understandings of the threats posed by the Western powers pushed for contrary international policies. The Soviet Union's economic troubles were creating incentives for all

32. Zubok, "Gorbachev and the End of the Cold War," 239.
33. Odom, *Collapse of the Soviet Military*, 155, 157; Adomeit, *Imperial Overstretch*, 496–498, 500.
34. In Beschloss and Talbott, *At the Highest Levels*, 163.
35. Alan Collins, *The Security Dilemma and the End of the Cold War* (New York: St. Martin's Press, 1997), 155–156; Meyer, "Sources and Prospects of Gorbachev's New Political Thinking," 142–144.
36. In Garthoff, *Great Transition*, 242; for similar expressions of this belief by New Thinkers, see 142, and also Collins, *Security Dilemma and the End of the Cold War*, 153–154; Wohlforth, *Elusive Balance*, 279; Sternthal, *Gorbachev's Reforms*, 153; *Europe Transformed: Documents on the End of the Cold War*, ed. Lawrence Freedman (London: Tri-Service Press, 1990), 343. These statements recognize the importance of the security dilemma to U.S.-Soviet relations, which is a view that old thinkers rejected.

Soviet leaders, regardless of ideological beliefs, to retrench internationally. Old thinkers' ideological differences with the United States created substantial countervailing pressures against retrenchment because of the security fears associated with a geopolitical retreat. In contrast, because New Thinkers viewed the Western powers in much more benign terms than did Soviet conservatives, the incentives pushing the former away from retrenchment were much smaller. In fact, New Thinkers' ideological similarities with the Western powers in some ways *reinforced* the effects of economic variables by creating incentives to integrate with Western economic and political institutions in order to help realize their goals of domestic liberalization. Because of New Thinkers' fairly benign view of the United States and its allies, these individuals did not feel the strong need to try to continue Cold War hostilities with the West like old thinkers did.

Old and New Thinkers' Foreign Policies

As previously discussed, there were a number of foreign policy changes initiated by Gorbachev and his associates that enjoyed widespread support (at least at the declaratory level) among Soviet decision makers from across the political spectrum. These policies included reducing the Soviet Union's commitments to the Third World, withdrawing from the war in Afghanistan, reducing the Soviet Union's strategic nuclear arsenal, and above all reducing defense spending.[37] Agreement between old and New Thinkers on these policies points to the importance of the Soviet Union's economic decline in the 1980s in forging foreign policy agreement.

There were, however, clear limits to this consensus. With regard to the necessity and appropriateness of Gorbachev's foreign policies that had the greatest impact on ending the Cold War, including the unilateral reduction of large numbers of Soviet weaponry and personnel from Eastern Europe and agreeing to allow German unification within NATO, there was fierce disagreement among Soviet decision makers that largely corresponded with these individuals' ideological beliefs. For example, although most Soviet conservatives claimed to recognize the need to reduce defense spending, their support for policies designed to realize this goal was highly conditional. The majority of old thinkers would only support Gorbachev's proposed cuts in military expenditures if the Americans agreed to equivalent reductions. Conservatives like Yazov, Akhromeyev, Ligachev, and Warsaw Pact armed forces Chief of Staff

37. The Soviet withdrawal from Afghanistan was a more hotly contested issue between old and New Thinkers than these other objectives. On conservatives' opposition to withdrawal, see Sarah E. Mendelson, *Changing Course: Ideas, Politics, and the Soviet Withdrawal from Afghanistan* (Princeton: Princeton University Press, 1998).

Anatolii Gribkov all agreed that (in the words of Yazov, writing in February 1988) "the limits of sufficiency [i.e., the limits of possible cuts in Soviet defense spending] are defined not by us but by the actions of the United States and NATO."[38]

To most old thinkers in the 1980s, the need to maintain parity between American and Soviet forces remained a greater determinant of their foreign policies than the Soviet Union's economic troubles.[39] Despite mounting evidence pointing to the great weakness of the USSR's economy, conservatives, according to Chernyaev, "were still dominated by an obsession with absolute parity that had squeezed the country dry in the preceding decades. And therefore it hardly occurred to anyone that we could give up the race, even though its senselessness . . . [was] obvious."[40] Akhromeyev resigned in protest over Gorbachev's announcement at the United Nations in December 1988 that he intended to withdraw unilaterally from Eastern Europe 5,000 tanks and 500,000 men,[41] and Akhromeyev and other conservatives believed that the disproportionate cuts of Soviet missiles agreed to in the Intermediate-range Nuclear Forces (INF) Treaty were a mistake.[42]

Conservatives' opposition to unilateral or disproportionate cuts in Soviet forces was not rhetorical or symbolic only, but had important policy implications. In fact, for most of the 1980s old thinkers were quite successful in blocking Gorbachev's initiatives that were designed to reduce Soviet defense spending and improve relations with the United States. According to Chernyaev, after the first three years of perestroika from 1985 to 1988, "the real activities of the military-industrial complex . . . had changed neither in style nor substance."[43] Or as William Odom, an expert on the Soviet military, explains: "Notwithstanding [evidence of the Soviet Union's great economic difficulties] Gorbachev did not succeed in compelling the military and VPK [the Military-Industrial Commission of the Council of Ministers] to begin perestroika within their own ranks. . . . In the spring of 1988 . . . Gorbachev saw that limiting strategic nuclear arms, reducing the armed forces, and withdrawing troops from eastern Europe

38. In Adomeit, *Imperial Overstretch*, 352.

39. Odom, *Collapse of the Soviet Military*, 94, 225; Chernyaev, *My Six Years with Gorbachev*, 80–81, 84, 90; Adomeit, *Imperial Overstretch*, 352; Savel'yev and Detinov, *Big Five*, 117, 129; Matthew Evangelista, *Unarmed Forces: The Transnational Movement to the End of the Cold War* (Ithaca: Cornell University Press, 1999), 315–318; Sternthal, *Gorbachev's Reforms*, 77, 120.

40. Chernyaev, *My Six Years with Gorbachev*, 84; see also Odom, *Collapse of the Soviet Military*, 94.

41. Odom, *Collapse of the Soviet Military*, 144; Adomeit, *Imperial Overstretch*, 352.

42. Odom, *Collapse of the Soviet Military*, 134. After retiring from politics, Gorbachev claimed that the "Ministry of Defense, knowing full well how difficult it was for the country to bear the arms race, in all of my years of working in Moscow, not once came up with a proposal for the limitation of the military or manufacturing of weapons" (in Sternthal, *Gorbachev's Reforms*, 45).

43. Chernyaev, *My Six Years with Gorbachev*, 193.

were beyond his power. He had reached the limits of his personal authority in overriding his military leaders while they continued to drag their feet."[44]

In December 1986, the military forced Gorbachev to renew nuclear testing because the United States had not reciprocated the Soviets' nuclear moratorium. Soviet arms deliveries to the Third World actually increased in the second half of the 1980s in comparison to the previous years.[45] The Five-Year Plan of 1988 approved increases in spending for a number of offensive weapons. Thanks to conservatives' defiance, the implementation of the strategic doctrine of "defensive-defense"—which was a central component of Gorbachev's attempt to end the confrontation with the NATO allies by eschewing offensive capabilities—was poor. Virtually until the time of the dissolution of the Warsaw Treaty Organization (WTO) in 1990, the military continued to train and base operational exercises on the presumption of a border-crossing counteroffensive.[46] Conservatives' opposition to disproportionate weapons cuts was instrumental in preventing an agreement with the Americans on the Strategic Arms Reduction Treaty (START) while Gorbachev was in power.[47] Finally, some Soviet decision makers went to considerable lengths to sabotage the Conventional Forces in Europe (CFE) treaty with America. In the weeks prior to the signing of the treaty in November 1990, the Soviet military and its sympathizers moved massive numbers of weapons and equipment east of the Urals in order to reduce the amounts subject to reduction; provided Soviet negotiators with numbers for the amount of equipment liable to reduction that were much lower than the figures possessed by their Western interlocutors; and transferred three ground-force divisions from the army to the navy to exempt them from the treaty.[48]

All these outcomes could only damage Gorbachev's efforts to achieve a rapprochement with the NATO allies at a time when the Soviet Union was in great need of a relaxation of international tensions in order to reduce the economic burdens of high levels of military spending. Gorbachev recognized as much when he angrily confronted Defense Minister Yazov over conservatives' opposition to his policies: "What are you doing, still preparing to fight a nuclear war? Well, I'm not, and everything else follows from that. . . . If we still want to conquer the world, then let's decide how to arm ourselves further and outdo the Americans. But then

44. Odom, *Collapse of the Soviet Military*, 136.
45. Richard Herrmann, "Soviet Behavior in Regional Conflicts: Old Questions, New Strategies, Important Lessons," *World Politics* 44, no. 3 (April 1992): 452–457.
46. Gerard Snel, "'A (More) Defensive Strategy': The Reconceptualisation of Soviet Conventional Strategy in the 1980s," *Europe-Asia Studies* 50, no. 2 (March 1998): 218–219, 224, 229.
47. Sternthal, *Gorbachev's Reforms*, 111, 169, 178–179, 185, 187.
48. Evangelista, *Unarmed Forces*, 363. See also Chernyaev, *My Six Years with Gorbachev*, 307, 554.

that'll be it, and everything we've been saying about a new policy has to go on the trash heap."[49]

Additional evidence pointing to the importance of old thinkers' ideological beliefs to their policies is the fact that these individuals' opposition to Gorbachev's international decisions in some ways became more pronounced as the decade progressed, even though the Soviet Union's economic situation continue to worsen.[50] For example, starting in the spring of 1990, military leaders insisted that a representative of the armed forces be present in all security negotiations with the Americans. These representatives were significantly less cooperative than were Gorbachev, Foreign Minister Eduard Shevardnadze, and their allies.[51] "More than once," U.S. Secretary of State James Baker recollected, "I thought I had an agreement with Shevardnadze, only to see the Soviet military undo it the next time we met."[52]

Conservatives' opposition to Gorbachev's domestic and international reforms was so strong in the late 1980s that a key motivating factor for the creation of genuine democratic institutions in the USSR was to establish the means of circumventing the party's influence on policy.[53] Similarly, at several points during his tenure as general secretary, Gorbachev had to engage in deep purges of his opponents in the Politburo, Central Committee, and security agencies. It was only after Gorbachev replaced many of his conservative opponents and consolidated decision-making power in the hands of a few New Thinkers that the latter were able to realize their most revolutionary international objectives.[54]

---

49. In English, "Road(s) Not Taken," 263. The Soviet ambassador to America and later head of the International Department of the Central Committee, Anatoly Dobrynin, claims that despite the Soviet Union's economic troubles, if the Americans had not eventually reciprocated Gorbachev's concessions there "would have [been] no lack of support from the military-industrial complex" for "tough, militaristic" policies, including a "massive rearmament program." Gorbachev in this situation "would have been forced to continue the conservative foreign and domestic policies of his predecessors" (Anatoly Dobrynin, *In Confidence: Moscow's Ambassador to America's Six Cold War Presidents* [New York: Times Books, 1995], 611).

50. Zubok, "Gorbachev and the End of the Cold War," 239; English, *Russia and the Idea of the West,* 224; Evangelista, *Unarmed Forces,* 256–257; Cohen, "Introduction," xxiii, xxix, xxx.

51. Don Oberdorfer, *The Turn from the Cold War to a New Era: The United States and the Soviet Union, 1983–1990* (New York: Simon and Schuster, 1992), 404, 406–408.

52. James A. Baker, *The Politics of Diplomacy: Revolution, War, and Peace 1989–1992* (New York: George Putnam's Sons, 1995), 204; Sternthal, *Gorbachev's Reforms,* 191.

53. According to Shakhnazarov, "the VPK . . . resisted limitations on strategic weapons, reductions in the army, the withdrawal of troops from eastern Europe. . . . [There was] desperate resistance to any attempt to excessively reduce the swollen military budget. . . . Gorbachev could not overcome the resistance without leaning on the support of . . . [public] opinion" (in Sternthal, *Gorbachev's Reforms,* 115).

54. Odom, *Collapse of the Soviet Military,* 94, 110, 116, 137, 140–141, 393; Adomeit, *Imperial Overstretch,* 326–327, 337–338, 346, 515–516, 569; Jerry F. Hough, *Russia and the West: Gorbachev and the Politics of Reform* (New York: Simon and Schuster, 1990), 174; Archie Brown, "Power and Policy in a Time of Leadership Transition, 1982–1988," in *Political Leadership in*

Conservatives' refusal to support Gorbachev's most conciliatory policies toward the Western powers was perhaps most evident with regards to Germany's unification within NATO. In private sessions of Soviet leaders, Gorbachev's decision to approve this outcome was vehemently attacked by conservatives "as a betrayal of the country's most vital interests."[55] So great was the hostility to the unification of Germany and its continued membership in NATO that the final Soviet vote approving this outcome had to be taken in a special session outside the full Politburo, where opposition to this decision was too high.[56]

Conservatives supported two principal alternative policies to Gorbachev's decision to acquiesce to German unification within NATO. First, members of this group assert that they would have been much tougher negotiators over the German question than were Gorbachev and his advisors. Old thinkers claim that they would have, at a minimum, received much more money and more formal security guarantees from the Western powers in exchange for permitting a unified Germany in NATO, and at a maximum, they would have forced the Germans to choose between unification and membership in NATO.[57] These claims are credible. Almost all of the key decision makers in the Western powers agree that despite the USSR's economic troubles, the Soviets continued to possess significant leverage in the negotiations over Germany's future status.[58] If nothing else, the fact that the Soviet Union still had over 350,000 troops in East Germany in 1990 assured this. American and German leaders were very worried that the Soviets would attempt to exchange a crisis-free agreement on German unification for Germany's exit from NATO precisely because they knew this tactic had a good chance of succeeding.[59]

---

the Soviet Union, ed. Archie Brown (London: Macmillan, 1989), 189–195, 204, 207; Sternthal, *Gorbachev's Reforms*, 159–160.

55. Gerhard Wettig, "Moscow's Acceptance of NATO: The Catalytic Role of German Unification," *Europe-Asia Studies* 45, no. 6 (1993): 963. See also Evangelista, *Unarmed Forces*, 256, 260, 315, 317–319, 361–362; English, *Russia and the Idea of the West*, 218; Adomeit, *Imperial Overstretch*, 491.

56. Sigal, *Hang Separately*, 76; Beschloss and Talbott, *At the Highest Levels*, 271.

57. Bennett, "Trust Bursting Out All Over," 201; Brooks and Wohlforth, "Economic Constraints and the End of the Cold War," 302, 304; Zubok, "Gorbachev and the End of the Cold War," 228; Dobrynin, *In Confidence*, 627, 630–631; interviews with former Soviet officials Valery Boldin (Gorbachev's chief of staff) and N. S. Leonov (a deputy director of Soviet intelligence), available at http://www.mershon.ohio-state.edu/Resources/OldProjects/endcoldwar/transcriptdir.htm.

58. Hannes Adomeit, "Gorbachev and German Unification: Revision of Thinking, Realignment of Power," in *Soviet System*, ed. Dallin and Lapidus, 469; Philip Zelikow and Condoleezza Rice, *Germany Unified and Europe Transformed: A Study in Statecraft* (Cambridge, Mass.: Harvard University Press, 1997), 69, 154, 161, 172, 196, 246, 273; George Bush and Brent Scowcroft, *A World Transformed* (New York: Alfred A. Knopf, 1998), 241, 300.

59. Bush and Scowcroft, *World Transformed*, 241, 300; Zelikow and Rice, *Germany Unified and Europe Transformed*, xi, 148, 161, 172, 196, 248. If the Soviets did attempt to separate German

New Thinkers rejected this plan of bargaining. Instead of threatening reprisals or even demanding significant sums of money in exchange for approving German unification within NATO, "Gorbachev [handed] over the key to German unity . . . [and] for all practical purposes he [did] so *unconditionally.*"[60] As long as Germany's unification was accomplished by peaceful means and the Western powers gave the Soviet Union assurances that Soviet interests would be protected (more about these assurances below), Gorbachev and his advisors were willing to accede to a unified Germany within NATO with surprisingly little resistance given the putative stakes involved. Both scholars and the decision makers involved in the negotiations over Germany are in agreement that these talks were extraordinarily smooth. This would not have been the case if old thinkers had governed the Soviet Union throughout the 1980s.

Second, it must be remembered that Soviet leaders could have chosen to address their declining influence in Eastern Europe by essentially doing nothing. In other words, instead of explicitly acquiescing to American demands with regards to a unified Germany within NATO, the Soviets could have attempted simply to muddle through with essentially status quo policies in the hope that things would "work out" for the best. Doing nothing to address the issue of German unification was, in fact, the dominant strategy of a majority of old thinkers. Based on an analysis of archival evidence and interview data, Hannes Adomeit (a leading authority on German-Soviet relations) concludes that if the Soviet Union had been governed by conservatives in 1989–90, Soviet policies on the subject of German unification would have been ones of "obstructionism, procrastination, and delay. Nothing would have changed."[61]

I do not mean to assert that muddling through with status quo policies was a viable strategy in the long run for the prevention of German unification within NATO. Eventually, revolutionary forces on the ground in East Germany and throughout Eastern Europe were very likely to overwhelm the deteriorating Soviet position. But the fact that German unification within NATO was the most likely eventual outcome given power realities does not mean that acquiescence to this position was the policy that Soviet decision makers were most likely to adopt, especially in the

---

unification and NATO membership, the Americans were prepared to oppose this gambit and try to force the Soviets to capitulate (Zelikow and Rice, *Germany Unified and Europe Transformed*, 246, 252). U.S. leaders were, however, far from certain that they would succeed in these efforts, as the sources cited in this footnote clearly reveal.

60. Adomeit, *Imperial Overstretch*, 488 (emphasis in original). Before Gorbachev agreed to German unification within NATO, Germany had committed to the Soviet Union roughly only seven billion DM in guaranteed loans and grants.

61. Ibid., 326. See also 491, 498; Sigal, *Hang Separately*, 49, 56, 76; Zelikow and Rice, *Germany Unified and Europe Transformed*, 179, 245, 261; Beschloss and Talbott, *At the Highest Levels*, 178, 186.

short run. Despite the Soviet Union's failing economy, most conservatives continued to oppose Gorbachev's policies that ultimately approved of a unified Germany within NATO.

Old and New Thinkers' policy differences concerning German unification were important. At a minimum, allowing German unification in exchange for Germany's exit from NATO would have created very different security structures in Europe than we see today. Moreover, if conservatives had been able to extract sufficient funds in exchange for agreeing to Western proposals, perhaps the Soviet Union's disintegration could have been delayed or even prevented (though the latter is unlikely). Probably most alarming, if Soviet conservatives were allowed to continue to drag their feet over the German issue, an incendiary situation could have developed in which popular forces in Germany directly confronted Soviet troops. The great dangers associated with scenarios like this one are clear.

Ideological differences between New and old thinkers explain their policy disagreements. Most Soviet conservatives remained convinced that the NATO allies were highly aggressive states dedicated to the destruction of the Soviet Union. To acquiesce to German unification in NATO was simply too great a danger for many old thinkers to allow despite the economic incentives pushing for this outcome. Ligachev expressed conservatives' fears when he told the February 1990 Central Committee Plenum that "it would be unpardonably short-sighted and a folly not to see that on the world horizon looms a Germany with a formidable economic and military potential. . . . The time has come to recognize this new danger [of a "new Munich"]. . . . It is not too late."[62]

Most New Thinkers were not nearly as concerned about the revolutionary international changes taking place in the late 1980s and early 1990s. This does not mean that Gorbachev and his supporters had no misgivings about these developments. The historical record is clear that New Thinkers, even some of the most liberal like Shevardnadze, were initially anxious about the ramifications for Soviet security created by German unification within NATO.[63] This should not be surprising given the massive transfer of power that accompanied Germany's unification, the fact that the Soviet Union's postwar security structures had been predicated on the division of Europe, and the enormous sacrifices made by the Soviets to defeat Nazi Germany. The key point for our purposes is that because of their ideological similarities with the Western powers, New Thinkers, unlike most conservatives, ultimately could be assured that a unified Germany in NATO

62. In Adomeit, *Imperial Overstretch*, 490–491. See also 510–511, 536–537; Odom, *Collapse of the Soviet Military*, 159, 170–171, 181–182; Zelikow and Rice, *Germany Unified and Europe Transformed*, 179–180, 261; Chernyaev, *My Six Years with Gorbachev*, 44, 273; Nichols and Karasik, "Civil-Military Relations under Gorbachev," 33–34, 39–40, 47–48.
63. Wallander and Prokop, "Soviet Security Strategies in Europe"; Zelikow and Rice, *Germany Unified and Europe Transformed*, 421.

was not a significant threat to the Soviet Union. "The most important thing for Gorbachev [on the subject of German unification]," as Chernyaev recalled, "was that he regarded the process of unification as a democratic national movement. From his standpoint it was quite legitimate, quite consistent with . . . New Thinking, and therefore opposing [it meant] . . . opposing his own philosophy for which he began perestroika."[64] Gorbachev was able to take the "risk" of substantially reducing Soviet armaments, as well as withdrawing Soviet troops from Eastern Europe, because he believed that "nobody would attack us even if we disarmed completely."[65] Without New Thinkers' belief that Germany's unification in NATO did not represent a significant threat to Soviet interests, the negotiations resolving the issue that lay at the heart of the Cold War rivalry would not have gone nearly as smoothly as they did.[66]

American Foreign Policies and the End of the Cold War

There can be no doubt that relative power concerns played an important role in shaping American policies toward the Soviet Union in the 1980s. A prominent theme of Reagan and his advisors in the 1980 presidential election and throughout his first four years as president was that increases in Soviet capabilities and geopolitical influence over the previous decade had placed America's security in greater peril than it had been at any time since the end of the Second World War.[67]

In order to protect America's security from the Soviet threat, Reagan and his advisors adopted a three-pronged strategy that had a single end: to maximize the United States' relative power position in relation to the USSR. They proposed the largest peacetime military budget in American history, tried to exhaust Soviet capabilities by engaging in a policy that

64. In Wohlforth, *Cold War Endgame*, 70. Gorbachev reports that he told Romanian dictator Nicolae Ceauşescu in December 1989 that because the revolutions in Eastern Europe "had a clearly democratic character . . . there was no reason to fear the collapse or the end of socialism" (in Jacques Lévesque, "The Emancipation of Eastern Europe," in *Ending the Cold War: Interpretations, Causation, and the Study of International Relations*, ed. Richard K. Herrmann and Richard Ned Lebow (New York: Palgrave Macmillan, 2004), 123).

65. Chernyaev, *My Six Years with Gorbachev*, 45–46, 235–360. See also *Witnesses to the End of the Cold War*, ed. William C. Wohlforth (Baltimore: Johns Hopkins University Press, 1996), 5, 37; Adomeit, *Imperial Overstretch*, 517, 521, 533, 536; Odom, *Collapse of the Soviet Military*, 95, 157.

66. Key Soviet leaders including Gorbachev, Shevardnadze, Chernyaev, and Alexander Bessmertnykh (who succeeded Shevardnadze as Soviet Foreign Minister in 1991) have explicitly agreed with this statement. Zelikow and Rice, *Germany Unified and Europe Transformed*, 331, 332, 342, 344, 472; Beschloss and Talbott, *At the Highest Levels*, 165.

67. Alexander Haig, *Caveat: Realism, Reagan, and Foreign Policy* (New York: Macmillan, 1984), 220, 224; Ronald Reagan, *An American Life* (New York: Simon and Schuster, 1990), 552; Oberdorfer, *Turn from the Cold War to a New Era*, 32; Beth Fischer, *The Reagan Reversal: Foreign Policy and the End of the Cold War* (Columbia: University of Missouri Press, 1997), chap. 2.

was tantamount to economic warfare, and aided indigenous forces that opposed Soviet control and influence in various regions around the world, including the Solidarity movement in Poland, the Mujahedin in Afghanistan, the Contras in Nicaragua, and UNITA in Angola. By substantially increasing America's relative power, leaders in the Reagan administration hoped to create a set of international incentives that were so strong that they left Soviet decision makers little choice but to behave in ways that were less threatening to American security.[68]

Despite the importance of relative power concerns to America's key leaders during the Reagan presidency, it would be a mistake to understand the Reagan administration's policies toward the Soviet Union primarily as a function of realist thinking. Reagan and his most influential advisors never viewed the Soviet threat in geopolitical terms alone, but instead stressed the ideological motivation behind the Soviet menace. In fact, very often to key officials, such as Reagan, Secretary of Defense Caspar Weinberger, and Secretary of State George Shultz (who replaced Alexander Haig in 1982), Soviet power was understood in a particularly threatening light *because of* Soviet leaders' profound ideological differences with the Western powers.[69] For example, Shultz repeatedly claimed both to Western audiences and his Soviet interlocutors that the United States could never have a "normal" relationship with the USSR if the ideological gap separating the two states remained unchanged: "Only when the Soviets changed human rights practices and recognized the importance of these rights to their own society could Soviet-American relations change at the deepest level."[70] Or as Reagan himself asserted: "All of us need to be better informed about the unchanging realities of the Soviet system. We are in a long-term twilight struggle with an implacable foe of freedom." "We cannot assume that their ideology and purpose will change; this implies enduring competition."[71]

---

68. Garthoff, *Great Transition*, 29.
69. Keith Shimko's content analysis of the statements made by Reagan, Weinberger, and Shultz (among others) reveals that these individuals, in a clear majority of the time, attributed Soviet motivation to Marxist-Leninist ideology. Keith Shimko, *Images and Arms Control: Perceptions of the Soviet Union in the Reagan Administration* (Ann Arbor: University of Michigan Press, 1991), 67–69, 87–89, 105–108.
70. George Shultz, *Turmoil and Triumph: My Years as Secretary of State* (New York: Charles Scribner's Sons, 1993), 586; see also 398, 528, 574, 582, 586, 762, 888, 1012, 1132.
71. Both in Shimko, *Images and Arms Control*, 107. The president expressed a related belief after the Geneva Summit when he stated to Gorbachev that "an improvement of the human condition within the Soviet Union is indispensable for an improvement in bilateral relations with the United States" (in Freedman, *Europe Transformed*, 219). Similarly, Undersecretary of State for Political Affairs Lawrence Eagleburger stated: "The Soviets [are] not only our rival, but the rival of a humane world order. . . . Our rivalry, then, must continue as long as our two nations remain true to the principles upon which they were founded" (in Fischer, *Reagan Reversal*, 19). See also Richard Pipes, "Can the Soviet Union Reform?," *Foreign Affairs* 63, no. 1 (Fall 1984): 47, 48, 59.

Consistent with the claims that the superpowers' geopolitical enmity was to a significant extent a product of their ideological differences, Reagan and his advisors asserted that if the ideological rivalry between the United States and USSR could be overcome, the power-political conflict would substantially come to an end. For example, Paul Nitze, the president's arms control negotiator with the Soviets, wrote: "The rest of the world would welcome [institutional and ideological] reforms and such internal progress [in the Soviet Union]. They would make the Soviet Union in many ways a stronger competitor but, hopefully, a less paranoid and more cooperative one."[72] More important, Reagan and others frequently stated that increasing democratization and respect for human rights in the Soviet Union would lead to a much better relationship with America.[73]

Leaders in the Reagan administration did more than simply assert the centrality of ideological differences as a key cause of the U.S.-Soviet rivalry. They also based their policies on the implications of this belief. A prominent objective of American foreign policies in the 1980s (and since the beginning of the Cold War, for that matter)[74] was to use external pressure to try to change the core ideological principles of the Soviet regime: from a totalitarian state dedicated to Marxism-Leninism to a more democratic one founded on central tenets of political liberalism. In the 1983 top-secret National Security Decision Directive (NSDD)-75, Reagan officials asserted that reducing the ideological distance dividing the superpowers was a preeminent U.S. interest. The directive stated that a critical objective of U.S. foreign policy was "to promote . . . the process of change in the Soviet Union toward a more pluralistic political and economic system in which the power of the privileged ruling elite is gradually reduced. The U.S. recognizes that Soviet aggressiveness has deep roots in the internal system."[75]

72. Paul Nitze, "Living with the Soviets," *Foreign Affairs* 63, no. 2 (Winter 1984/85): 372.
73. Reagan, *American Life*, 682, 714; Lou Cannon, *President Reagan: The Role of a Lifetime* (New York: Simon and Schuster, 1991), 787, 790. Richard Pipes (Soviet specialist on the National Security Council) similarly asserted that "the key to peace . . . lies in an internal transformation of the Soviet system" (Pipes, "Can the Soviet Union Reform?," 59). Jack Matlock, senior director for European and Soviet Affairs on the NSC staff, 1983–1986, and the ambassador to the Soviet Union, 1986–1991, summed up the president's views on this subject: "[Reagan] understood that the Cold War was ultimately about ideology. He saw both the arms race and geopolitical competition as symptoms of an ideological struggle, not its causes . . . [Reagan was convinced] that a more open Soviet Union with an informed and empowered public would not threaten the United States or its neighbors" (Jack F. Matlock, *Reagan and Gorbachev: How the Cold War Ended* (New York: Random House, 2004), 320; also xiv, 105, 131, 218, 295, 316).
74. Cf. Gregory Mitrovich, *Undermining the Kremlin: America's Strategy to Subvert the Soviet Bloc, 1947–1956* (Ithaca: Cornell University Press, 2000).
75. In *National Security Directives of the Reagan and Bush Administrations,* ed. Christopher Simpson (Boulder: Westview Press, 1995), 255). Pipes (NSDD-75's author) revealed in a startling manner how critical the goal of narrowing the ideological gap with the Soviet Union was to his thinking when he asserted that "Soviet leaders would have to choose between

Leveraging internal change in the Soviet Union was a preeminent objective to many key U.S. leaders because they believed that such shifts would likely result in more cooperative relations with America. As Soviet expert on the NSC staff and later the U.S. Ambassador to the Soviet Union, Jack Matlock, phrased it: "The crux of the problem was that the Soviet Union would have to change before the U.S.-Soviet relationship could improve fundamentally. If the Soviet Union stayed as it was, we could hope only to manage the mutual hostility, not to harmonize policies. . . . I thought that a U.S. strategy that encouraged internal Soviet change [therefore] made sense."[76]

The evolution of American leaders' views and behavior toward the USSR over the course of the late 1980s indicates the importance of the ideological distance separating the two states to these individuals. A longitudinal analysis of these years reveals that changing U.S. attitudes and policies toward the Soviet Union to the point where the key decision makers during the Reagan presidency were declaring the Cold War to be over corresponded most closely with ideological changes in the Soviet Union, and not with shifts in Soviet power, as realist theories predict.[77]

As late as February 1988, Secretary of State Shultz declared that he found it "difficult to believe that [America's] relations with the Soviet Union will ever be 'normal' in the sense that we have normal relations with most other countries." Thus "it seems unlikely that the U.S.-Soviet relationship will ever lose what always had been and is today a strongly wary and at times adversarial element."[78] A policy paper issued by the president the previous month reached similar conclusions.[79]

Yet by the time of the Moscow summit in May 1988, Reagan and some of his key advisors, including Shultz, adopted an entirely different tone than they had possessed for the previous seven years. At the summit, "a new theme developed: that of approval for Gorbachev and his works."[80]

---

peacefully changing their Communist system in the direction followed by the West or going to war. There is no other alternative and it could go either way" (in Garthoff, *Great Transition*, 12). (Pipes was subsequently rebuked for the starkness of this statement.) See also Pipes, "Can the Soviet Union Reform?," 48, 61; Alexander Dallin, "Learning in U.S. Policy toward the Soviet Union in the 1980s," in *Learning in U.S. and Soviet Foreign Policy*, ed. George Breslauer and Philip Tetlock (Boulder: Westview Press, 1991), 409.

76. Jack Matlock, Jr., *Autopsy on an Empire* (New York: Random House, 1995), 80–81. See also Baker, *Politics of Diplomacy*, 41; also Matlock, *Reagan and Gorbachev*, 105.

77. For a more detailed longitudinal analysis that compares the timing of changes in American leaders' attitudes and policies toward the Soviet Union during the Reagan and Bush administrations with shifts in Soviet power, behavior, and ideology, see Mark L. Haas, "U.S. Foreign Policies at the End of the Cold War: Reactions to Shifts in Soviet Power, Behavior, or Ideology?," paper presented at the American Political Science Association annual meeting, Chicago, September 2004.

78. In Garthoff, *Great Transition*, 340.

79. Ibid., 339.

80. Fitzgerald, *Way Out There in the Blue*, 456.

At this time, Reagan stated that his description of the Soviet Union as an "evil empire" belonged to "another time, another era," despite the fact that he had made the former statement just five years earlier.[81] Most surprising, when asked if he could declare the Cold War to be over, the president, albeit with a hesitation, answered: "I think right now, of course."[82] Reagan, Shultz, and Matlock, among others, would reassert this belief without hesitation in the next seven months.[83] Moreover, for the remainder of Reagan's time in office, no significant negative developments took place between the superpowers.[84] The two states were clearly on the road to developing normal relations, which both the president and the secretary of state said was a very unlikely outcome just months earlier.

Realist theories have difficulty explaining this remarkable, and rather sudden, transformation. When Reagan's views of the Soviet Union were revolutionizing, none of the major indices of power capabilities had been reduced anywhere near the point where they could plausibly explain this change. In terms of military hardware, little had changed since Reagan became president. In the Gorbachev and Reagan years, the Soviets had committed themselves to reducing weapons in only one category of weapons: intermediate-range nuclear forces, and the INF Treaty signed by the U.S. and USSR in December 1987 reduced Soviet nuclear arsenals by only four percent. Overall Soviet defense spending from 1985 to 1987 grew, according to contemporary CIA estimates, at a 4.3 percent per annum pace, which was the fastest rate of growth for a three-year period since the 1960s.[85] In December 1988, Gorbachev did pledge to decrease the Soviet armed forces in Eastern Europe by 500,000 men and 5,000 tanks. These proposed cuts significantly reduced the Soviets' ability to wage an offensive war in Europe. Even after this decision, however, the Soviet Union still possessed a significant advantage in conventional forces over NATO.[86] More important for our purposes, Reagan and other key U.S. leaders had declared the Cold War to be over well before Gorbachev made this commitment.

The Soviet Union's economy from America's perspective also remained fairly constant during the time that U.S. assessments of the Soviet danger were greatly changing. According to some CIA estimates, the Soviet

---

81. In Garthoff, *Great Transition*, 352, also 358.

82. In Fitzgerald, *Way Out There in the Blue*, 458.

83. Ibid., 467; Zelikow and Rice, *Germany Unified and Europe Transformed*, 19; Shultz, *Turmoil and Triumph*, 1131.

84. Garthoff, *Great Transition*, 368.

85. Noel E. Firth and James H. Noren, *Soviet Defense Spending: A History of CIA Estimates, 1950–1990* (College Station: Texas A&M Press, 1998), 100–102.

86. Even after this reduction, the WTO possessed two and a half times more tanks than NATO did in Europe, over twice as many armored vehicles, nearly three times as many artillery pieces, and twice as many combat aircraft (Mike Bowker, *Russian Foreign Policy and the End of the Cold War* [Aldershot: Dartmouth, 1997], 76).

Union's economy had even slightly improved during the period when American leaders were substantially downgrading the threat posed by the USSR.[87] Although long-term projections for the USSR's economy remained bleak, this assessment was a constant throughout the 1980s.

Similarly, by the time Reagan left office very few changes had been made in the Soviet Union's support of clients in the Third World.[88] Indeed, Soviet arms deliveries to Third World states actually grew in relationship to similar American efforts in the 1985–88 period, including to Afghanistan, Cambodia, and Nicaragua.[89] The result of these efforts was that in "important ways Soviet regional leverage in 1990 was greater than it had been in 1980."[90] Finally, it must be remembered that by the end of Reagan's presidency, the Soviet Union's empire in Eastern Europe remained intact, even if Gorbachev was reducing the number of Soviet troops present in the region.

The transformation in American leaders' attitudes toward the Soviet Union in the spring of 1988, to the point where Reagan and others concluded that the Cold War was ending, corresponded not with changes in Soviet capabilities (nor with alterations in the content of U.S. policymakers' ideological beliefs, which remained constant), but with a significant narrowing of the ideological distance dividing the superpowers that resulted from objectively revolutionary domestic changes in the Soviet Union. Gorbachev and fellow New Thinkers had initiated important domestic-ideological changes in the USSR before 1988, most notably the introduction at the plenary session of the Central Committee in January 1987 of competitive elections within the CPSU for party posts.[91] Nevertheless, the nature of Gorbachev's ideological objectives remained ambiguous, especially to foreign observers, for his first three years in power. As late as February 1988 Gorbachev repeatedly denied that he was dedicated to profound ideological changes in the Soviet Union. In a speech given by Gorbachev to a Central Committee plenum in this month, "every third phrase," according to Georgi Shakhnazarov, "could

87. The CIA estimated that from 1980 to 1985, the Soviet Union's national income grew at a rate of 1.8 percent. This figure was believed to have increased to 2.7 percent for the years 1985 to 1987 (Mark Harrison, "Soviet Economic Growth Since 1928: The Alternative Statistics of G.I. Khanin," *Europe-Asia Studies* 45, no. 1 [1993]: 146).

88. In February 1988, however, Gorbachev publicly pledged to remove Soviet troops from Afghanistan in a year's time. This was not an insignificant development. This change, however, was somewhat offset by an increase in aid to indigenous forces in Afghanistan who were sympathetic to the Soviet Union.

89. Herrmann, "Soviet Behavior in Regional Conflicts," 452–457.

90. Ibid., 461.

91. In June of 1987, the Politburo also approved two business laws that gave firm managers power to make some decisions independently of the centralized state economic bureaucracies. The laws, however, did not take effect until the beginning of 1988, and even Ligachev did not consider them a significant move toward a market economy (Odom, *Collapse of the Soviet Military*, 137).

have been used by those who argued that Gorbachev wished to do no more than 'touch up' socialism."[92] According to Archie Brown, one of the foremost experts on Soviet domestic politics during the Gorbachev era, it was not until the spring of 1988 that Gorbachev switched from "reformist to transformative change of the [Soviet] political system."[93]

Before 1988, key foreign observers did not believe that Gorbachev was dedicated to revolutionary ideological changes in the Soviet Union on the Western model. Shultz thought that at the end of 1987 Gorbachev was "still imprisoned by [Marxist-Leninist] ideology . . . Success . . . would depend on his willingness to abandon, not just modify, a failing system."[94] Similarly, Matlock (who was the most important advisor to Reagan on Soviet politics) was of the opinion as late as April 1988 (as was Reagan) "that Gorbachev seemed serious, but had not yet made a breakthrough to fundamental [domestic] reform." It was not until this month (for reasons discussed in detail below) that the U.S. possessed unambiguous evidence that "Gorbachev was finally prepared to cross the Rubicon and discard the Marxist ideology that had defined and justified the Communist Party dictatorship in the Soviet Union."[95]

The key change by which Gorbachev unambiguously demonstrated his commitment to replacing the Soviet political system with a much more liberal one came when he publicly laid out in April 1988 his domestic objectives to be voted upon at the upcoming Nineteenth Party Conference scheduled for June. The proposals constituted an institutional and ideological revolution in the Soviet Union. They included the establishment of competitive elections with secret ballots, term limits for elected officials, separation of powers with an independent judiciary, and provisions for freedom of speech, assembly, and the press.[96]

These institutional changes proposed by Gorbachev in the spring of 1988 were the catalyst that pushed many of America's most important decision makers, including Reagan, Matlock, Shultz, and National Security Advisor Colin Powell, to understand the depths of the ideological revolution taking place in the Soviet Union.[97] These individuals immediately recognized the significance of Gorbachev's 1988 proposals for both Soviet society and, more important for our purposes, the nature of the ideological distance dividing the two superpowers. According to Matlock, "As I read [Gorbachev's proposals on the eve of the Moscow summit beginning in late

92. Archie Brown, *The Gorbachev Factor* (Oxford: Oxford University Press, 1996), 175.
93. Ibid.
94. Shultz, *Turmoil and Triumph*, 1081.
95. Matlock, *Reagan and Gorbachev*, 295–296; also Matlock, *Autopsy on an Empire*, 91, 144; Sigal, *Hang Separately*, 25, 196; Fitzgerald, *Way Out There in the Blue*, 329.
96. Fitzgerald, *Way Out There in the Blue*, 454; Matlock, *Autopsy on an Empire*, 122; Adomeit, *Imperial Overstretch*, 351.
97. Fitzgerald, *Way Out There in the Blue*, 454, 459; Sigal, *Hang Separately*, 26; Cannon, *President Reagan*, 789; Reagan, *American Life*, 708.

May] and discovered one new element after another, my excitement grew. Never before had I seen in an official Communist Party document such an extensive section on protecting the rights of citizens or such principles as the separation of powers, judicial independence, and presumption of a defendant's innocence until proven guilty."[98]

The very next morning, Matlock informed Reagan and some of his closest advisors of these important developments. In the ambassador's words, Gorbachev's proposed institutional changes "contained the seeds of the liberation of the country"—"if they turned out to be real, the Soviet Union could never again be what it had been in the past." "[Specifically,] what had passed for 'socialism' in Soviet parlance had dropped from sight. What the [Party Conference proposals] described was something closer to European social democracy."[99]

It was shortly after Gorbachev made his domestic intentions clear that America's leaders began to assert that the Cold War was ending. This was not a coincidence. America's key leaders explicitly recognized the causal connection between domestic changes in the Soviet Union and a likely revolution in American-Soviet relations. As Reagan explained in a speech in London after the Moscow summit, the "democratic reform" that Gorbachev initiated in the Soviet Union, which included "such things as official accountability, limitations on length of service in office, [and] an independent judiciary," was ushering in "the hope of a new era in human history, and, hopefully, an era of peace and freedom for all."[100] As soon as Reagan and many of his key advisors became convinced that Gorbachev was dedicated to genuine democratic reform in the Soviet Union, the former began to view the Soviet Union, led by New Thinkers, as a trustworthy actor that would not be a significant danger to other states' safety.[101]

Gorbachev himself recognized that ideological changes in the Soviet Union on the Western model were central to the improvement in U.S.-Soviet relations in 1988. According to Chernyaev, "Gorbachev [in the early years of his tenure as general secretary] believed that we could end the Cold War mostly or exclusively through a process of disarmament, while putting aside all those other questions, such as human rights." "It was only later that Mr. Gorbachev accepted and even became convinced

---

98. Matlock, *Autopsy on an Empire*, 122.
99. Ibid.
100. In Fitzgerald, *Way Out There in the Blue*, 459.
101. Some hardliners in the Reagan administration, including Weinberger, Assistant Secretary of Defense Richard Perle, and Deputy CIA Director Robert Gates, continued to advocate the adoption of confrontational policies toward the Soviet Union throughout the 1980s. Both Weinberger and Perle, however, resigned in 1987. Moreover, it is interesting that in his memoirs, Gates ultimately attributes the end of the Cold War largely to the domestic changes initiated by Gorbachev (Robert M. Gates, *From the Shadows: The Ultimate Insider's Story of Five Presidents and How They Won the Cold War* [New York: Simon and Schuster, 1996], 380, 447, 450).

that without a solution to the human rights problem the Cold War could not be brought to an end, and a new relationship with the United States could not be built."[102] Only when major ideological changes in the Soviet Union in 1988 on the Western model accompanied Gorbachev's arms-control offensive of the previous three years did the Americans begin to believe that the superpowers' relationship was changing at its most fundamental level.

The importance of domestic-ideological changes in the Soviet Union to the development of U.S. foreign policies continued after George Bush became president in January 1989. The transition between the Reagan and Bush administrations in this area was not a seamless one, however. Although the most important decision makers in the Reagan White House, including Reagan and Shultz, had declared the Cold War to be over,[103] the key leaders of the Bush administration, including the president, Secretary of State James Baker, and National Security Advisor Brent Scowcroft, were much more cautious in their assessments of the international situation. Bush was less conservative than Reagan, which made the new president more vulnerable to criticisms from certain factions of the Republican Party if he were to move too quickly in improving relations with the Soviets. Bush and his advisors also recognized the significant impact that rhetoric would likely have on the development of America's policies toward the Soviet Union. As Scowcroft recollected: "Once you say the Cold War is over, you can never take it back. You can only say it once."[104] Once these words were publicly spoken, the pressure for massive cuts in defense spending would become overwhelming. This fact created powerful incentives for caution while the Bush administration got its bearings. Soviet officials labeled this period of U.S. foreign policy from January to May 1989 as "the pause" in the progress of American-Soviet relations.[105]

102. In Wohlforth, *Witnesses to the End of the Cold War*, 166, 95, respectively. On several occasions Gorbachev told the Politburo that without political liberalization and an increased respect for human rights in the Soviet Union, hostility with the United States and its allies would not end. According to Gorbachev: "We had to think long and hard to grasp that human rights are . . . universal . . . and to understand that [without democracy] we'd never achieve real trust in foreign relations" (in English, "Road(s) Not Taken," 266). See also English, *Russia and the Idea of the West*, 219, 221–222; Eduard Shevardnadze, *The Future Belongs to Freedom* (New York: Free Press, 1991), 54–55, 57–58, 123, 126.

103. Garthoff, *Great Transition*, 467; Zelikow and Rice, *Germany Unified and Europe Transformed*, 19.

104. In Zelikow and Rice, *Germany Unified and Europe Transformed*, 20.

105. Incentives pushing for increasing levels of cooperation with the Soviets were in fact already at work in the first months of 1989. Reagan's declarations that the Cold War was over helped to create widespread public optimism in both the U.S. and its European allies that U.S.-Soviet enmity was at an end (for public opinion polls revealing these beliefs, see: Oberdorfer, *Turn from the Cold War to a New Era*, 294, 323; Fitzgerald, *Way Out There in the Blue*, 559; Charlotte Saikowski, "Voters' Evolving Security Views," *The Christian Science Monitor*, July 27, 1988, 3). An important consequence of these favorable views was that the political pressures for cuts

Once the Bush administration completed an intensive review of the developments in the Soviet Union, the president and his closest advisors were inclined to continue to develop much more cooperative relations with the USSR. For example, in an NSC meeting in May 1989, Condoleezza Rice, a Soviet expert on the NSC staff, said that the world was entering a new era that would allow the United States to move "'beyond containment' to almost the reverse of containment, the encouragement of Soviet integration into the Western economic and political community."[106] Implicit in this assertion was the belief that the Cold War was over. If it was time to move "beyond containment," then the Cold War rivalry that necessitated the containment policy must have ended. President Bush agreed with these ideas so much that they became the core of his commencement speech at Texas A&M University on May 12. The speech was meant to announce America's strategic objectives vis-à-vis the Soviet Union.[107]

This position was not just rhetoric. Key U.S. leaders believed America should take bold steps in order to improve relations with the USSR. In May 1989, the president ordered Secretary of Defense Dick Cheney and Admiral William Crowe, chairman of the Joint Chiefs of Staff, to come up with a plan that proposed equal numbers of American and Soviet military personnel in Europe at a level 20 percent smaller than current U.S. numbers (the previous plan, developed after a two-year debate, called for much smaller cuts of 5 to 10 percent[108]). Moreover, Bush instructed that these changes should be "front-loaded" in such a way that the bulk of the troop reductions would happen sooner rather than later.[109] In order to implement these changes, Bush overrode his military advisors' recommendation for a more cautious approach (Crowe claimed the cuts would "make a mockery of forward defense and jeopardize the [NATO] alliance").[110] According to Scowcroft, "We hoped . . . [the conventional forces proposal would] demonstrate both to the Soviets and the Europeans

---

in defense spending were growing increasingly more powerful at the time Reagan left office (E. J. Dionne, "Poll Finds Public Favors Sharp Cut in Arms Funds," *The New York Times*, March 12, 1989, 24). Public pressure, as well as urgings to the new administration in the first months of 1989 from Reagan, Margaret Thatcher, Helmut Kohl, François Mitterrand, and U.S. Senators to increase the level and pace of cooperation with the Soviets, had an impact on Bush leaders. According to contemporary U.S. officials' accounts, both Baker and Scowcroft pushed for the adoption of "bold ideas aimed at satisfying public desire for new approaches" with the USSR (R. Jeffrey Smith, "Arms Cuts Gain Favor as Anxieties Ebb," *The Washington Post*, May 8, 1989, A1;" Beschloss and Talbott, *At the Highest Levels*, 49–50, 76).
106. Oberdorfer, *Turn from the Cold War to a New Era*, 347.
107. Beschloss and Talbott, *At the Highest Levels*, 69.
108. Smith, "Arms Cuts Gain Favor as Anxieties Ebb."
109. Beschloss and Talbott, *At the Highest Levels*, 75, 77–78.
110. Ibid., 76.

that we were serious, forward-looking, and prepared to take some risks to move East-West relations to a new plane."[111]

In the summer of 1989, Bush instructed Baker and Scowcroft to negotiate with the Soviets a massive reduction in existing stocks of chemical weapons in the two superpowers.[112] What was most significant about these proposals was that verification of the disposal of chemical weapons is very difficult to obtain. Yet Bush told Scowcroft that he was not terribly concerned about the Soviets cheating on the agreement. This view stood in stark contrast to Bush's reasons for opposing a less ambitious chemical weapons treaty with the Soviet Union in 1984 when he was vice president.[113] The Soviets were quick to realize this important change in the American position. As Sergei Tarasenko, Shevardnadze's personal aide, told his boss about Bush's proposal: "This is really something new and important. The Americans are no longer ... so obsessed with our cheating."[114]

Probably most surprising, so great was Baker's trust of Shevardnadze and Gorbachev, that instead of attempting to loosen Soviet control over Eastern Europe, the secretary of state in December 1989 actually approved a possible Soviet invasion of Romania for the purpose of quelling potential violence by Romanian citizens against the toppled Ceauşescu regime.[115] This decision "was a remarkable reflection of a basic shift in outlook toward seeing the Soviet Union as a force contributing to positive change in the world rather than assuming it to be a permanent source of destabilization and threat. It would have been hard to find a more striking example reflecting American recognition of the end of the Cold War."[116]

Power variables no doubt explain some of these favorable views and policies by the Bush administration. Most important, Gorbachev's December 1988 pledge to remove unilaterally 500,000 military personnel and 5,000 tanks from Eastern Europe reduced substantially the Soviet military threat to the NATO states.

Although this change was very significant, in other important dimensions of power, the Soviet Union's position remained largely unchanged in 1989. Soviet leaders continued to support regimes around the globe that were hostile to American interests, including Cuba, Nicaragua, and Afghanistan. "As late as September [1989]," as Michael Beschloss and Strobe Talbott explain, "one could still fairly argue that Gorbachev had not seriously changed Soviet behavior around the world [in Third World

---

111. Bush and Scowcroft, *World Transformed*, 74.
112. Beschloss and Talbott, *At the Highest Levels*, 120–121; Garthoff, *Great Transition*, 385.
113. Beschloss and Talbott, *At the Highest Levels*, 120.
114. Ibid.
115. Thomas Blanton, "When Did the Cold War End?," *Cold War International History Project Bulletin* 10 (March 1998), virtual archive, 4. http://wwics.si.edu/index.cfm?fuseaction=library.document&topic_id=1409&id=382.
116. Garthoff, *Great Transition*, 408.

states]."[117] Rice stated in a meeting with U.S. officials that "we keep telling them to knock it off, but the Soviets are still putting military equipment into every nook and cranny of the Third World. I think we've got to re-ask ourselves the tough question: What are the tangible differences from the old days?"[118] Finally, although the long run projections for the Soviet economy remained bleak, in 1989 the USSR was still experiencing positive economic growth, at least according to Western estimates (1.5 percent of GNP).[119]

According to Bush administration officials' own accounts, domestic-ideological changes in the USSR, and not shifts in Soviet power, were the key variable pushing these individuals to believe that the U.S.-Soviet relationship was, as Baker put it in September 1989, on the verge "of a whole new world."[120] American decision makers believed that the greater the ideological convergence between the Soviet Union and the United States, the less hostile the USSR would be to U.S. interests. For example, according to President Bush in May 1989, it was necessary to move beyond containment to the integration of the Soviet Union into the Western political and economic system because of the "full scope of change taking place . . . in the Soviet Union."[121] Or as the president explained at another time in the same month, as the Soviet Union changed domestically in terms of solidifying democracy, "our doctrine need no longer be containing a militarily aggressive Soviet Union."[122]

Baker saw the March 1989 election of a Soviet Congress of People's Deputies (which was the most democratic election in Russia's history) as powerful evidence that America was dealing with a very different type of Soviet Union than in previous years.[123] Similarly, an important turning point in Baker's views of Soviet intentions occurred in a July 1989 meeting with Shevardnadze in Paris. The key to the talks was not a breakthrough on any substantive issue. Instead, the negotiations were critical because they helped convince Baker that Shevardnadze was genuinely committed to domestic liberalization in the Soviet Union. From that point on, Baker saw Shevardnadze as a trustworthy person who was dedicated to transforming the U.S.-Soviet relationship from rivalry to partnership.[124] Consistent with this view, in testimony before the Senate in early

117. Beschloss and Talbott, *At the Highest Levels*, 105; see also Bush and Scowcroft, *World Transformed*, 134.
118. In Beschloss and Talbott, *At the Highest Levels*, 105.
119. Kotz and Weir, *Revolution from Above*, 43, 75; Åslund, *Gorbachev's Struggle for Economic Reform*, 17.
120. In Beschloss and Talbott, *At the Highest Levels*, 121.
121. In Oberdorfer, *Turn from the Cold War to a New Era*, 348.
122. Ibid., 352.
123. Beschloss and Talbott, *At the Highest Levels*, 45–47.
124. Baker, *Politics of Diplomacy*, 135–142; Chollet and Goldgeier, "Once Burned, Twice Shy?," 161–162.

October 1989, the secretary of state recognized that Gorbachev and fellow New Thinkers had made "an extraordinary effort at internal reform" that constituted a "true revolution." America's policies, he continued, should be designed to help domestic reform in the USSR succeed since "our own national interest . . . does not exist in isolation from the events taking place in the Soviet Union."[125]

Even Scowcroft, whose mantra was to judge states by their capabilities and not their intentions, placed great emphasis on the effects of domestic-ideological changes in the Soviet Union to America's security. In fact, for the national security advisor the key to understanding future Soviet foreign policies and the likelihood of ending the Cold War was to be found in Soviet domestic politics. As Scowcroft put it, "What was the internal situation in the Soviet Union? What were [Gorbachev's] relations with the conservatives, and what was his staying power? *These questions . . . remained at the forefront of every [American] policy decision related to eastern Europe.*"[126]

The importance of ideological convergence between the superpowers to American leaders continued after 1989, which was a watershed year for the USSR in terms of its power-projection capabilities. In the fall of this year, Soviet leaders chose not to try to prevent the revolutions that swept across Eastern Europe. By abandoning the "Brezhnev Doctrine" (which asserted the Soviet Union's obligation and right to protect the survival of socialist regimes in the states in Eastern Europe), Gorbachev was taking a major step toward the abandonment of the USSR's empire in this region.

Nineteen eighty-nine also marked the last year that the Soviet Union experienced positive economic growth. In 1990, the USSR's GNP declined by 2.4 percent. The Soviet economy did even worse in 1991, falling by 12.8 percent.[127] The CIA was aware of these numbers at the time.[128]

There can be little doubt that these trends in the Soviet Union's relative power had important effects on America's key decision makers' perceptions of the Soviet threat. The more the USSR's relative power and geopolitical influence declined, the smaller the Soviet Union's ability to challenge U.S. interests. Moreover, there is evidence suggesting that after 1989, the Americans were adhering to a core tenet of offensive realism: the more the relative power balance shifted in America's favor, the greater their negotiating demands became. As President Bush declared to West German Chancellor Helmut Kohl in a meeting in February 1990 with regard to Germany's unification and continued membership in the Atlantic alliance: "The Soviets are not in a position to dictate Germany's

125. In Garthoff, *Great Transition,* 386.
126. Bush and Scowcroft, *World Transformed,* 39 (emphasis added).
127. Kotz and Weir, *Revolution from Above,* 75.
128. Beschloss and Talbott, *At the Highest Levels,* 374.

relationship with NATO. What worries me is talk that Germany must not stay in NATO. To hell with that! We prevailed, they didn't. We can't let the Soviets clutch victory from the jaws of defeat."[129] Similarly, on the START talks the Americans were very inflexible. Their dominant negotiating strategy was to "sit back, pocket what the Kremlin had to offer, and wait for more."[130]

However, to claim that shifts in relative power were the primary determinant of America's policies toward the Soviet Union in 1990 and 1991 significantly inflates the extent and importance of the USSR's relative power decline as it was understood by America's key decision makers at the time. With regard to the international event that probably mattered most to America's leaders in the years before the Soviet Union's collapse: the unification of Germany with continued membership in NATO, America's key decision makers firmly believed that the Soviet Union continued to possess significant influence. Consequently, the Americans believed that the Soviets had the ability to damage U.S. interests in these areas, if they chose to do so. As Philip Zelikow and Condoleezza Rice explain on this subject: "No senior officials in either Washington or Bonn believed . . . that the USSR [did not possess] significant leverage over events in Central Europe. Moscow could force the German people to choose between unification and membership in NATO, channeling the surging tide for unity against the supporters of the alliance. Moscow could also force the German people to choose between respecting the Soviets' wishes or precipitating a major international crisis." It is for these reasons that "no one doubted that the road to unification still led through Moscow."[131]

Consistent with the belief that the Soviets continued to possess significant influence over events, Bush and his key advisors did not primarily attribute the key developments after 1989 that were so beneficial to America's security, including a unified Germany in NATO, to America's dominant relative power position. Instead, *American officials consistently and unequivocally attributed favorable outcomes to the fact that a party dedicated to the liberalization of the Soviet Union's political and economic system was currently in power.* As long as New Thinkers continued to govern, the Americans were optimistic that the Soviets would cooperate. If conservatives once again took control, the Americans (as well as their European allies) believed that outcomes would most likely be very different, despite the Soviet Union's continued economic problems.[132]

Scowcroft, for example, asserted that domestic politics in the Soviet Union created "a window of opportunity" for the United States that

129. In Bush and Scowcroft, *World Transformed*, 253.
130. Beschloss and Talbott, *At the Highest Levels*, 119, 117; Garthoff, *Great Transition*, 423.
131. Zelikow and Rice, *Germany Unified and Europe Transformed*, 196. See also xi, 69, 154, 161, 172, 246, 273; Bush and Scowcroft, *World Transformed*, 241, 300.
132. Bush and Scowcroft, *World Transformed*, 216, 222, 229, 238, 271, 275, 495, 563.

allowed America to advance its interests in Europe. As long as New Thinkers were in power, the chances were good that cooperation would proceed. Thus "it was in our interest to do what we could to prolong the tenure of Gorbachev and the Soviet reformers, men who through perestroika and glasnost had set these changes in motion. . . . We had to move quickly and carefully to make the most of the favorable climate before Gorbachev left, or was forced from, the scene."[133] Zelikow and Rice, who were central to the negotiations pushing for the unification of Germany, used nearly identical language to describe the situation. According to their account, "top American officials believed from the beginning of 1990 onward that they were operating within a narrow window of opportunity. If the process of German unification could not be completed very soon, [conservatives could come to power in the USSR and thus] the United States and the FRG might find themselves dealing with a different kind of Soviet government and a more dangerous international environment."[134] Even if the Soviet Union's failing economy left Soviet leaders very little choice but to capitulate to U.S. positions, America's key decision makers did not believe this to be the case at the time.

The widespread belief among Bush administration officials that the Cold War was ending due to Gorbachev's domestic revolution helps explain Bush's strategy of negotiating with the Soviet leader. The President almost always tried to settle various outstanding Cold War disputes by trying to reassure the Soviets rather than coercing them with America's power superiority.[135] In order both to reassure the Soviets and bolster New Thinkers' domestic position, in 1989–1990 the Americans made new proposals on START, CFE, and chemical weapons talks; offered a number of concessions to ease trade restrictions on the Soviet Union; promised not to engage in polemics with regards to the Soviet Union's deteriorating position in eastern Europe and the Soviet republics[136]; and engineered a number of policies that were designed to increase the Soviets' confidence that a unified Germany's membership in NATO would not threaten Soviet security.[137]

133. Ibid., 205–206.
134. Zelikow and Rice, *Germany Unified and Europe Transformed*, 241.
135. Thomas Risse, "The Cold War's Endgame and German Unification (A Review Essay)," *International Security* 21, no. 4 (Spring 1997): 168–179.
136. For details on the preceding points, see Beschloss and Talbott, *At the Highest Levels*, 154–157, 164, 188–189; Zelikow and Rice, *Germany Unified and Europe Transformed*, 190–191, 196–197, 241.
137. The most important of these assurances were commitments by Germany not to develop or possess nuclear, chemical, or biological weapons, the promise that current German borders were inviolable, the pledge that non-German NATO forces would not be deployed in the former territory of East Germany, and the provision of ceilings on the level of military forces that Germany and other countries could deploy in Central Europe. NATO leaders also agreed that their states would abide by a pledge of no first use of nuclear weapons, promised to eliminate nuclear-tipped artillery shells in Europe, committed Germany to limit the size of

Gorbachev and his advisors were impressed with these policies. Georgi Arbatov, a Soviet expert on the United States, claimed that Bush's economic proposals meant "the end of economic warfare" between the superpowers.[138] Gorbachev and his allies also repeatedly claimed that the Western powers' security initiatives with regard to Germany and NATO were crucial to their ability to allow this state to be unified and remain in the Atlantic alliance.[139]

This analysis does not mean to imply that the Americans met the Soviets halfway in the negotiations that settled the outstanding issues of the Cold War. The Soviets clearly did much more compromising than the U.S. Instead, the key points are: (1) U.S. leaders believed the Cold War to be over because of Gorbachev's and New Thinkers' domestic liberalization; and (2) this view was critical to convincing the Americans that Gorbachev could be persuaded to end amicably remaining Cold War disputes.[140] Hence the adoption by the U.S. of primarily reassuring rather than coercive policies. As Baker explained after he left office: "The nature of perestroika and glasnost and the sympathy that these reforms engendered among Western public opinion really allowed the United States and its allies to treat this former adversary, the Soviet Union, as a partner rather than as a defeated foe . . .."[141]

This choice was important. Consistent hard-line U.S. policies could have facilitated old thinkers' attempts either to try to force the Germans to choose between unification and NATO membership, or to muddle through in Eastern Europe the best they could in an attempt to maintain the status quo (as explained, the most likely outcome of this latter strategy was that the Soviet Union's deteriorating position in Eastern Europe would have been eventually overwhelmed by local revolutionary forces). Thus without the reassuring policies by the Americans that accompanied the trust and low-threat levels created by Gorbachev's domestic liberalization, outcomes very likely could have evolved in ways that were much less favorable to U.S. interests.

In sum, despite the Soviet Union's significant economic troubles in the late 1980s and early 1990s, the United States' most important decision makers were of the opinion that U.S.-Soviet relations would continue to be very cooperative only as long as a liberalizing party was governing the

---

its military, and agreed to transform NATO from an anti-Soviet military alliance to a post-Cold War political coalition that promised to have close, cooperative relations with its former enemies.

138. Oberdorfer, *Turn from the Cold War to a New Era*, 378.

139. Zelikow and Rice, *Germany Unified and Europe Transformed*, 331–332, 342, 344, 472; Wohlforth, *Cold War Endgame*, 22, 58.

140. Cf. Thomas Risse, "Let's Argue!: Communicative Action in World Politics," *International Organization* 54, no. 1 (Winter 2000): 1–39.

141. In Wohlforth, *Cold War Endgame*, 18.

USSR. If a party dedicated to different domestic-ideological objectives assumed power in the Soviet Union, a much more confrontational and hostile relationship was believed likely to follow. Zelikow and Rice recount the American point of view when they write: "The Cold War could not have ended and Germany could not have been unified without the Soviet Union's renunciation of [Marxism-Leninism and its principles of] conflict and class struggle in Europe."[142] To the most important decision makers in both America and the Soviet Union, the substantial reduction in the ideological distance dividing them over the course of the 1980s was the key cause of their dramatic reductions in threat perceptions, which were central to allowing the Cold War to end in the largely cooperative manner that it did.

142. Zelikow and Rice, *Germany Unified and Europe Transformed*, 369.

Conclusion

The central purpose of this book has been to develop a causal logic that explains how the degree of ideological differences dividing states' leaders is likely to shape their perceptions of threat and consequent foreign policy choices, and then to test the hypotheses generated by this causal logic against the evidence of great power relations during critical periods over the last two centuries. The evidence, on the whole, supports these predictions. In each of the case studies, there is a strong correspondence between changes in the degree of ideological differences dividing decision makers across states and their perceptions of threat and consequent international behavior. The more similar leaders' ideological beliefs, the less threatening their relations tended to be; the more dissimilar decision makers' ideologies, the more threatening their interactions.

This correspondence between the size of the ideological gap dividing states' leaders and their perceptions of threat and foreign policy behavior should not be dismissed as either a spurious relationship or primarily the product of variables omitted from my analysis. Three facts increase our confidence in the centrality of ideological distances to the formulations of politicians' foreign policies during critical times over the past two hundred years. First, process tracing overwhelmingly supports this assertion. In each of the periods examined, the key decision makers of the era consistently attributed enmity or amity toward other actors in the system based on the degree of ideological differences dividing them. Because leaders' private statements on this subject mirrored their public ones, decision makers' use of ideological language should not be discounted as mere rhetoric that was primarily designed to further objectives of a non-ideological nature.

Second, leaders' perceptions of threat and consequent foreign policy choices corresponded very closely with objective domestic-ideological changes in one or more states. Alterations in no other variable corresponded as closely with changes in threat and behavior. This includes shifts in the international distribution of power. Politicians' perceptions of threat and consequent international policies quite often did not alter when power variables were changing in substantial ways, or perceptions of threat and behavior often changed to a significant degree when power variables were largely constant. These last findings are corroborated by the fact that politicians' threat perceptions and resulting foreign policy preferences often varied starkly by party affiliation (for examples, see Table 3). If states' positions in the international distribution of power are the key cause of leaders' security choices, we should not find systematic partisan variation in policies because a state's relative power position is constant for all its members.

Finally, the evidence supports the predictions of the causal mechanisms developed in Chapter 1. Most powerful were the conflict-probability and demonstration-effects mechanisms. In every system examined, there was a clear correspondence between the ideological distance dividing states' leaders and their assessments of the likelihood of international conflict and domestic subversion. The evidence also supports the predictions of the communications causal mechanism, though not as robustly as the other two. In the periods of history examined, there was no significant example of diplomatic misunderstanding among ideological allies. Conversely, in those instances when actors dedicated to rival ideological objectives had no immediate aggressive intentions toward one another, they frequently had difficulty in conveying the benign nature of their ambitions (e.g., Tsar Nicholas's relations with Britain when led by Whigs, Soviet signals to Britain and France from 1934 to 1938, and British signals to the USSR in 1941). This difficulty in communicating obtained frequently despite the use of "costly signals" in the communications process. The problem for testing the predictions of this mechanism is that instances of benign intent among ideological adversaries were relatively rare. Consequently, there were relatively few opportunities for leaders dedicated to rival legitimating principles to misunderstand one another's objectives.

Claiming that the degree of ideological differences dividing leaders was a critical determinant of states' international policies does not mean either that the content of the different ideologies examined had no important international effects, or that ideological variables always superseded the effects of relative power concerns on outcomes. I discussed the principal conditions under which power variables are likely to trump the effects of ideology—as well as various rejoinders and caveats to these instances—in Chapter 1.

[212]

With regard to issues of ideological content, two patterns of outcomes are particularly important. Large ideological differences dividing leaders translated into high levels of threat regardless of the content of these individuals' ideological beliefs in virtually all cases.[1] Substantial ideological similarities among decision makers, however, were more likely to result in stable amicable relations under some ideological conditions than others. For example, although relations between the Soviets and Chinese communists were very cooperative in the late 1940s and especially the 1950s, ultimately this condition was more unstable than cooperative relations among liberal regimes in the twentieth century or among the absolutist monarchical powers in Europe for much of the nineteenth century. Similarly, although mutual dedication to fascist principles helped to push Germany and Italy into an alliance in the 1930s, the levels of trust between these states' leaders was not as deep as that exhibited in other ideological communities. In sum, although my hypotheses were largely confirmed regardless of the content of the ideologies in question, these findings were most robust for liberal and monarchical regimes. Intolerant ideologies, such as fascism, or perfectionist ideologies that prescribed a single leader of the transnational ideological movement, such as Marxism-Leninism, tended to temper—though without eliminating—the effects of ideological affinity on leaders' behavior over the course of their relations.[2]

THEORETICAL IMPLICATIONS

In addition to demonstrating the centrality of ideological distances to states' security policies, my argument and findings generate three prominent theoretical implications for the study of international relations. First, the causal logic offers a potential explanation for the findings of numerous (largely quantitative) studies that indicate the systematic importance of regime type in international relations. Scholars have found that both democratic and autocratic regimes tend to ally with states of their own regime type;[3] that states' alliance portfolios tend to alter after regime

1. The most prominent exception to this pattern occurred when leaders dedicated to different ideological objectives aligned against even greater ideological threats. I list these instances in the next section.

2. Cf. Stephen M. Walt, *The Origins of Alliances* (Ithaca: Cornell University Press, 1987), 33–37. Other than Sino-Soviet relations after 1957, the only other prominent examples from the case studies of leaders adopting consistently hostile behavior toward actors with which they shared important ideological objectives were Nazi Germany's hostility to Britain and France even when the latter were governed by conservatives, and Lord Palmerston's policies toward France after 1837. In the large majority of the cases, decision makers' presumption of amity toward those dedicated to similar ideological beliefs tended to be well founded.

3. Suzanne Werner and Douglas Lemke, "Opposites Do Not Attract: The Impact of Domestic Institutions, Power, and Prior Commitments on Alignment Choices," *International Studies*

changes;[4] that both autocratic and democratic states tend to have peaceful relations with polities of their regime type;[5] and that leaders of virtually all regime types have through the centuries repeatedly attempted to export forcibly particular domestic institutions.[6] Decision makers have been especially prone to engage in this last behavior in the most threatening international security environments. By demonstrating how a high degree of ideological similarities among states' leaders will create a low threat environment in which decision makers possess important common international and domestic interests, I offer a comprehensive argument that helps to explain these policies and outcomes.

Second and related to the previous point, the evidence indicates that political liberalism's impact on states' relations is not as unique as many democratic peace theorists claim. Instead, increasing ideological similarities among leaders are likely to result in decreasing perceptions of threat regardless of the content of the ideologies in question. Thus relations among monarchical states during the Concert of Europe (especially among Austria, Prussia, and Russia) and Sino-Soviet relations from 1949 to 1958 were just as cooperative as relations among liberal-democratic states in the twentieth century. In the contemporary system, we should similarly expect various illiberal groups (e.g., Islamic fundamentalists) to band together.

Once again, these claims do not mean that the content of political liberalism (or other ideologies for that matter) has no important, independent effects on states' relations. After all, there have been numerous wars among monarchical states, but few (if any) among liberal democracies. Similarly, although the relationship between China and the Soviet Union from 1949 to 1958 was just as cooperative as relations among the liberal-democratic powers after World War II, the Sino-Soviet Alliance was much more brittle than the NATO coalition. Liberalism's unique behavioral prescriptions no

---

Quarterly 41, no. 3 (September 1997): 529–546; Randolph Siverson and Juliann Emmons, "Birds of a Feather: Democratic Political Systems and Alliance Choices in the Twentieth Century," *Journal of Conflict Resolution* 35, no. 2 (June 1991): 285–306; Mark Peceny, Caroline C. Beer, and Shannon Sanchez-Terry, "Dictatorial Peace?" *American Political Science Review* 96, no. 1 (March 2002): 15–26.

4. Randolph M. Siverson and Harvey Starr, "Regime Change and the Restructuring of Alliances," *American Journal of Political Science* 38, no. 1 (February 1994): 145–161.

5. Zeev Maoz and Nasrin Abdolali, "Regime Types and International Conflict, 1816–1976," *Journal of Conflict Resolution* 33, no. 1 (March 1989): 3–35; Zeev Maoz and Bruce Russett, "Alliance, Contiguity, Wealth, and Political Stability: Is the Lack of Conflict among Democracies a Statistical Artifact?" *International Interactions* 17, no. 3 (1992): 245–267; Arvid Raknerud and Havard Hegre, "The Hazard of War: Reassessing the Evidence for the Democratic Peace," *Journal of Peace Research* 34 (1997): 385–404.

6. John M. Owen, "The Foreign Imposition of Domestic Institutions," *International Organization* 56, no. 2 (Spring 2002): 375–409; Suzanne Werner, "Absolute and Limited War: The Possibility of Foreign-Imposed Regime Change," *International Interactions* 22, no. 1 (July 1996): 67–88.

doubt contributed to these differences. Nevertheless, the point remains that different ideological communities in the last two hundred years exhibited similar tendencies as relations among liberal leaders, even if these outcomes were not as stable as liberal interactions. A more comprehensive explanation of political ideologies' effects in international relations than that provided by democratic peace studies is necessary to explain all these outcomes.

Finally, the argument and evidence in this book are suggestive of ways in which power and ideology combine to affect outcomes.[7] The case studies point to three general types of ideological relationships among the great powers' leaders (see Table 3). First (Scenario 1), decision makers from different states can be dedicated to very similar ideological objectives that make them close ideological allies. Second (Scenario 2), different states' leaders can possess important ideological similarities *and* differences (thereby preventing as close of an ideological relationship as in Scenario 1), but still believe that some other state represents a greater ideological danger than they do to one another. Finally (Scenario 3), states' key decision makers can be both divided by very large ideological differences and view no other regime as a greater ideological danger. Power variables will have very different effects on leaders' policies toward particular states depending upon into which one of these three ideological groupings their relations fall.[8]

Relative power concerns will have the smallest impact on decision makers' international policies when the ideological differences dividing them are small (Scenario 1). In this situation, leaders will not see members of their ideological community as significant threats to their most important security concerns. Instead, they will tend to trust one another and believe that they share important international and domestic interests. These views will allow ideological allies to escape from the pernicious effects of the security dilemma as a source of international conflict and instead create a "security community." Members of a security community rule out the use of force as a means of settling disputes, and instead possess stable expectations of peaceful change. They neither fight one another nor expect to do so, and instead engage in security cooperation.[9] Relations among Austria, Prussia, and Russia for much of the nineteenth century, Sino-Soviet relations from 1949 to 1958, and among the Western

---

7. The following ways in which power and ideological variables combine to shape outcomes stand in addition to those discussed in Chapter 1.

8. The following analysis of leaders' policies in Scenarios 1 and 2 assumes that states with which decision makers share important ideological objectives do not engage in behavior that destroys these individuals' presumptions of amity (e.g., Germany's invasion of Czechoslovakia in March 1939).

9. Cf. Emanuel Adler and Michael Barnett, eds., *Security Communities* (Cambridge: Cambridge University Press, 1998), especially chaps. 1 and 2.

democracies since the Second World War meet these requirements of a security community.

This analysis does not mean that regimes within an ideological community will have harmonious relations or that they will no longer have important conflicts of interests. Instead, ideological similarities place limits on states' disputes that allow them to continue their close security relations. Despite lasting conflicts of interest, members of an ideological community continue to base their policies on the expectation of the peaceful settlement of disputes.

Relative power concerns acquire greater saliency in the second of the two ideological scenarios described above, namely when leaders in States A and B share important ideological similarities and differences, but believe that their counterparts in State C are a significantly greater ideological threat. In this situation, decision makers in A and B will not be as threatened by increases in the other's relative power position as realists would likely predict. Because leaders in A and B will believe that they have the same principal international enemy in State C, they will view relative power shifts in the other's favor as potentially benefiting their interests. Moreover, the existence in the system of a greater ideological threat will tend to obscure the potential dangers that A and B pose to one another, thereby resulting in higher levels of trust and cooperation than we would otherwise expect.

Decision makers in States A and B in Scenario 2, however, will be much less trusting of one another's intentions than in Scenario 1. Consequently, the independent effects of power variables on states' policies will be more prominent. Probably most important, the problem of uncertainty and the effects of the security dilemma will be noticeably more evident to states' relations under these conditions. Despite the existence of State C, leaders in A and B will be willing to fall behind one another only so far in terms of relative capabilities before they begin to take steps to maintain their place in the international distribution of power. Thus, for example, conservatives in Britain and France significantly increased defense spending throughout the 1930s so as not to fall behind Germany too far in terms of relative power, while they continued to believe that Hitler would very likely be a reliable bulwark against the Soviet Union. Similarly, Tsar Nicholas in the second half of the Concert of Europe was willing to ally with Britain against a greater ideological threat, France under Louis-Philippe's rule, but the tsar was adamant that Britain's influence in the Near East not significantly increase.

Relations among leaders who possess important ideological similarities and differences, but believe that some other state represents a greater ideological danger than they do to one another, operate within a world characterized by the tenets of defensive realism. In this world, leaders remain guarded about others' intentions, but they do not make worst-case assumptions about them. Relative power concerns play an important role in politicians' security calculations, but leaders primarily seek only to maintain their state's relative position in the international distribution of power; they are "defensive positionalists," not "power maximizers." Although decision makers recognize the possibility of war among them, they remain optimistic that hostilities can be avoided.

Relative power concerns have the greatest impact on states' security policies in Scenario 3, when the ideological differences dividing states' leaders are substantial, and there is no greater ideological danger in the system to obscure their antipathy. This is the world described by offensive realism. In these systems, the security dilemma will have perpetual and profound effects on leaders' international policies. Decision makers will tend to make worst-case assumptions about one another's intentions, and they will view security as extremely scarce and contested. In order to protect their state's interests, politicians will engage in power-maximizing strategies, up to and including preventive war against anticipated enemies. Relations between Revolutionary France and the old regime powers in the 1790s, and both Nazi Germany's and the Soviet Union's relations with the other great powers, fall into this category.

The preceding analysis indicates that different realist theories are likely to be upheld only in particular ideological contexts. My argument thus helps resolve a key divide among realist theories: when leaders are most likely to be guided by the prescriptions of either offensive or defensive realism.

POLICY IMPLICATIONS

The evidence presented in the empirical chapters generates a number of policy implications for the protection of states' security. First, whether or not decision makers should adopt deterrent or reassuring strategies toward particular states should depend largely on the degree of ideological differences dividing them. Because reassuring policies are unlikely to blunt significantly ideological rivals' enmity toward one another, appeasement strategies in these circumstances will tend to increase states' vulnerabilities without a compensating increase in security. Even when being appeased, leaders dedicated to opposing ideological objectives are likely to continue to view one another as subversive dangers to their domestic authority. Moreover, because ideological rivals will tend to understand one another's intentions as malign, they will be inclined to view any concessions made by others as temporary ones that are forced upon them by circumstance. Attempts to communicate the opposite positions are likely to be unsuccessful.

Table 3. The Connection Between Leaders' Ideological Relationships and Their Security Policies

Type of Ideological Relationship	Examples from the Case Studies	Security Relations Characterized by:
1. States' leaders are dedicated to similar ideological objectives	The old regime powers during the 1790s; Austria, Prussia, and Russia during the Concert of Europe; Britain and France from 1830 to 1848; PRC-Soviet relations before 1958; the Western democracies since 1945; Soviet "New Thinkers" and the Western democracies	Security Community
2. States' leaders possess important ideological similarities and differences, but believe another regime represents a greater ideological danger	British and French conservatives' relations with Nazi Germany; British and French socialists' relations with the USSR in the 1930s; Tsar Nicholas's relations with Britain from 1830 to 1848; British Tories' attitudes toward the absolutist monarchies in relation to revolutionary, democratic states during the Concert of Europe	Defensive Realism
3. States' leaders are divided by large ideological differences, and no other regime is a greater ideological danger	The relations between revolutionary France and the old regime powers in the 1790s; Tsar Nicholas's relations with the July Monarchy in France; British Whigs' relations with the absolutist monarchies during the Concert; Nazi Germany's relations with the USSR; British and French conservatives' relations with the USSR and Western socialists' relations with Germany and Italy in the 1930s; the USSR's relations (when governed by orthodox Marxist-Leninists) with all "capitalist" states	Offensive Realism

Deterrent strategies against states with which decision makers share important ideological objectives run the opposite risks. Because members of an ideological community will tend to view one another as likely allies, coercive policies in these circumstances not only create important opportunity costs of foregone cooperation, but increase the likelihood of unnecessary and unwanted conflict. For example, Mao's hostile rhetoric and policies against the Soviet Union after 1957 not only destroyed the Sino-Soviet alliance, but set in motion the events that ultimately led to a state of acute enmity between the two communist powers. China after 1957 was as a result made less secure than when Mao based his policies toward the USSR on common ideological beliefs.

Second, because increasing ideological similarities among states' leaders will tend to benefit these individuals' domestic and international interests, decision makers will confront powerful incentives to help their ideological allies come to power in other states. The means available to realize this objective vary significantly, from economic and diplomatic support of one's international ideological allies to forcible regime exportation by armed combat.

The use of military force to bring about regime change is obviously a riskier strategy than alternatives. Because forcible regime exportation will most likely make conflicts significantly more costly than will more moderate war-fighting objectives, leaders should consider very carefully if the likely gains in security resulting from an increase in the ideological similarities uniting them will outweigh the costs and risks associated with prolonging and deepening hostilities. For example, the security benefits for the United States of compelling by military force a nuclear-armed Soviet Union to renounce its communist system of governance for a more liberal regime would certainly have been smaller than the costs created by this strategy.

This example notwithstanding, the evidence is clear that a strategy of forcible regime promotion has been very effective in increasing great power peace and cooperation at critical points in history, including the Bourbon restoration in France after the Napoleonic Wars and the forced conversion of Japan and Germany to liberal regimes after the Second World War. Moreover, if states at various times had followed with more determination a policy of regime exportation, the course of great power relations would most likely have been substantially changed for the better. Perhaps the most notable instance in which great powers did not pursue with sufficient resources policies of forcible regime promotion to their long-run detriment occurred during the Russian civil war of 1918–20 after the Bolsheviks seized power. Britain, France, the United States, and Japan all sent troops to Russia to aid the counter-revolutionary forces, but they sent far too few to realize their objective. This irresolute intervention only further alienated the Bolshevik rulers and convinced them that their enmity to the Western powers was justified. Once leaders decide that the likely gains of forcible regime change outweigh the costs associated with this strategy, half-hearted measures to realize this goal should be avoided.

Similarly, in the aftermath of a successful regime change, decision makers in other states would be wise to remember that these political changes, at least in the short run, are often tenuous. To help keep their ideological allies in power in a new regime, foreign leaders should continue to provide economic and diplomatic support to this state, and they should certainly avoid actions that threaten the new regime's security.

These latter actions can only undermine the domestic legitimacy of the very group that the foreign powers have an interest in protecting. Thus, for example, the great powers in the years following the Bourbon restoration went to considerable lengths to avoid conflicts with France in order to help solidify the Bourbons' domestic power.

Politicians, however, have not always remembered these warnings. French hostility to Weimar Germany in the 1920s and insufficient support by Britain and America helped to undermine German liberals' authority, which facilitated Hitler's rise to power. Since the end of the Cold War, the Western democracies have expanded the NATO alliance to Russia's border. Because many Russians view NATO expansion as a threat to Russia's security, this outcome has weakened the credibility and thus the domestic power of Russian liberals, who based much of their claim to leadership on the assertion that the Western powers are both benign and trustworthy.

Contemporary American decision makers would do well to remember both these lessons. This book offers support to George W. Bush administration officials' claims that a liberal-democratic Iraq is likely to be much more supportive of American interests than alternative regimes. Yet the Americans must be certain to dedicate sufficient resources both to realize and sustain this very difficult objective. Only time will tell if they heed this advice.

IDEOLOGY AND CONTEMPORARY U.S. FOREIGN POLICY

The argument presented in this book helps us understand two of the most important dimensions of contemporary American foreign policies: why U.S. leaders remain committed to exporting liberal ideology and institutions to other states; and why fundamentalist Islamic groups, such as Osama bin Laden's al Qaeda network, are so fiercely hostile to America.

America's leaders since its founding have claimed a great interest in the spread of liberal institutions and values, and a majority of U.S. presidents since Woodrow Wilson have actively engaged in democracy promotion through economic, diplomatic, and military means. The current president, George W. Bush, is one of the most forceful proponents of this position. Bush has repeatedly emphasized the importance of spreading liberal ideology in the Middle East, South Asia, China, and Russia as central objectives of his administration.

Scholars have frequently dismissed these statements and actions as, at best, either sops to an idealistic American public or mere rhetoric to cloak more power-centered goals, and, at worst, dangerous moralistic crusades that are deleterious of American interests.

These views are mistaken. Because decreasing the ideological differences among states tends to increase their safety, American leaders' long-standing, bipartisan interest in democracy promotion exemplifies not naive utopianism, but a sophisticated understanding of both which states are most likely to be enemies and allies, as well as a key foundation upon which U.S. security rests.[10]

With regard to Islamic fundamentalist organizations like al Qaeda, U.S. decision makers must be very clear about the ultimate source of these groups' enmity to America and its allies. According to many Islamic fundamentalists' own accounts, their hostility toward the Western powers in general and the United States in particular does not result primarily from these states' policies, including various forms of neo-imperialism and their support of Israel. Instead, Islamists' hostility toward the Western powers results from the profound ideological differences dividing the two groups. For example, in the writings of the Egyptian philosopher Sayyid Qutb, whose ideas inform al Qaeda's core doctrines, "the complaints about American policy are relatively few and fleeting. . . . [Qutb's] deepest quarrel was not with America's failure to uphold its principles. His quarrel was with the principles. He opposed the United States because it was a liberal society, not because the United States failed to be a liberal society."[11] As Qutb himself explained, the conflict between the Western powers and fundamentalist Muslims "remains in essence one of ideology."[12]

Qutb and his current followers in al Qaeda (which one scholar of Middle Eastern politics labels "the ideological organization par excellence")[13] fear the continued spread of the Western states' domestic principle of the

10. President Bush expressed these points in a speech to the United Nations on September 21, 2004: "Our security is not merely found in spheres of influence, or some balance of power. The security of our world is found in the advancing rights of mankind. . . . [The] advance of liberty is the path to both a safer and better world." Available at http://www.cbsnews.com/stories/2004/09/21/world/main644795.shtml. Bush is a firm believer not only in the centrality of ideological distances to leaders' choices of allies and enemies, but in the power of demonstration effects: liberalism's success in a few states in a given region will make it easier for this ideology to continue spreading. Hence one of the main motives for establishing liberal regimes in Iraq and Afghanistan. As the president explained in his 2004 convention speech: "I believe in the transformational power of liberty. The wisest use of American strength is to advance freedom. As the citizens of Afghanistan and Iraq seize the moment, their example will send a message of hope throughout a vital region . . . And as freedom advances . . . nation by nation, America will be more secure and the world more peaceful." Available at http://www.washingtonpost.com/wp-dyn/articles/A57466-2004Sep2.html. Or as he asserted in his Second Inaugural: "The survival of liberty in our land increasingly depends on the success of liberty in other lands. The best hope for peace in our world is the expansion of freedom in all the world. America's vital interests and our deepest beliefs are now one . . . [Advancing liberalism] is the urgent requirement of our nation's security." Available at: http://www.npr.org/templates/story/story.php?storyId=4460172

11. Paul Berman, "The Philosopher of Islamic Terror," *New York Times Magazine*, March 23, 2003, 29.

12. Ibid., 56.

13. Michael Doran, "The Pragmatic Fanaticism of al Qaeda: An Anatomy of Extremism in Middle Eastern Politics," in *September 11, Terrorist Attacks, and U.S. Foreign Policy*, ed. Demetrios James Caraley (New York: Academy of Political Science, 2002), 61.

separation of church and state, which subverts fundamentalists' objectives of creating theocracies throughout the Islamic world.[14] In large part to prevent this ideological subversion, Qutb and his modern-day followers remain committed to *jihad* (holy war) against America and its allies, as well as against secular Islamic states.

Because of al Qaeda's ideological objectives and the demonstrated ruthlessness of its members, there can be no compromise with these individuals. This does not mean, however, that the solution to the conflict from America's perspective should be solely a military one. An important component of America's strategies designed to defeat al Qaeda should be policies designed to demonstrate the superiority of political liberalism in comparison to rival systems of belief. Part of this effort should be an informational campaign designed to publicize efforts by the United States and its allies over the last fifteen years to protect the lives and liberties of Muslim peoples in Kuwait, Somalia, Bosnia, Kosovo, Afghanistan, and Iraq. The United States should also devote considerable resources across the Islamic world to improving human rights, including women's rights, to combating poverty, to spreading secular education and respect for law, and to realizing a just compromise in the Israeli-Palestinian conflict. An important component of the solution to America's current ideological conflict should be an attempt to win the hearts and minds of members and sympathizers of al Qaeda. Although many are no doubt beyond conversion, perhaps such a strategy can siphon off a significant level of support for this group.

With regard to America's relations with the other key actors in the system, China, Russia, and the established liberal-democracies in Europe and Japan, I make straightforward predictions. Despite the crisis in the relationship between the United States and its liberal-democratic allies (particularly France and Germany) in the months preceding the American-led attack on Iraq in March 2003, common ideological beliefs among these states' leaders will likely continue to push them into low-threat relationships with the expectation of the peaceful settlement of disputes. Illiberals in China and Russia, in contrast, are likely to view the United States as substantially greater threats to both their domestic and international interests. Substantial tensions between the United States and the other liberal powers are therefore likely to be relatively short-lived, as will be cooperative, crisis-free relations with authoritarian China.[15]

14. Bernard Lewis, *The Crisis of Islam: Holy War and Unholy Terror* (New York: Modern Library, 2003), 159; Paul Berman, *Terror and Liberalism* (New York: W. W. Norton, 2003), 79–80, 82, 90–92, 95, 117–118, 183, 190.

15. For details on how these predictions have been confirmed based on the great powers' balancing policies toward the United States since the end of the Cold War, see John M. Owen, "Transnational Liberalism and U.S. Primacy," *International Security* 26, no. 3 (Winter 2001/2002): 117–152. In brief, illiberal China has responded to American unipolarity by greatly increasing its military spending since 1995, while defense spending in the other liberal powers (including Germany and France) has remained essentially constant since the early 1990s.

Other Systems To Investigate

The five periods of history examined in the case studies are not the only ones that my argument can help explain. Other important relationships in which the degree of ideological differences dividing leaders likely had critical effects on outcomes include the Peloponnesian Wars between Athens and Sparta in the fifth century B.C., the wars of religion in Europe in the sixteenth and seventeenth centuries, Anglo-American relations in the last decades of the nineteenth century, and U.S.-Soviet relations at the beginning of the Cold War.

One period worthy of additional study, during which this book's hypotheses were consistently violated, is the decades leading up to the First World War and the relations then between the great powers. This system actually represents a double violation of my argument: close ideological allies (Germany and Russia) viewed one another in highly threatening terms, and ideological enemies (the Western democracies and Russia) formed alliances well before combat began.

There was in the pre–World War I system a great deal of ideological sympathy between Russian and German leaders, as well as significant ideological aversion between British and French decision makers on one side and Russian leaders on the other. A number of factors combined to overwhelm both tendencies. These factors included widespread social Darwinist beliefs throughout the great powers; growing pan-Slavism in Russia; the simultaneous power-political rise of Germany and Russia; the presence of revisionist aims in all the continental powers; British and French fears of the recreation of the Russo-German entente because of the latter's ideological similarities (which increased the incentives for the former to come to terms with Russia before Germany did); British and French leaders' general lack of concern of ideological subversion to Russian principles (which decreased the barriers to an alliance);[16] and growing fears among the Germans, especially the kaiser, that a revolution in Russia that would end the Russian monarchy was inevitable in the relatively near future.[17]

Taken together, these factors made the pre–World War I system unique. A detailed examination of this period would, however, provide further insight into the conditions under which my argument is and is not likely to explain states' core security policies.

---

16. Notice that these last two ideological conditions were very different than in the 1930s, which helps explain why Britain and France adopted very different alliance policies before the two world wars.

17. On many of the above points, see Roderick R. McLean, *Royalty and Diplomacy in Europe, 1890–1914* (Cambridge: Cambridge University Press, 2001).

CONCLUSION

This book began with the observation that the study of ideology in international relations is one of the most contested topics in the literature. Scholars continue to differ substantially in their understandings of how ideologies affect states' foreign policies and the extent that they do so. By developing detailed causal mechanisms revealing how the degree of ideological differences dividing states' leaders is likely to shape their threat perceptions, and then testing the hypotheses generated by this causal logic against the evidence offered by great power relations at critical times over the last two hundred years, I have added clarity to these debates.

Ideological variables did not, of course, account for every important policy adopted by the great powers in the periods examined. But the consistency with which ideologies affected leaders' most important security policies in these cases cannot be ignored. It is simply impossible to understand the central developments of these periods without taking into account the impact of the ideological distances dividing leaders on outcomes. Given the importance of political ideologies to the evolution of great power relationships in the past, both scholars and policy makers alike would be ill-advised to discount the likely effects of these variables to the future development of international politics.

Index

Aberdeen, George Hamilton Gordon, Earl of, 95
Adamthwaite, Anthony, 130
Adomeit, Hannes, 192
Adrianople, Treaty of, 78
Afghanistan, 3, 30, 187, 195, 199, 204, 221–22
Akhromeyev, Sergei, 178, 184, 187–88
alliances
  failure to form, due to ideological antipathy, 53, 82, 121–26, 129–30, 174–75
  with ideological allies, 16–18, 29, 51, 88–90, 95, 98–102, 107, 148–58, 214–16, 222
  with ideological enemies, 28–30, 102–4, 108, 135, 137–40, 174–75
  with ideological rivals against equal or greater ideological threats, 30, 86–88, 94–98, 112–15, 128, 131–32, 216–17
Alexander I
  opposition to liberals, 83–84, 89
  policies toward Ottoman Empire, 78–84
  policies toward Poland, 76–77
  relations with other great powers, 84–85
  See also Russia: in the Concert of Europe
Al Qaeda, 3, 220–22
Amiens, Treaty of, 61, 70–72
Anderson, Matthew, 88
Andropov, Yuri, 180n12
Angola, 195
appeasement
  in the 1930s, 105, 121–22, 125, 127, 129, 133–34, 138
  in relation to ideological enemies, 217

Arbatov, Georgi, 209
aristocratism, 42–44, 46–47
Austria
  in the 1790s, 40, 43–45, 47–53, 65–67; foreign policies: importance of ideological distances, 43–44, 47–52; puzzles for realism, 48
  in the 1930s, 112, 115, 133
  in the Concert of Europe, 74–77, 79, 81–82, 85, 88–90, 92n53, 93, 95, 100, 214–15

Baker, James, 190, 202, 204–5, 209
balance of power. *See* realism
balance-of-threat theory, 21–22, 120
Baldwin, Stanley, 124, 128
Bandung Line, 160, 169
Beck, Ludwig, 112–18. *See also* Germany: in the 1930s; Germany: foreign policies of German resistance
Beschloss, Michael, 185n30, 204–5
Bessmertnykh, Alexander, 194n66
Bezborodko, Alexander Andreevich, 69
Bin Laden, Osama, 3, 220
Blomberg, Werner von, 116–17
Blondel, Jules, 134n93
Blum, Leon, 125n61, 130n78, 132–34
Bonnet, George, 124, 126
Bosnia, 222
Bosporus and Dardenelles, 79–81, 100
Bourbon restoration, 23, 75, 92, 219–20
Brauchitsch, Walther von, 115
Brezhnev Doctrine, 206
Brissot de Warville, 48, 51, 53–54

Cornell Studies in Security Affairs

A series edited by Robert J. Art, Robert Jervis, *and* Stephen M. Walt

A Grand Strategy for America by Robert J. Art
Political Institutions and Military Change: Lessons from Peripheral Wars by Deborah D. Avant
Japan Prepares for Total War: The Search for Economic Security, 1919–1941 by Michael A. Barnhart
Flying Blind: The Politics of the U.S. Strategic Bomber Program by Michael E. Brown
Citizens and Soldiers: The Dilemmas of Military Service by Eliot A. Cohen
The Origins of Major War by Dale C. Copeland
Pivotal Deterrence: Third-Party Statecraft and the Pursuit of Peace by Timothy W. Crawford
Military Organization, Complex Machines: Modernization in the U.S. Armed Forces by Chris C. Demchak
Whole World on Fire: Organizations, Knowledge, and Nuclear Weapons Devastation by Lynn Eden
Innovation and the Arms Race: How the United States and the Soviet Union Develop New Military Technologies by Matthew Evangelista
The Purpose of Intervention: Changing Beliefs about the Use of Force by Martha Finnemore
A Substitute for Victory: The Politics of Peacemaking at the Korean Armistice Talks by Rosemary Foot
The Wrong War: American Policy and the Dimensions of the Korean Conflict, 1950–1953 by Rosemary Foot
The Best Defense: Policy Alternatives for U.S. Nuclear Security from the 1950s to the 1990s by David Goldfischer
Storm of Steel: The Development of Armor Doctrine in Germany and the Soviet Union, 1919–1939 By Mary R. Habeck
America Unrivaled: The Future of the Balance of Power edited by G. John Ikenberry
The Meaning of the Nuclear Revolution: Statecraft and the Prospect of Armageddon by Robert Jervis
Fast Tanks and Heavy Bombers: Innovation in the U.S. Army, 1917–1945 by David E. Johnson
Modern Hatreds: The Symbolic Politics of Ethnic War by Stuart J. Kaufman
The Vulnerability of Empire by Charles A. Kupchan
The Transformation of American Air Power by Benjamin S. Lambeth
Anatomy of Mistrust: U.S.-Soviet Relations during the Cold War by Deborah Welch Larson
Planning the Unthinkable: How New Powers Will Use Nuclear, Biological, and Chemical Weapons edited by Peter R. Lavoy, Scott D. Sagan, and James J. Wirtz
Cooperation under Fire: Anglo-German Restraint during World War II by Jeffrey W. Legro
Dangerous Sanctuaries: Refugee Camps, Civil War, and the Dilemmas of Humanitarian Aid by Sarah Kenyon Lischer

About the Author

MARK L. HAAS is an Assistant Professor in the Political Science Department and the Graduate Center for Social and Public Policy at Duquesne University. He formerly was a National Security Fellow at the Olin Institute for Strategic Studies and an International Security Fellow at the Belfer Center for Science and International Affairs, both at Harvard University.